GETTYSBURG'S
Confederate Dead

Pvt. Elijah Amick, 15th South Carolina, Kershaw's Brigade,
mortally wounded on July 2, 1863.

Gregory A. Coco

Savas Beatie
California

Originally published by Thomas Publications in 2003.

Library of Congress Control Number: 2022938622

First Savas Beatie Edition, First Printing

ISBN-13: 978-1-61121-654-7
eISBN: 978-1-954547-56-8 (Savas Publishing)

SB

Savas Beatie
989 Governor Drive, Suite 102
El Dorado Hills, CA 95762
916-941-6896
www.savasbeatie.com
sales@savasbeatie.com

Savas Beatie titles are available at special discounts for bulk purchases by corporations, institutions, and others. For more details, please contact contact us at sales@savasbeatie.com or visit www.savasbeatie.com for more information.

In memory of 1/Lt. John R. Stowe, 1st Cavalry Division, USA.

— A casualty of the Vietnam War. —

This book is dedicated to four individuals who, over the last 140 years, made the greatest efforts to ensure that Gettysburg's Confederate dead would not be forgotten. They are:

DR. JOHN W. C. O'NEAL: For his early work, between 1863 and 1866, in gathering the names of Confederates buried on the battlefield and in the hospital sites around Gettysburg. Also, for his care of their graves, replacing headboards, and diligent work in finding and sending remains back to their families in the South.

DR. RUFUS B. WEAVER: For the supreme task of finding, identifying, boxing, and shipping 3,320 remains to the South between 1871 and 1873. But, especially, for the fact that even as a Northerner, he treated his mission as a sacred trust, and was ever aware that his work for "the lamented dead" was of great importance to so many thousands of grieving relatives.

KATHLEEN GEORG HARRISON: For her long hours of labor spent compiling, clarifying, and comparing the names and units of more than 1,000 Confederates in Dr. O'Neal's "Physician Handbooks," "Record Book," and other lists he made, to those in Dr. Weaver's shipment notes, thereby bringing order to what was once chaos. Without Kathy Harrison's interest and her endeavors in the 1970s, this book would never have been started.

ROBERT K. KRICK: For the many years of intense and difficult research in compiling a "Gettysburg Death Roster," which contains the names and units of nearly 4,700 Southerners who were killed or mortally wounded in the famous battle. He called his work "a memorial of sorts, with connotations verging on sentimentality," but Bob Krick surely underestimated the importance of his project. It was necessary and useful, it is respected, and is highly appreciated by the Civil War community. Historian Krick will be thanked and cited, long after we all, like those Confederates, pass from existence.

The Gregory A. Coco Collection

by Savas Beatie

A Strange and Blighted Land: Gettysburg: The Aftermath of a Battle

On the Bloodstained Field:
Human Interest Stories of the Campaign and Battle of Gettysburg

A Vast Sea of Misery: A History and Guide to the Union and Confederate
Field Hospitals at Gettysburg, July 1-November 20, 1863

Confederates Killed in Action at Gettysburg

Wasted Valor: The Confederate Dead at Gettysburg

A Concise Guide to the Artillery at Gettysburg

Killed in Action: Eyewitness Accounts of the Last Moments
of 100 Union Soldiers Who Died at Gettysburg

Rebel Humor: 120 stories of the
Comical Side of Confederate Army service, 1861-1865

War Stories: A Collection of One Hundred Fifty Little-Known
Human Interest Stories of the Campaign and Battle of Gettysburg

The Civil War Infantryman: In Camp, on the March, and in Battle

Two Confederate Officers Remember Gettysburg:
Col. Robert M. Powell, 5th Texas Infantry, Hood's Texas Brigade & Capt. George Hillyer, 9th Georgia Infantry

The grave of Pvt. Oscar W. Covin in Magnolia Cemetery.

CONTENTS

Preface 9

Acknowledgments 11

Part
  I   Those Lamented Dead.. 13
  II Where Defeated Valor Lies 27
       The Roster of Gettysburg's Identified Confederate Burials 33

Appendix
  I   Burial Roster Notes 112
  II The Number of Confederate Wounded 115
  III A Register of Gettysburg Confederate Burial Sites 116
  IV Were Any of the Confederate Dead Left Behind? 124
  V Elliott's Map 126

PHOTO CREDITS

PREFACE

THE subject of the Confederate burials at Gettysburg first caught my interest in the late 1970s when Kathleen Georg Harrison, now chief historian of the Gettysburg National Military Park, introduced me to a project she was working on in her free moments. At that time, Kathy Harrison was preparing a compilation of all Southerners who were interred in identified graves in the Gettysburg area, and remained there throughout the years from 1863 to 1873. By way of her efforts, I became fascinated with, not only the Confederates who had been left behind in Pennsylvania when General Robert E. Lee's Army retreated, but also with the burial sites themselves. Kathy eventually finished the work but did not publish the list. Later, in 1990, I attempted to tell a small portion of this story, without a roster, in a book called *Wasted Valor*. This book, *Gettysburg's Confederate Dead*, was written to narrate the basic story of the removal of the Southern dead, and to provide researchers with a comprehensive alphabetical roster of the identified burials as well.

Color Corporal Solomon S. Page, Co. D, 59th Georgia, mortally wounded
on July 2, is buried in Harrisburg Cemetery, Harrisburg, Pa.

(RG)

The grave of Capt. John T. Green, Co. I, 8th Virginia Infantry,
Glenwood Cemetery, Washington, D.C.

"Offered up his life as a sacrifice in the 'Lost Cause' in the memorable charge made by
Pickett's Division in the Battle of Gettysburg on the third day of July 1863. Aged 27 years."

ACKNOWLEDGMENTS

THE long process of completing a detailed list of the identified or "known" Confederates who died and were buried at Gettysburg, could not have been finished without hours of help from some very generous people. To bring the story and roster to light, it was necessary to conduct a period of tedious research, including the preparation of an initial catalog of approximately 1,100 3" X 5" index cards. These cards had to be assembled to begin the process of organization. Each card eventually contained between seven to fifteen separate bits of information, and all had to be typed into a computer to form a clear and readable list. This was the moment I knew I needed some real assistance. The person who came to my aid in this transitional step was Tina M. Adams, a co-worker and friend at the Gettysburg National Military Park. It was pretty evident then that I was not qualified to accomplish this computerized creation of the roster. However, due to Tina's skills and dedication, she pressed on through a long and very laborious chore. With her format in place, the book finally began to take shape. So, for your kind and best efforts Tina, I am very thankful, and forever in your debt.

A surprise awaited me as the first edit of Tina's 65-page roster neared completion. As I studied and verified each line, it was obvious that I had underestimated how much additional research was needed to make the list nominally accurate. There were errors everywhere, not from Tina's typing, but in many of the Confederate soldiers' names, units, ages, dates of death, and places of burial. Each page was found to contain between fifty to one hundred inaccuracies or questions needing corrections or answers. Frankly, after realizing the need for so much unexpected retyping, I decided it would not be fair to ask Tina to do any more. That's when Cindy L. Small came to my rescue. She volunteered to make the thousands of changes, and in the process, eventually had to add 300 more names and the attendant information to the list, pushing it up to eighty pages. The work on this roster never seemed to end, especially with the difficulty of manipulating the multiple columns across the computer screen. Never daunted, Cindy kept at it, and became an expert in Confederate burial sites at Gettysburg, while saving the project from implosion and oblivion. So to you Cindy, I shall be grateful through all my years, and although I will try, it will be impossible to ever repay you.

Besides Tina and Cindy, there were several other people who assisted in the completion of this book. Robert Gale offered his vast collection of Gettysburg burial location photographs to me for inclusion in these pages. I only regret that we used so few of his images, but the roster just took up too much space. John Heiser and Scott Hartwig were patient and always responded positively to my numerous requests during the countless hours I spent "holed up" in the Gettysburg National Military Park library. Locally too, Ben Resnick, Ryan Stouch, Kathy Harrison, Greg Goodell, Anthony Nicastro, Tim Smith, Jerry Bennett, and superintendent Brian A. Kennell of Evergreen Cemetery, were very helpful. Also helpful were Gary Beaver, G. Thomas LeGore and Richard Clem in Maryland; Robert B. Bradley in Alabama; Paul Sledzik in Washington D.C.; David W. Vaughan, Greg White, and Thomas B. Ray in Georgia; Donna Woods and Jane Montz in Texas; Clarence W. Hollowell, Jr. in North Carolina; Jean E. Bishop, Gus Johnson and Jeannie Civlichoski in Connecticut; and Thomas W. Howard, Michael Wagenhauser, Lewis Leigh, Jr. and Gregory F. Taylor in Virginia. To all of you, and to the staff at Thomas Publications, (Dean Thomas, Jim Thomas, Sally Thomas, Andy DeCusati, Kay Eyler, and Truman Eyler) many, many thanks for your exertions on my behalf, as well as your kindnesses, and continued friendships.

Gregory A. Coco
Bendersville, Pa.
March 1, 2002

(RG)

The grave of Pvt. Jefferson B. Jessee, Co. C, 37th Virginia Infantry,
Hollywood Cemetery, Richmond, Va.

I

THOSE LAMENTED DEAD

"It is hard to think of so many of our warm-hearted, brave Southern youths now sleeping beneath the cold clods of Pennsylvania. We can only hope that the day is not far distant when we may bring their dead bodies back to their native soil."[1]

A POET once wrote that the bravest battles are not fought on the battlefield, but in the hearts of parents who have lost a son in war.[2] It must have been this way for the mother of 18-year-old Sgt. Thomas Booker Tredway, of the "Chatham Greys," 53rd Virginia Infantry. Tredway died on July 13, 1863, from wounds received in combat on July 3 at Gettysburg. His body was first interred in a cornfield on Jacob Schwartz's farm, a U.S. field hospital facility in use for several weeks in July and August of 1863. Then in 1872, his skeletal remains were collected and shipped with others to Hollywood Cemetery in Richmond, Virginia. Looking back now, it appears doubtful that Tredway's mother ever knew any of this, but we do have evidence that she never got over his loss. She even tried to keep up a small glimmer of hope that he would one day return. This was proven about 1910, when Tredway's sister, Pattie, wrote:

> "We never knew the particulars of his death, but heard afterward that the fatal bullet struck him while bending over the body of his wounded colonel whom he was endeavoring to assist.... My mother spent long days and nights awaiting his return, and even long after...every footstep on the porch outside her door and every unusual noise in the night made her think it was 'Tom' coming home."[3]

Tredway's story was not unusual, and was just one of many that grew out of the carnage of Gettysburg. With a total of probably close to 5,000 Confederates who are believed to have been killed or to have 'died of wounds' in that battle alone, stories like Tredway's would always abound. So many Southern men were gone, while uncertainty and anguish fermented in their hometowns, as families waited for news, whether it be good or bad. The mother of Captain Oliver Mercer of the 20th North Carolina may have said it best when she wrote to a Gettysburg resident the sadness she felt while searching for what was left of her son's body. "Oh! we have lost so much.... [He was] a brave, noble boy in the full bloom of youth, and my heart yearns to have his remains, if they can be found, brought home to rest in the soil of the land he loved so well. I need your assistance and I am confident you will aid me."[4] Like many over time, Mrs. Mercer finally gave up all prospects of ever seeing her son alive again. Therefore, in the end, her only comfort, akin to other relatives of the Confederate dead, was the knowledge that her son, and their sons, brothers, fathers, and friends had received some medical care before death, and then were provided with a marked, secure, and permanent grave. It did not seem much to ask, considering the terrible sacrifices that had been made. Yet, the bodies of these soldiers were on the enemy's land, and the difficulties only began with the knowledge of that reality.

Such feelings of helplessness were expressed often in the months and years following Gettysburg's battle, and surely after every other of the thousands of engagements that took place during the Civil War. And while those appeals may or may not have been heard elsewhere, in Pennsylvania, a series of events, combined with the efforts of a few individuals, started a chain reaction that in the end, somewhat moved events in a direction to satisfy the desperate wishes of this grieving population.

Somehow, even before the end of 1863, the word began to trickle down into the states of the Southern Confederacy, that there was a chance, even a real possibility, that with patience and the right contacts, a family could actually recover the body or remains of a cherished loved one, lost and buried in Pennsylvania. There are some accounts in the historical record which relate how a few Confederates were, in fact, moved to their homes quite soon after the battle. These were rare exceptions, but, they still did occur. A few examples can even be found in this book's roster, as you can see under the names of Captains Samuel Gray and Isaac Stamps. Such cases were definitely not the rule, and usually involved families of soldiers who had wealth or some friendly connections in the United States. It would be unique to find an account of a poor family in some "Deep South" state making the attempt to claim a son's body. And since a large segment of General Lee's army was made up of enlisted men with backgrounds of limited means, there is little doubt that many parents from this strata of the culture never took away, nor had shipped home, the remains of their offspring.

The need to fulfill so many urgent and heart-stricken requests brought forth the concern and services of a handful of men in the Gettysburg area who, early on, assisted in the retrieval of Confederate soldiers' corpses or skeletal remains. Although there were others lesser known, such as John G. Frey who died in 1866, one of the first and most notable names to be associated with these tasks was Samuel Weaver, a local photographer who was fifty-one years old in 1863. In a letter dated December 27, 1865, to the mother of Captain George Bedinger, 33rd Virgina, Weaver regretfully explained that he had been unsuccessful in his efforts to locate her son's grave, and added that "I was appointed by Governor [Andrew] Curtin on Sunday a week after the battle to go over the battle field and the hospitals and get all the names of the Penn[sylvanians] that was mark[ed] on the field...and whilst I was taking the names...I took the names of all the marked graves both Federal and Confederate."[5] Hence, we can ascertain from his statement, that even as soon as a few weeks after July 12, Weaver

Samuel Weaver.

likely had a workable list containing, if his words were true, possibly as many as 1,000 to 1,300 Confederate grave sites located across a sizable portion of Adams County. The reason the figure 1,000 to 1,300 is used here is because out of the possible 5,000 Southern soldiers who are now believed to have lost their lives during the battle, or afterwards due to wounds, only that number ended up being buried and marked by their comrades, or had died in Union hospitals where their graves were accounted for by Federal authorities. Weaver, as one of the agents for Governor Curtin, later went on to be employed in supervising the exhuming of the bodies of Union soldiers who were casualties of the battle, for interment into Gettysburg's new Soldiers' National Cemetery. In the culmination of this work, Weaver reported on March 19, 1864, that "we examined more than three thousand rebel graves."[6] His register likely came forth from these activities as well.

The importance of such a list to the relatives of these dead Southerners can easily be imagined. It could be said that "every name on that list [was] a lightning strike to some heart, and breaks like thunder over some home, and falls a long black shadow upon some hearthstone."[7] Still, such a record was also a ray of hope to those who sought to bring home to rest a few bones as a tangible or physical reminder of a beloved son, brother, husband, or father. Weaver must have understood this, because in concluding the above letter to Mrs. Bedinger, he added, "If any of your friends wishing any information & will let me know..., I will attend to these requests with promptness." Weaver's efforts on behalf of these Southern families probably began slowly through the winter of 1863-64 and picked up in tempo throughout the next seven years, until his untimely death in early 1871. Since it is impossible to know how many Confederate remains he personally attended to in those first years, it is fair to say that when the war ended in May 1865, his activities in this realm likely expanded. Eventually, Weaver must have acquired quite a respected reputation throughout the South, because shortly before his death, the Ladies Memorial Association of Charleston was in contact with him regarding the removal of South Carolina's dead from the environs of Gettysburg.

Doctor John William Crapster O'Neal was a second individual who, during the same time frame as Weaver, also played a prominent part in the early identifying, collecting, and shipment to the South of Confederate remains. A native of Virginia, Dr. O'Neal was born in Fairfax County in April, 1821, making him 42 years old at the time of the battle. He attended college in Gettysburg, and later in Maryland where he received his

(ACHS)

Dr. John O'Neal.

and so on. For example, on the above page alone he lists 28 names, along with their companies and regiments, plus most of their dates of death. He also describes an additional "27 graves unknown," which were behind the barn on the Jacob Schwartz's farm.

(GAC)

At least 55 Confederate soldiers were buried behind Jacob Schwartz's barn in Mt. Joy Township.

medical degree in 1844. Dr. O'Neal's practice of medicine began in Hanover, Pennsylvania, where he married Ellen Wirt on September 14, 1846. By 1850 Ellen and John O'Neal had resettled in Baltimore. Thirteen years later, in February, 1863, the couple moved to Gettysburg, where Dr. O'Neal continued in private practice, but also accepted an appointment as Adams County's official physician.[8]

No one can really be sure when Dr. O'Neal first took an interest in the thousands of dead Confederates whose graves dotted the countryside in a 20-mile arch around Gettysburg. Perhaps his attention to these unfortunate men stemmed from youthful days spent as a boy in Virginia, or his many years in Baltimore, or simply from the difficult hours he spent in caring for some of them as wounded soldiers far from home, and in enemy country. Although there was always speculation, no one in those days ever tried to discredit Dr. O'Neal by implying he was a traitor, (although he was in the minority as a Democrat), or even a "Southern sympathizer." He seemed to have had a reputation as a kind man and a good physician, even though Dr. O'Neal once said to a reporter in 1905, "You know in those days there were people who didn't like me...." However, what can be gleaned from his private papers is that in the months directly following the battle, Dr. O'Neal began to write down the names and locations of Confederate graves he encountered while on his rounds as a busy country doctor making "house calls." Throughout his travels around the county, he carried with him a little diary-like journal called the "Physician's Hand-Book of Practice." And on the pages of these books, throughout the years 1863 and 1864, intermingled with home remedies, patients' names and ailments, and fees collected and due, one can find entries such as,

Due to the absence of most of Dr. O'Neal's private papers, it is impossible to know to what extent he was able to use his own growing list of Confederate burial sites to assist aggrieved families in the South. Some documentation exists, however, to suggest that Dr. O'Neal was very involved in these proceedings. At times, he may have even included with his letters, hand-drawn maps suggesting the exact spot where a grave could be found. In one case, a North Carolina woman who was searching for the body of her son wrote to Dr. O'Neal in August, 1866, that her local newspaper had printed, "welcome intelligence to many bereaved Southern hearts that you have cared for the graves of many of our Confederate dead at Gettysburg, replaced headboards and prepared a list of names." This one sentence tells us a lot about the doctor, including the fact that Dr. O'Neal was gaining his own reputation across a large area of the country. We can feel, too, that it would have been hard for a man like Dr. O'Neal to ignore such agonizing pleas, and surely he did not. One former Union soldier said of the doctor that he had "a heart filled with the milk of human kindness and the spirit of brotherly love." This writer also remembered that the deceased men in gray "especially appealed" to the doctor. "They had no friends here. They had fallen

15

on a field hostile to them," and he "made it his duty, as far as he could, to preserve a record of these graves that their friends might some day carry what was left to rest in the soil of the land of their birth."[9]

Unfortunately, very few letters still exist that were written by Dr. O'Neal to people he assisted in the recovery of Confederate remains. But from those extant, one may clearly perceive the doctor's true character and generous nature. He was polite, interested, and concerned, and it is obvious he never let the magnitude or the tragic nature of these circumstances be used to profit from the desperation and grief of others. In fact, the work done on behalf of distraught relatives and friends of these soldiers was probably billed too low for the amount of time and trouble attending it. In one case, for instance, Dr. O'Neal located and prepared for shipment what was left of the body of Lt. Valentine W. Southall, 23rd Virginia Infantry. On August 10, 1869, he wrote to Joseph W. Southall with this message and the total charge for his services:

Sir,

Today I had exhumed & packed the remains of Lt. Southall. The wounded bone is wrapped in paper & packed [on] top of box which you can examine.

The box I send by Morson's Express. The expenses are,

For digging	1.50
For horse & wagon	1.50
For Box	1.75
Postage & gates about	.50
	$5.25

which amount I shall require to be paid the express office when the box will be delivered.

For your kind courteous manner of correspondence please except[sic] thanks.

Very respectfully
J. W. C. O'Neal[10]

(GFT)

The grave of Lt. Southall in the family cemetery at their home "Selma," near Amelia, Virginia.

It is plain to see from this note, and the minor expenses itemized on the enclosed statement, that Dr. O'Neal had no intention of defrauding or victimizing this family he had consented to help.

Since the burial list that Weaver compiled and mentioned in his letters has never been found, it remains to be seen if he truly produced an accurate register of the 1,000 to 1,300 Confederates believed to have had marked or identified graves in the Gettysburg area. Meanwhile, in Dr. O'Neal's case, we do have the opportunity to inspect a smaller registry of the Southern graves he discovered. These, remember, were burials still visible and had identifying marks. They were scattered about the battleground or on farmsteads which had been employed as field hospitals in the weeks following the fighting in Pennsylvania. From his jottings, one can surmise that, following his initial surveys, Dr. O'Neal periodically revisited many of the concentrations of burial sites. While we cannot know for sure, the date "October 1864" crops up enough in his notes to cause one to believe this was a time he may have made a repeat inspection of the grave sites. There is positive proof that Dr. O'Neal inspected the Confederate burials in May 1866 because those documented assessments still exist.

In any event, by the early summer of 1866, Dr. O'Neal must have made his last tour of the field and was ready to "advertise" to the world that he had catalogued the names and burial locations of hundreds of Confederates. On June 23, 1866, the editor of the Gettysburg *Compiler*, Henry J. Stahle, issued a receipt to Dr. O'Neal for five dollars in cash, paid by the doctor to have a "just revised" list published in the *Compiler*, of the "marked Confederate dead." This roster had been printed twelve days earlier on the front page of the newspaper. In his introductory remarks concerning Dr. O'Neal's project, Stahle explained:

The list has been gotten up for the purpose of enabling relatives to recover their dead with certainty, thus saving them the trouble and expense of a fruitless search after those not marked. Dr. O'Neal has no direct or indirect interest in this matter, and is moved only by a common feeling of humanity.

Covering several long columns of type, the register consisted of approximately 600 names and units. By no means was it a perfect portrayal of the number of General Lee's men who occupied shallow graves on and off the Gettysburg battlefield. Dr. O'Neal's "muster roll of the dead" was filled with scores of errors, not because of carelessness, but simply because of how well or how indifferent the graves had been marked by comrades or

Union hospital attendants. Also, three full years had passed since the headboards or other identifying marks had been placed over the bodies. In that span of time, the ravages of nature had rendered names and other markings difficult or often even impossible to decipher. Many of the entries on Dr. O'Neal's register were incomplete, such as the examples of "Lt. Blume," "Corp Bede," or "_____Scrabbs, North Carolina." Some consisted of only initials, as in "W C G," "J.W.P., 11th Georgia," or "W.A. of N.O." There were other anomalies too, like "Sergt._____Bolt," and "Capt. _____ _____ 52nd North Carolina." Yet, on the positive side, it was still possible, using Dr. O'Neal's list as a starting point, to establish the whereabouts of any one of more than 500 Confederate graves resting in that vast and unfamiliar area consisting of thousands of acres of battlefield and old hospital sites.[11]

Sometime just prior to or shortly after the above 1866 list was published, Dr. O'Neal must have collected all of his notes on Confederate burials, along with his "Physician's Handbooks," and any other materials he had accumulated on the subject. He then combined all of the data in a large and permanent ledger or "record book." Eventually, in 1943, his daughter donated this valuable book to the Gettysburg National Military Park, where it remains to this day. At that time, Dr. O'Neal had been dead for 30 years, but the good deeds he had accomplished for his fellow Americans, now reunited and fighting World War II, were still being recognized and appreciated.[12]

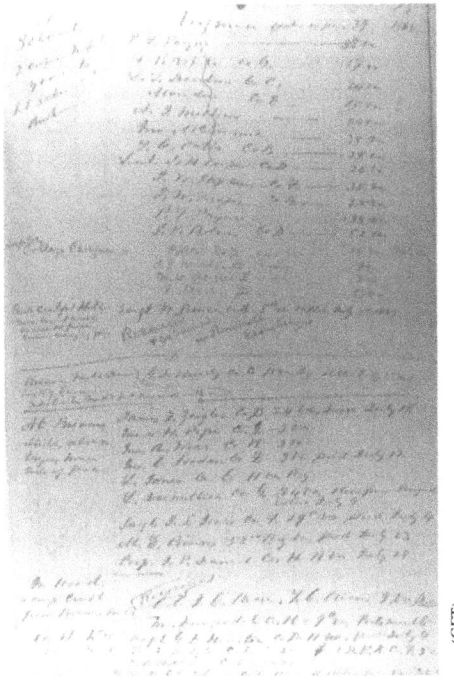

(GFT)

A page from Dr. O'Neal's Confederate burial journal.

As the months and years passed following the 1865 surrenders of Confederate armies in Virginia, North Carolina, Georgia and elsewhere, the rate of letters coming to Weaver, Dr. O'Neal and others, requesting assistance in recovering the bodies and remains of Southern soldiers in the Gettysburg area, must have begun to gradually diminish. This was only normal, as interest in the war took a backseat to the common concerns of everyday life. This wasn't to say that the men still lying in those shallow graves were forgotten. It was just a plain reality that for most Southerners, bringing back a beloved son or husband from Pennsylvania was simply beyond the ways and means of the average family. While collecting individual remains likely waned in these years, a new idea began to gather momentum. This was the belief that the states of the old Confederacy should attempt to gather the bones of each and every Southern soldier in the North and return them for a proper burial in their native land. Following the war, the United States government began the slow but methodical process of collecting the remains of Union soldiers for reinterment in any one of the many national cemeteries recently established across the country. This did not go unnoticed in the South, especially when the national government made no provisions to relocate Confederate dead in these hallowed places.

It cannot be pinpointed exactly when this "movement" or idea of returning the dead to the South began to take shape. Likely, it sprung up simultaneously in several Southern states, possibly along with the formation of various "Ladies Memorial Associations." These associations were postwar organizations which developed, not only to honor the Confederate "cause" and its former soldiers, but also to care for Southern graves, and to give women a voice or a semblance of power that they otherwise lacked in the repressive, male-dominated society of the nineteenth century. Or, perhaps the stories that began to circulate in the South of "Yankee" farmers vowing to plow up the graves of Confederates lying buried on their farms, finally stirred up the passions of the Southern populace. News of grave desecration was usually given in first-hand "reports" by visitors coming back from places in the North, particularly Gettysburg or Sharpsburg, Maryland. The following is a good example. It was written in the Columbus, Georgia *Daily Enquirer* in 1866. The source was Leonard Jones who had just returned from Pennsylvania where he had traveled to locate the body of his deceased father, Col. John A. Jones, formerly of the 20th Georgia Infantry. In one paragraph of the article concerning Colonel Jones, the correspondent gave his readers a startling bit of information, "Mr. Jones informs us that the field where were buried the Confederate dead of Gettysburg, has been put in cultivation, and the mounds and headboards have been leveled by the harrows which prepared the ground for wheat." Other examples of this type of reporting were sometimes even more sensational, which was obviously meant to, and surely would have, incite the anger of most patriotic Southerners. An article in the Hawkinsville, Georgia *Dispatch* certainly propagated these feelings. It began in the same fashion as usual, stating, "Having been informed by a person who has visited the spot...," then continued, "that unless removed by fall, the owners of the ground [where our Georgians are buried] have given notice that they 'intend ploughing up the land and grinding the bones for fertilizing purposes,....'" The writer added that the Savannah Memorial Association "asks each of her sister associations in the State to come forward at once and assist her in removing these remains to a resting place on her own soil."[13]

For fear that the reader could get the wrong impression of all of this, it is only fair to explain that not all Northerners felt that the bones of these now dead enemy soldiers should be so heartlessly treated. For example, Dr. Rufus Weaver, who eventually moved more than 3,000 remains to the South from Gettysburg, wrote in late 1871 that he had "met with some very kind and humane persons during my work this Summer. In those cases, the graves had been noted and cared for & respected by the land owner and especially so were Mr. [Josiah] Benner and [John] Cunningham. Whilst both are (one for certain) I think Republicans, yet they were deeply interested in all the dead on their land and not a grave had been disturbed." In point of fact, much of the same disregard was happening in parts of the Southland. In 1869, for instance, Russell H. Conwell, a recently discharged Union soldier, took a trip across the territory of the old Confederacy, and occasionally found instances where the graves of Southern soldiers were being ignored, neglected, or even abused. Once, while in the area of Fort Harrison, which stood southeast of Richmond, he witnessed a farmer plowing up a twenty-acre field that had been a graveyard for many of the Confederates killed in action while manning a sector of the defenses of that city. Skulls and other bones were scattered everywhere, and some of these remains were even being carted away for fertilizer. When asked about the desecration, the farmer replied that this section of land was "now the richest piece he had," and said, "[I] didn't put 'em there nohow."[14]

So to return to the subject, it was indeed true that some citizens of the North wanted to provide the Confederate dead of Gettysburg with a cemetery of their own in Pennsylvania. Even John Seymour, the brother of Horatio Seymour, the governor of New York, had a desire to have this come to fruition. In 1864, he wrote to a prominent Gettysburg attorney, Moses McClean, proposing to purchase land near Seminary Ridge for a Confederate cemetery.[15] But a New York newspaper, the *Express*, may have been one of the first forums to voice a real solution, however unpopular a crusade it might have seemed to people north of the Mason and Dixon Line. Less than a year after the great battle, this paper's editors, after hearing the claims that the Rebel dead were to be plowed up and made into fertilizer, declared that "in accordance with the laws of civilized warfare," it was only proper to pay respect to the "buried remains, even of our enemies." Continuing, the editorial pointed out that when the war was over, and "calm reflection [is] unbiased by heated passion, [a] piece of ground should be set aside, and such of the bodies as are recognizable..., should have a separate burial, and a headboard, though it be but rough wood, should designate the name and regiment, if known. The foe who so bravely contested the famed battle of Gettysburg, certainly need a better fate than the burial of a dog."[16]

On February 2, 1864, one of Gettysburg's newspapers, the Adams *Sentinel*, printed some interesting and thoughtful comments which somewhat mirrored what the New York article hoped to convey. In a piece entitled "The Rebel Dead," the *Sentinel* made a clear presentation of the same idea.

> There appears to be considerable feeling in and around Gettysburg that a place be set apart for the burial of the Confederate dead who are now buried promiscuously over the battlefield, or in the vicinity. The recent rains have washed the places where they are buried, and the bones are exposed; besides, which, in a short time the land will be put under cultivation, and no trace of their last resting-place will be left. Common humanity would dictate a removal to some spot, not in or about our own National Cemetery, but the purchase of ground somewhere, where Southern friends may, when the rebellion is crushed, and all is peace, make their pilgrimage here. Our state should not make the purchase, nor should it be expected; but if Southern people should express the desire and would carry it to completion, we should say — let it be done for the sake of our common humanity. The hostility of the dead has ceased; and let there be a spot where a father, a mother, a sister or brother, can visit their last resting place, 'when this cruel war is over.'

To say the least, this article was written in a very generous spirit, especially when one considers that it was published during what would become the bloodiest and most destructive year of the American Civil War. To what extent it brought the editors criticism is not known, but one response to their sympathetic prose was sent to the paper from a woman in Washington, Pennsylvania. "Our paragraph met the eye of a lady," they noted, "...who...says: 'The sentiments you express in regard to the "Confederate Dead," are humane, magnanimous, and to my mind, very patriotic.'" And enclosed within her letter was a poem, which the Sentinel set to type:

Oh! choose ye a place where the dead may rest,
And gather their bones from the field,
On their nameless graves let the sod be press'd,
For Death has their mission sealed.

Ye Southern dead, what a mournful past —
Three years so grim and gory —
Oh, would ye had clung to the dear old Flag,
For HERS WAS OUR EQUAL GLORY!

But the past, the past, we may not recall,
The past so fraught with sorrow,
Then let us pray that for each, for all,
There may speed a peaceful morrow.

Yes, choose ye a spot where the dead may sleep,
Nor storms their bones uncover,
A spot where their lov'd ones may come and weep,
'When this cruel war is over.'[17]

During the early years following the end of hostilities, while thousands of Confederates slowly moldered into the earth of Pennsylvania, various factions sought to determine the right course to follow in regard to their "heroic dead." On several occasions, General Lee was questioned, or made comments on this serious and important subject. After all, the men who occupied those lonely graves had been his soldiers and had lost their lives under his command. Though General Lee normally tried to avoid anything that had to do with the late war, he always showed strong feelings when it came to the slain soldiers of the South. In March of 1866, Lee remarked to the chairman of a Richmond memorial association, that the "graves of the Confederate dead will always be green in my memory, and their deeds be hallowed in my recollection." Later, to one of his former officers, Lee voiced his opinion that the war should be forgotten, and it was best to "aid our noble and generous women in their efforts to protect the graves...of those who have fallen, and wait for better times." When it came specifically to his men entombed at Gettysburg, Lee at first was not "in favor of disturbing the ashes of the dead, unless for a worthy object, and I know of no fitter resting-place for a soldier than the field on which

he has nobly laid down his life." In time, however, General Lee came to soften his stance on this belief when he learned "that the Confederates were being neglected at Gettysburg." He said, "If the people of the States are ready to receive these remains, it is but right and proper that they should be returned there for final interment, and it would be a source of gratification to the people of the States to be thus able to care for their dead."[18]

General Lee's adversary at Gettysburg, General George G. Meade, had his own feelings about what to do about the Confederate dead on the historic battlefield. In a speech delivered in the summer of 1869, General Meade asked that his "feeble voice" be added to the debate on the subject.

When I contemplate this field, I see here and there marked with hastily dug trenches the graves in which the dead with whom we fought are gathered.... Above them a bit of plank indicates simply that these remains of the fallen foe were hurriedly laid there by the soldiers who met them in battle. Why should we not collect them in some suitable place?... Some persons may be designated...to collect these neglected bones and bury them without commemorative monuments, but simply indicate that below sleep the misguided men who fell in battle for a cause over which we triumphed.[19]

Elsewhere in his remarks, Meade made a reference to using the government's resources if necessary to complete this task. Nothwithstanding, when all was said and done, the Federal government never became involved in this controversy. But in an odd way, the Commonwealth of Pennsylvania did. In 1871, Major Henry Kyd Douglas, an ex-Confederate soldier who had once been a staff officer under General Thomas "Stonewall" Jackson, and had suffered a wound near Culp's Hill during the battle, came to Pennsylvania. He lobbied for a bill to be introduced in the legislature that would appropriate funds to have "all the confederate soldiers interred at Gettysburg and other points in Adams and Franklin counties...removed to Washington Cemetery located in Hagerstown, Maryland and properly buried." The legislature acted on the bill and voted to set aside $3,000 to be disbursed for that purpose. In the end, nothing ever came of this good gesture, because by 1871, other plans which had earlier been put into motion, finally began to take shape to solve the problem forever.[20]

The rise of the "Ladies Memorial Associations" throughout the South had a huge impact on how individual Southerners viewed deceased Confederate soldiers in their midst, and elsewhere. But for these societies, which brought attention to the plight of the dead, most citizens would probably have quickly put the war and its casualties out of sight and out of mind. Within a relatively short time following the war's end, these groups began to raise money and pressure state governments to allocate funds for the removal of Southern soldiers from the Gettysburg community. Since Samuel Weaver had always shown respect for the Confederate dead, and had the experience necessary to complete the task, (he had disinterred more than 3,500 Union soldiers from the field to the new national cemetery), in 1870, he was called upon to assist in this endeavor. After meeting personally with several women from Charleston, South Carolina, and Baltimore, and overcoming various difficulties that presented themselves on the battlefield itself, Weaver was ready to begin work on this complicated and challenging project. Unfortunately, before he could start the actual disinterments, a freak railroad accident took his life on February 10, 1871.

In the wake of this unexpected setback, the members of the Charleston association turned to Weaver's thirty-year-old son, Dr. Rufus Weaver. Although disinterested at first in their proposition because of his own busy career, Dr. Weaver was definitely qualified to undertake such a difficult business. He was a medical doctor with specialized training in the human anatomy, and had access to his father's notes and records. He was also familiar with the environs of Gettysburg and its battlefield and surrounding farms, because it was his community, and he had assisted his father during the Union reinterments. But it is understandable that Dr. Weaver would have preferred to turn from their request.

Dr. Rufus B. Weaver.

(ACHS)

In 1862, after graduating from Pennsylvania College, Rufus Weaver immediately went to work to obtain a Master of Arts degree, which he completed in 1865. In that same year, Weaver enrolled in a special course in practical anatomy at the University of Pennsylvania. (His interest in this subject may well be traced back to the year he watched his father inventory the bones of thousands of Union soldiers). Then from 1868 through 1870, Weaver finished a general medical course at the University of Pennsylvania, and a clinical course at the Jefferson Medical College. Furthermore, between 1865 and 1869, Dr. Weaver was a Demonstrator of Anatomy at The Pennsylvania Medical School, and a Prosector of Anatomy at the Hahnemann Medical College in Philadelphia. In 1869 he married Madeline L. Bender, and at the time his father died, after years of study, he was just settling into his teaching profession.[21]

When the pressure to accommodate the wishes of several of these associations did not subside, Dr. Weaver finally consented in early 1871 to gather the remains of the dead. Therefore, during the spring, summer and early fall of that year, when his teaching duties were not as heavy, Dr. Weaver collected and shipped 385 skeletons to the South. On May 10, 1871, seventy-four of these remains arrived in Charleston by ship from Baltimore for the Ladies Memorial Association of that city. All were South Carolinians who were recovered from the Gettysburg battlefield and the military hospital cemetery in Chester, Pennsylvania. The majority were reinterred in Charleston's Magnolia Cemetery. Later, on August 21, and September 24, another 101 remains of Georgians killed at Gettysburg, sent by Dr. Weaver, were reburied in Laurel Grove Cemetery, under the direction of the Ladies Memorial Association of Savannah, Georgia. And by October, Dr. Weaver had directed 137 sets of remains to Raleigh, North Carolina, to be buried in Oakwood Cemetery by the members of the Wake County Ladies Memorial Association. This shipment was made up exclusively of men from the Old North State. An association member described their plight thusly: "The thirsty soil of Gettysburg drank in some of the best blood of North Carolina...." During that same summer, 73 individual soldiers, also part of the 385, were boxed and delivered to their families in Maryland and elsewhere in the South. In all likelihood, Dr. Weaver was probably responsible for the bulk of those shipments as well. All of the arrivals of the crated remains from Gettysburg were attended by large and respectful parades and ceremonies at each of the three cemeteries named above. Dr. Weaver's fee for the labor of disinterment, the box itself, the shipment cost, record keeping, and his professional expertise in sort-

This section in Magnolia Cemetery holds the 74 South Carolina dead sent there by Dr. Weaver in 1871.

Oakwood Cemetery in Raleigh, where 137 North Carolina dead are interred.

(AMN)

(RG)

ing and identifying each set of bones, probably added up to about $3.25 per body, which is what he later quoted to the secretary of the Hollywood Memorial Association of the Ladies of Richmond.[22]

It was no easy task for Dr. Weaver to locate, exhume, box, and ship 385 soldiers' remains to cities and other lesser known localities throughout the South. The work was complicated, hot, and dirty, and often had to be rushed to beat the spring plantings. Dr. Weaver frequently toiled 15 to 20 hours a day. He and his crew generally started their labors before daybreak, because so much had to be accomplished ahead of the farmers coming to their fields. Dr. Weaver personally supervised the opening of each grave and handled all of the remains himself. "In the absence of boxes," [coffins], said Dr. Weaver, "it required one with Anatomical Knowledge, to gather all the bones;...and, regarding each bone important and sacred as an integral part of the skeleton, I removed them so that none might be left or lost." In the evening, after mealtime, Dr. Weaver arranged, labeled, and then wrote out a permanent record of every grave uncovered that day.[23]

There were other problems too. On some farms, the landowners refused to allow the bodies to be carried away without cash changing hands. Dr. Weaver generally did not succumb to these extortions and called such actions "depraved and degraded." But at one homestead north of Gettysburg, Dr. Weaver met his match in the guise of a young farmer named V. Oliver Blocher. When the bones of Lt. Col. David Winn, 4th Georgia, were exhumed, Blocher kept for himself "a gold plate and teeth" from that officer's skull. He would not let Winn's family have the dental set unless he was paid ten dollars. After making several futile trips to see Blocher and his father, David, to attempt to persuade them to give up the gold plate, Dr. Weaver finally re-

lented and paid five dollars to close the deal. The plate was then sent to Georgia to join the colonel's bones. Needless to say, this story found its way into the press, where David and Oliver Blocher received fairly harsh treatment. Words like "foul, faithless wretche[s]," "barbaric and unprincipled greediness," and "vile scum of humanity," were used freely to describe the actions and the character of these two Pennsylvania agriculturists.[24]

(DWV)

(RG)

Lt. Col. Winn was finally sent home after nearly 10 years in the North. (Inset) Winn's grave in Laurel Grove.

21

As autumn approached in that first year of exhumations, and after Dr. Weaver had concluded his shipments to Savannah, Raleigh, Charleston and elsewhere, he set aside time to catch up on correspondence he was too busy to answer over the summer. One of the letters Dr. Weaver penned stands out for the information it provides on future activities he hoped to pursue. The letter was dated October 9, 1871, and was addressed to the secretary of the Ladies Memorial Association of Savannah. In it Dr. Weaver makes the comment that he trusts her organization "will be able to procure aid enough to enable you to send for your unknown dead in the spring. I will be engaged in [Philadelphia] until early spring when I will be happy to return the remaining comrades to their native soil. I have sent to Raleigh about 140 North Carolina remains, and anticipate exhuming all her unknown dead next spring." From these words, we can see that Dr. Weaver's early work for the three associations involved only "known" or identified Confederates from Georgia, North Carolina, and South Carolina. In the same letter, he attempts to "drum up" support for continuing these efforts, which would give himself more business, by drawing into the equation one of Georgia's sister states from the extinct Confederacy.

"It seems very strange to me," mused the doctor, "that Virginia who is so near and whose known list is not so great as yours[,] does not recall her dead. I have learned that they [have] ample means to accomplish the work and not to do so is paying a very poor and uncharitable compliment to her dead. I have sent South all the State lists and none but you, N. C. & S. C. have done anything. None of the others have even taken account of the lists as far as I know. If all could see what I have seen and know what I know, I am sure that there would be no rest until every Southern father, brother and son would be removed from the North."

In closing his remarks, Dr. Weaver expressed that he "was especially gratified...to hear that all I have done has been approved by you and that all the work most conscientiously done by me has gained your confidence.... Please let me hear of the boxes as I am desirous to know how they reached you. They are always clean and neat when I give them in charge of the Steamer Co."[25]

The inclusion of Virginia's dead in the mission to return Southern remains to their homeland was not a new idea. In fact, the Hollywood Memorial Association of the Ladies of Richmond had, for some time, been hard at work trying to raise funds to attend to this duty. The Virginia General Assembly assisted the organization by appropriating $1,000 for the project. But it was not enough. The $3.25 per body needed by Dr. Weaver

to provide his services, made it necessary for the Memorial Association to collect more money. Voluntary contributions from the public helped, but fell far from the goal. Despite this shortfall of cash, which would come back to haunt both parties, the secretary of the Hollywood Association wrote to Dr. Weaver on November 8, 1871. In this letter, Elizabeth Brown told the doctor that her organization was "now ready to enter into arrangements & make contracts for the removal of the Confederate Virginia soldiers from Gettysburg to Richmond." Yet prior to the settlement of a final agreement between Dr. Weaver and the Hollywood Cemetery people, a change was made which further complicated the mediations. Since their earlier talks, the women of the association decided they wanted to have removed, not just the Virginians, but *all* of the Southerners still buried at Gettysburg.

In the meantime, Dr. Weaver, anxious to fix a solid contract with the Richmond group, sent ahead in February, 1872, the names of 400 Confederates he was prepared to collect and ship to Hollywood as soon as the weather permitted. This number was only an inconsiderable portion of the bodies still in the ground, but it may have been his subtle way to get them to act. The agreement had to be finalized, because if the digging did not begin soon, crops would be planted, and the farmers would deter any invasion of their fields.

Since the association's treasury contained only $4,000, it needed to know the amount of money that would have to be forthcoming to complete the project. To figure the total, a true count of the Confederates still buried at Gettysburg was critical. To obtain a firsthand appraisal, the association sent Charles Dimmock, an engineer and former captain in the Confederate Army, to Pennsylvania to study the situation. After an extensive tour of the battlefield and its surroundings, Captain Dimmock reported that there were approximately 2,500 remains to be exhumed. This meant the association officers needed to raise a minimum of $8,000 to pay Dr. Weaver upon completion of the shipments. That news must have come as a shock, but what was most influential in the outcome of these negotiations, was what Captain Dimmock had to reveal about the condition of many of the graves and burial trenches he had visited. All over the countryside, Dimmock was saddened to find mistreatment and outright desecration of hundreds of Confederate remains, where in places, the sun-bleached and crumbling bones of Southern soldiers lay everywhere exposed to view. Dimmock's startling discovery, and his praise for the reputation of Dr. Weaver, eventually won over any hesitations on the part of the Hollywood Memorial Association. With no further delay, the doctor was instructed to begin work, commencing immediately with the soldiers who were still identified. As additional funds became available, Dr. Weaver could continue his operations by recovering the graves of the unknowns. This order came none too soon, because the spring of 1872 was then in full bloom.[26]

For the next two years, from April 19 to September 10, 1872, and from April 9 to October 3, 1873, Dr. Weaver and his team opened graves and gathered Confederate remains. The majority of the work proceeded much as it had in 1871. The conditions were about the same, and Dr. Weaver was still periodically troubled by farmers trying to exploit families for payment, by holding hostage the bones of their relatives. His only real impediment though, was the elusive factor of time. Dr. Weaver was always restricted by too much to do, and too few hours in a day. He always understood one thing — once the crops began to grow, it would be nigh unto impossible to get into the fields to retrieve remains. Nonetheless, along with these daily chores and problems, there must have been an element of mystery and fascination hovering over all. And surely there was the satisfaction gained by doing good deeds for people who were still uncertain of the fate of a beloved father, son, husband, or brother. Correspondingly, just the process of opening each and every grave had to be interesting for a specialist in anatomy. But perhaps the job sometimes lost its excitement, when we consider how grim and mundane it may have become even to unlock the secrets of thousands of sealed tombs. Yet the dead always beckoned. The burial trenches, some containing upwards of 20 to 40 soldiers, were certainly a challenge. Over almost ten years, the individual bones became jumbled and tangled in the rotting uniforms and creeping roots of plants and trees. Around and amongst the damp clothing and broken skulls, cracked ribs, and encrusted femurs and other bones, were the little trinkets of what remained of the lives of so many young men. There were tarnished and dented brass buttons;

One of the Confederate burial trenches opened by Dr. Weaver southeast of Gettysburg.

pocket knives; coins; ragged chunks and pieces of letters; diaries, and testaments; percussion caps; an occasional belt buckle or timepiece; combs and toothbrushes; a rusty and dented canteen; and once, a whole musket; and, of course, bullets. The bullets were always there because most of these fellows had been infantrymen — fighting soldiers who had carried weapons and ammunition. But the shallow, musty graves held in them other bullets too, and jagged shell fragments, which told not of lives lived, but of death and destruction, and lives lost. For inevitably, the skeletons enshrouded what had killed them, whether bullet or shell, lead or iron. The bones almost always gave up the history, the last moments of a man. This history could be traced by unnatural holes, by scrapes and cracks and indentations that marred the otherwise smooth surfaces of the once-living material. Dr. Weaver missed none of it. He knew their stories; he could have told their tales. But the doctor chose never to write of it, of this phase, the physiology and psychology of violent death. His men opened the graves, and he collected, and sorted, and labeled, and packed the bones, all that was left of the "sacred machine," and he let it go at that.

Over the eleven or so months of 1872 and 1873 that Dr. Weaver was employed by the Hollywood Memorial Association, he prepared six separate shipments which traveled from Gettysburg to Richmond. All of the bones were packed into wooded boxes or crates. Identified soldiers, about 300, were placed in small, individual boxes. The larger boxes were big enough to hold, on the average, about 10 or 12 sets of remains. Eventually, approximately 2,600 Confederates made the trip to Virginia in these oversized boxes. The bigger crates normally contained the "unknowns." Sometimes "identified" soldiers were also included in these larger boxes. Weaver knew this, but since he could not tell them apart from the unknowns, he labeled them as such, within the collective.

The six shipments to Richmond, and the dates they left Gettysburg, are listed below. Included is the fee owed to Dr. Weaver for each lot.

Number 1.	June 13, 1872	708 remains	$2,300
Number 2.	August 3, 1872	882 remains	$2,866
Number 3.	September 10, 1872	683 remains	$2,219
Number 4.	May 17, 1873	333 remains	$1,082
Number 5.	June 28, 1873	256 remains	$ 832
Number 6.	October 11, 1873	73 remains	$ 237
Total		2,935 remains	$9,536 [27]

When he started the exhumations in mid-April, Dr. Weaver had hoped to deliver the first shipment of boxes to the officers of the association by May 15, 1872, in time for Richmond's Memorial Day. Unable

The section for Gettysburg's Confederate dead in Hollywood Cemetery.

to meet this deadline, the doctor persisted hard at work to complete two more shipments before fall. By the end of October, Weaver had returned to Philadelphia to resume his teaching duties at the medical college. At this juncture in his career, he had accomplished a great deal for the Southern people. Besides the remains sent to Charleston, Raleigh, Savannah, and elsewhere in 1871, Dr. Weaver had, in 1872, forwarded more than 2,200 additional bodies to Richmond. Regretfully, most of his labors went monetarily unrewarded. Previously, the Hollywood Association had sent a payment of $2,800, but by the close of the year, they still owed Weaver $4,585.

Curiously, this debt did not appear to have concerned Dr. Weaver when he began a new round of exhumations in the spring of 1873. But as the obligation grew, so did the association's inability to pay. The organization lost its confidence and slowly began to disintegrate following the early 1873 death of Captain Dimmock, who had been a steadying influence on the group. The stability of the organization was further affected when most of its funds disappeared "through mishandling by the firm entrusted to look after them." It is plain that the busy doctor never really knew how bad the situation had become. Even though he was somewhat aware of the associations plight, Dr. Weaver must have thought it temporary, for he persevered

with the shipments through October. But things never got better. By the end of 1873, he was still owed over $6,000 from the Hollywood Memorial Association, which, by then, was essentially defunct. And because the group had never been incorporated, that left no future chance for a legal settlement. Therefore, Dr. Weaver, for all intents and purposes, had to give up any claim for reimbursement.[28]

Although Dr. Weaver hardly expected to ever see his money, one can feel from the following words that apparently the doctor never forgot the sting of the loss he was forced to accept. This comes through in his reply to an 1887 letter from Dr. John O'Neal. Dr. O'Neal had written earlier to question Dr. Weaver in regard to an appeal from the family of Captain J.H. Moore, 11th Mississippi, a Gettysburg fatality. Dr. O'Neal had first sought help from the old Hollywood Association, but it was uncooperative. After giving Dr. O'Neal the information he needed, Dr. Weaver added these comments:

"However, I can understand all lack of interest in such inquiries, and so can you, when I tell you that the Association yet owe me, for that great work, including interest, over ($11,000) eleven thousand dollars! You have had an extensive correspondence with the friends of the Confederate dead and I judge that, from your acquaintance with many prominent personages of the South, most probably you might be just the one to exercise a favorable consideration in behalf of my interest in the above debt." Coincidentally, several years after this letter was composed, the old Hollywood Association was reactivated, and Weaver resubmitted his claim. Not unexpectedly, the members were astonished at the size of the bill, which few of them even knew existed. But in fairness to their memory, the association did try to satisfy the delinquent account, and in the end paid Dr. Weaver a portion of the debt.[29]

There is no evidence that Dr. O'Neal, who died April 24, 1913, was able to assist his old friend in any further recovery. So for his years of dedication and service, in honor of the thousands of Confederates he saved from oblivion at Gettysburg, Dr. Weaver went to his grave on July 14, 1936, still owed considerable money. Hopefully, the appreciation the good doctor received from the families he helped in bringing their boys home, was enough to offset the distress he felt at such a lingering injustice.

"Gather the corpses strewn
O'er many a battle plain;
From many a grave that lies so lone,
Without a name and without a stone,
Gather the Southern slain."[30]

NOTES

1. Rufus B. Weaver, Title quote from a letter to Mrs. E.L. Campbell of Savannah, Ga., dated Philadelphia, Oct. 9, 1871, in the files of the Gettysburg National Military Park library. Hereafter cited as "GNMP."

Judith W.B. McGuire, *Diary of a Southern Refugee During the War*. New York, N.Y., 1867. The quote is in the entry for July 14, 1863.

2. Joaquin Miller.

3. Maud C. Clement, *War Recollections of the Confederate Veterans of Pittsylvania County Virginia, 1861-1865*. Account by Pattie Booker Tredway Watson. Lynchburg, Va., c. 1960, pp. 83-84.

4. James K.P. Scott, *The Story of the Battles of Gettysburg*. Harrisburg, Pa., 1927, pp. 178-179.

5. Samuel Weaver, Letter to Mrs. C.B. Bedinger, dated Gettysburg, Dec. 27, 1865, in the files of the GNMP library.

6. David Wills, *Revised Report of the Select Committee Relative to the Soldiers' National Cemetery....* Harrisburg, PA, 1865, p. 149.

7. Adams (Pennsylvania) *Sentinel*. Article "Killed and Wounded," no author, issue date unknown, copy in author's files.

8. John W. C. O'Neal, Papers in the library of the GNMP, and his file and "Physician's Handbooks" in the Adams County (Pennsylvania) Historical Society (ACHS). Also, the Gettysburg *Compiler*, July 5, 1905, pp. 2-3.

9. Scott, op cit, pp. 178-179.

10. O'Neal, Letter to J.W. Southall in the C.S. burial files of the GNMP library.

11. O'Neal, Personal papers at the ACHS. Also Gettysburg *Compiler*, June 11, 1866, p. 1.

O'Neal, "List of Marked graves of Confederate Soldiers lying on the Battleground. Taken in May 1866." Original located in the archives of the GNMP.

12. Gettysburg *Times*. Article in the Dec. 3, 1943 issue.

O'Neal, "Record of Confederate Burials: The Journal of Dr. John W.C. O'Neal, M.D." Transcribed by Kathleen R. Georg (Harrison) in May 1982. Original located in the archives of the GNMP.

13. Columbus (Georgia) *Daily Enquirer*. Article in the Dec. 25, 1866 issue.

Hawkinsville (Georgia) *Dispatch*. Article in the July 6, 1871 issue.

14. Rufus B. Weaver, Letter to Mrs. R. L. Campbell, op cit.

Russell H. Conwell, (J.C. Carter, Ed.) *Magnolia Journey*. University, Ala., 1974, p. 31.

15. Denise Carper and Renae Hardoby. *The Gettysburg Battlefield Farmstead Guide*. Friends of the National Parks at Gettysburg (FNPG), Gettysburg, Pa., 2000, p. 8.

16. Gettysburg *Compiler*. Article in the April 11, 1864 issue.

17. Adams *Sentinel*. Article and poem in the March 15, 1864 issue. The poet was identified only as "A.S.M."

18. Douglas S. Freeman, *R.E. Lee, A Biography*. Vol. 4. New York, N.Y., 1962, pp. 436-437.

Confederate Veteran. Nashville, Tenn., 1901, Vol. 9, p. 198.

19. Gettysburg *Compiler*. Article in the July 16, 1869 issue.

20. Hagerstown (Maryland) *Daily News*. Article in the Feb. 21, 1876 issue, entitled, "Removal of Confederate Dead."

21. Wendy C. Burbage, "Re-interment of the South Carolina Dead from Gettysburg." *UDC Magazine*, June 1989, # 8, p. 15.

W.C. Storrick, Rufus B. Weaver's "Chronology Sheet," written Nov. 16, 1943; copy in the files of the GNMP library.

Cyrus Lieberman, Letter to the Editor, in the "Readers Forum," *Civil War Times Illustrated*. April, 1961.

22. Papers of the "Ladies Memorial Associations," of Charleston, Raleigh, Wake County, N.C., and Hollywood Cemetery of Richmond, in the archives of The Museum of the Confederacy, Richmond, Va. Copies in the GNMP library.

"Report of the Ladies Memorial Association of Raleigh, NC." # 5, 1902, p. 1. Copy in the library of the GNMP.

23. Rufus B. Weaver, Copy of a letter to Maj. Robert Stiles, March 8, 1892, in the files of the GNMP library.

24. Rufus B. Weaver, Letter to Mrs. R.L. Campbell, op cit.

Savannah Morning News. Article in the Dec. 26, 1871 issue, entitled, "A Disgraceful and Shameless Act."

25. Rufus B. Weaver, Letter to "Mrs. R.L. Campbell," op cit.

26. Mary H. Mitchell, *Hollywood Cemetery: The History of a Southern Shrine*. Richmond, Va., 1985, pp. 83-86.

Edward G. Richter, "The Removal of the Confederate Dead from Gettysburg." *Gettysburg Magazine*. Dayton, Ohio, 1990, Issue 2, pp. 114-115.

27. Storrick, "Information received...in letter from Dr. Rufus B. Weaver, (date not recalled)." Written Nov. 5, 1935. Copy at GNMP library.

Rufus B. Weaver, "Statement of Indebtedness," in his "Confederate Burial/Shipment Notes," at the archives of The Museum of the Confederacy, Richmond, Va. Copies are in the files of the GNMP library.

28. Mitchell, op cit, pp. 87, 90-92.

Richter, op cit, pp. 114-115.

Richmond *Times-Dispatch*. An article by Thomas W. Howard, entitled "Gettysburg Dead," in the Jan. 14, 1994 issue, p. E6.

29. Rufus B. Weaver, Letter to Dr. John W.C. O'Neal, written from Philadelphia and dated Feb. 19, 1887. A copy of the original, then in the possession of O'Neal's daughter, Mrs. J.T. Huddle, was made by Frederick Tilberg, Nov. 11, 1943; a duplicate of his copy is in the files of the GNMP library.

Richmond *Times-Dispatch*. Thomas Howard article, op cit. The exact figure Weaver was paid is unknown, but it may have been about $4,000.

30. Father A.J. Ryan, "The Deathless Dead." Third stanza of the poem. *Confederate Veteran*. Nashville, Tenn., 1900, Vol. 8, p. 504

SUGGESTED READING

For further information on the subject of the removals of Confederate remains from Pennsylvania, the following books and articles could be helpful and are recommended.

Coco, Gregory A. "Wasted Valor: The Confederate Dead at Gettysburg." *Gettysburg Magazine*. Dayton, Ohio, July 1, 1990, Issue 3, p. 95.

Coco, Gregory A. *Wasted Valor: The Confederate Dead at Gettysburg*. Gettysburg, Pa., 1990.

Krick, Robert K. *The Gettysburg Death Roster*. Dayton, Ohio, 1993.

Mitchell, Mary H. *Hollywood Cemetery: The Story of a Southern Shrine*. Richmond, Va., 1985.

Richter, Edward G. "The Removal of the Confederate Dead From Gettysburg." *Gettysburg Magazine*. Dayton, Ohio, Jan. 1, 1990, Issue 2, p. 115.

The grave of Capt. William W. McCreery,
Assistant Inspector General, Pettigrew's Brigade,
killed in action July 1, 1863.
Oakwood Cemetery, Raleigh, NC.

II

Where Defeated Valor Lies

"Gather their scattered clay,
Wherever it may rest;
Just as they marched to the bloody fray —
Just as they fell on the battle day —
Bury them breast to breast."

A. J. Ryan

THIS roster of the identified Confederate burials of Gettysburg was, in the main, compiled using Robert Krick's "Gettysburg Death Roster," Kathy Harrison's "Confederate Burials at Gettysburg: A Compilation," Dr. John O'Neal's "Journal of Confederate Burials" and his "Physician Handbooks," and Dr. Rufus Weaver's burial site notes and shipment lists. For a long time, I have collected information on known Confederate burials anywhere it could be found. Some of those sources include the various state and federal military service rosters now in print, also the standard published Civil War works on diaries, letters, memoirs and regimental histories, as well as many unpublished manuscripts, all too numerous to mention. This roster is fundamentally a useful source, but I'm certain it needs additional work to make it more complete and accurate. After much consideration, it would appear that the task to make such a list flawless is probably an impossible one due to the inherent nature of the subject. Consequently, a perfect record will doubtfully ever be accomplished.

The following roster of Southern soldiers is an attempt to give the researcher an alphabetical listing of the correct name, rank, initial burial, and final interment of about 1,400 out of approximately 5,000 men who died as a result of the Battle of Gettysburg. This roll covers *only* the Confederates whose *graves were marked or identified* by their comrades, on the field or in hospitals, or by federal authorities who buried the corpses if they did not survive their wounds while in U.S. hands. The roster also registers the age and date of death, if known. Be forewarned, this data was often difficult or impossible to obtain or confirm and, therefore, is highly suspect. Finally, where some particular quote was pertinent to a soldier or his grave site, it was included for the "human interest" content. If additional space were available, more of this personal material could have been added, such as the type of wound, last words, etc.

To guide the reader through the roster, and to gain more from its composition, an orientation may prove helpful.

☞ To begin, as mentioned earlier, there will be inaccuracies found within the list. For instance, where a soldier's name or unit was written by Dr. O'Neal, Dr. Weaver, or any other compiler, and could not be found to match the military record, an attempt was made to try and identify the man or his regiment. Full responsibility is accepted for mistakes resulting from this process. If anyone can correct any of these errors, please write to me via Thomas Publications.

☞ The title of this roster, "Where Defeated Valor Lies," comes from a line in the 1867 poem, *Ode At Magnolia Cemetery*, by Henry Timrod.

☞ All dates are in the 1800s, unless otherwise specified.

☞ The diamond symbol ♦ lets the reader know to go to Appendix I for auxiliary information on the soldier.

☞ For descriptions of some of the Gettysburg area burial sites mentioned in the roster, as well as their locations, see Appendix III.

☞ Dr. Weaver's shipment "Box Numbers and Letters" should be explained. In Part I, it was demonstrated that when Dr. Weaver sent the 2,965 remains to Hollywood Cemetery in Richmond, he placed them in small, individual, wooden boxes, and larger "collective" boxes. Each box was numbered, such as "1-171." The "1" stands for the shipment date, which in this illustration was June 13, 1871. The second figure, "171" is the soldier's personal identifying number, which here was Pvt. Robert Steele, 5th Virginia. If a third number is present, it is merely a way to isolate each soldier within a group. Boxes with "4-Y," "2-C-Miss," or the like, are used basically the same way. Except in these cases, they are collective designations. That is, several remains were shipped together in one box or boxes. As a means to an end, the box marks were also expected to aid people at Hollywood in finding the grave of an individual soldier or one containing several sets of remains. Within Dr. Weaver's papers there is a crude diagram of the Gettysburg section of that cemetery. It appears that by using Dr. Weaver's method, one could presumably locate a relative or friend, or at least get fairly close to the piece of ground he lay in. Admittedly, his system was confusing and more complicated than necessary; this was probably due to his use of identical letters or numbers in the various shipments, even though the dates were different. Today, one may visit the Gettysburg Section, which is in the north end of the cemetery, and stand in a sea of small stone markers. Many of these stones have designations on them which correspond to Dr. Weaver's inventory structure.

☞ This brings us to what are called the "State Lots." Dr. Weaver often found areas where, for example, ten men had been buried, and at one time the graves were all marked. Then, for some reason, the headboards or other markers were destroyed or removed, or the site was plowed over. In this situation, the doctor wrote in his ledger, "List of those whose graves can be identified but not separately. These can be packed in boxes, each box having marks on it to indicate, from the list which will be sent, the respective remains in each box. These are buried in separate 'state' lots and not promiscuously." The soldiers who ended up on Dr. Weaver's "state lots," are designated as such in the roster.

☞ Since the names and locations of all identified Confederates were first kept in the personal notes of Samuel Weaver, Dr. O'Neal, and Dr. Weaver, this roster could have either kept that information in their own words, or paraphrased the data contained therein. I chose to paraphrase most of their material to save space and to make it easier to understand. However, anything in quotation marks duplicates the exact words or phrases they used.

☞ You will note the use of the words "possibly" and "probably" in describing many burial sites. When very sure that the site was correct, "probably" was inserted. When only "pretty sure" of the accuracy, "possibly" was the choice.

☞ Within the roster are the names of a few Confederates whose bones are specimens in the National Museum of Health and Medicine. Most of these human artifacts are located in the Otis Historical Archives, of the Armed Forces Institute of Pathology, in Washington, D.C.

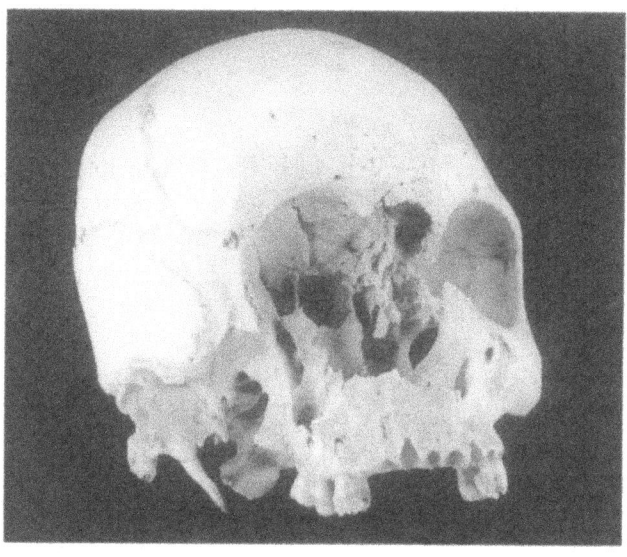

(NMHM)

The skull of Gibson Bowles, 42nd Virginia, is now in a museum. The rest of his skeleton is at Mt. Olivet Cemetery, Frederick, Md.

☞ In a rare instance, a soldier might be designated with two first names such as "Richard or Samuel Manning." This lets you know it was not possible to tell which man occupied that particular grave. Usually both were casualties, and the original name on the headboard was indistinct. Similarly, a soldier may be designated with two final burial sites, as in the examples of Private Stone, and Captains Burkhalter and Stamps. This could indicate the man was later moved to a second location, or, simply, a mistake was made. For instance, Captain Stamps was returned to Mississippi in December, 1863 by his wife, Mary. In 1872, Dr. Weaver reported that he sent the captain's remains to Richmond in Box 2-C. Probably what happened, was that nine years later when Dr. Weaver saw the discarded original headboard at the site, he assumed that one of the bodies in the ground nearby belonged to Captain Stamps.

Two of the small burial lot markers in Hollywood Cemetery that indicate box inventory numbers used by Dr. Weaver.

☞ This roster is mainly concerned with the known Confederate burials of the Battle of Gettysburg. But the reader will encounter the names of casualties from actions at Hanover, Hunterstown, and Fairfield, Pennsylvania, also Westminster, Frederick, Hagerstown, Falling Waters, and Williamsport, Maryland. Since these skirmishes were part of the Gettysburg Campaign, some of the dead are included so that researchers may benefit ·from that information as well.

☞ Incorporated within the roster are the names of Confederates believed to have been inadvertently buried by Samuel Weaver as Union soldiers in the Gettysburg U.S. National Cemetery. It is likely this happened. After all, Dr. Rufus Weaver mistakenly sent a couple of Federal soldiers to Hollywood Cemetery categorized as Southern remains, such as Marylander John H. Jester. Naturally, it is impossible now to verify, with any certainty, if these soldiers in the National Cemetery are indeed Confederates.

☞ Between 1872 and 1873, Dr. Weaver transferred six shipments to Richmond, totaling 2,935 remains. We have his records for four of these lots. Unfortunately, the paperwork on the last two shipments, Numbers five and six, has been lost. The total number of remains in shipments five and six, was 329, but the sites from which they were removed, and the identities of any, are not known. These men could have come from about 20 areas that had Confederate burials present, but evidenced no recoveries. Some of those places included the Almshouse, Camp Letterman, and Bream's Mill, and the farms of Adam Butt, George Culp, John Slyder, Jonathan Young, George Bushman, Samuel Johns, and Michael and John Crist. Finally, the missing fifth and sixth shipments' lists may have held the names of many of the 230-plus Southerners who once had marked graves, but are not presently on Dr. Weaver's catalog as ever having been disinterred as identifiable remains.

In conclusion, the reader should know that the following roster will be adjusted as new material becomes available. Any information that can add to, or correct any burial, will be thankfully accepted. Just mail your facts to me in care of Thomas Publications. If you just have a question about the roster, please include a self-addressed, stamped envelope, for a reply. Thank you.

Greg Coco

This may be the grave of Eli Green, 14th Virginia, in the U.S. National Cemetery at Gettysburg.

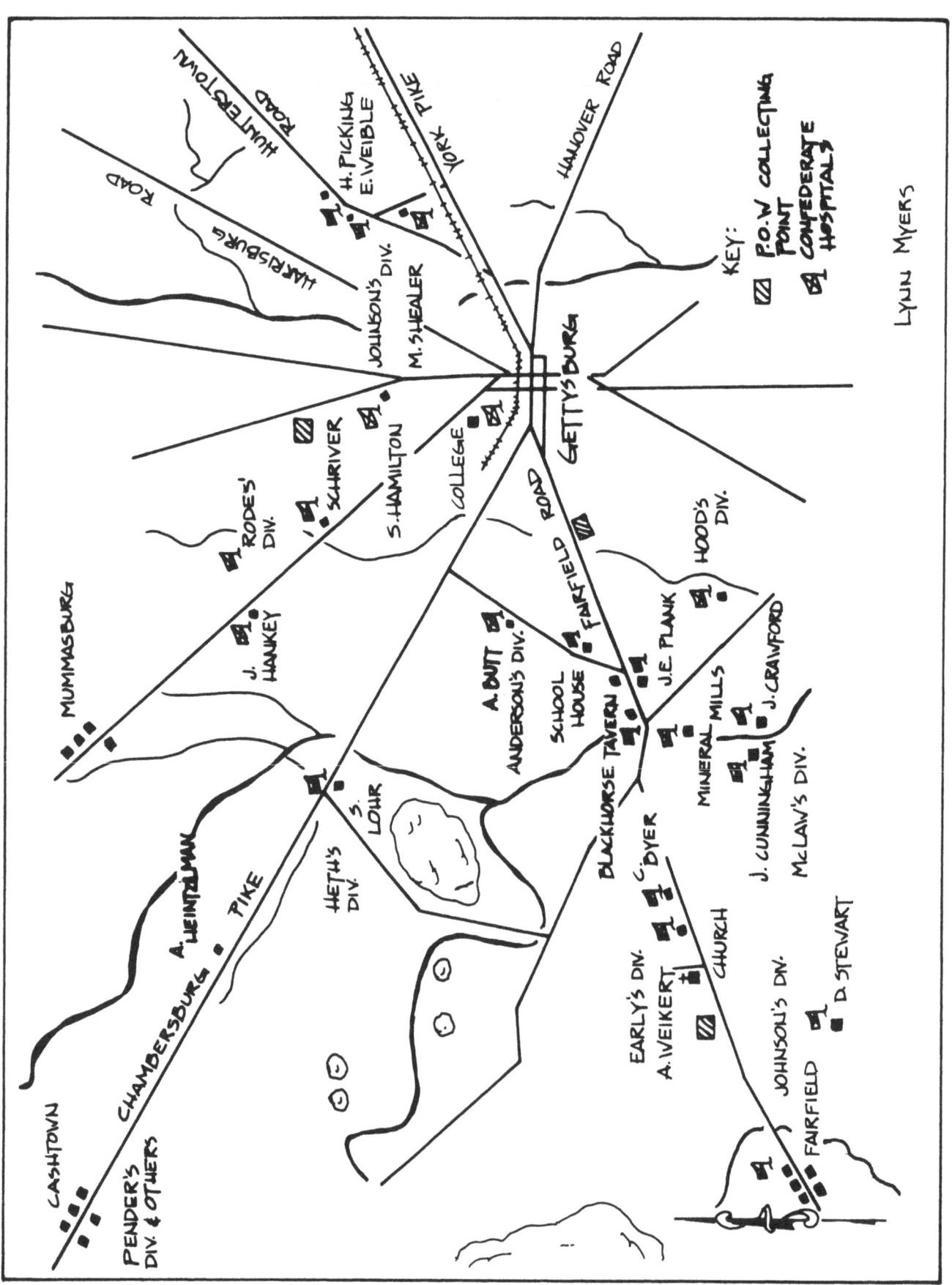

LYNN MYERS

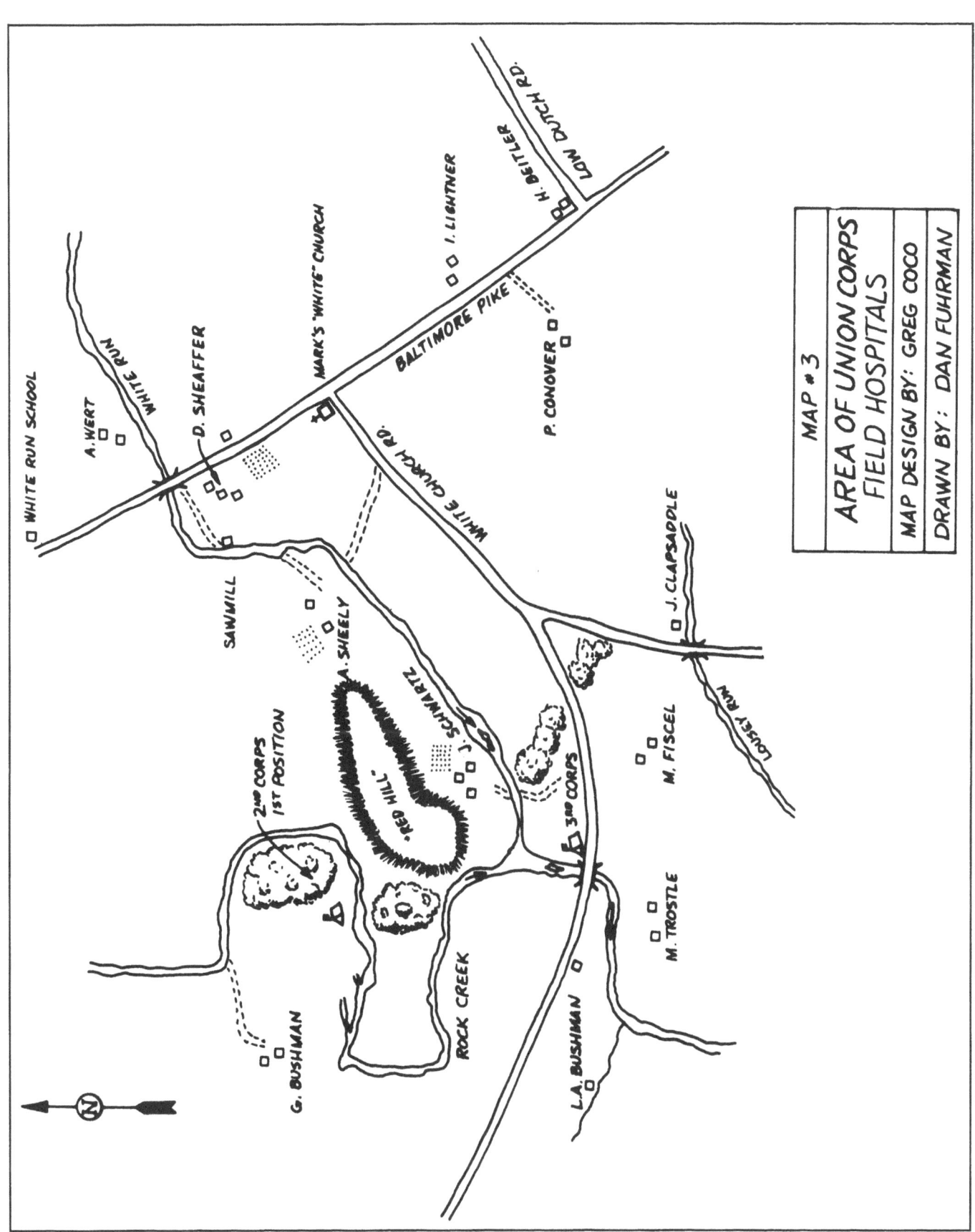

MAP #3

AREA OF UNION CORPS
FIELD HOSPITALS

MAP DESIGN BY: GREG COCO

DRAWN BY: DAN FUHRMAN

31

(RG)

The grave of Maj. Donald McLeod, 8th South Carolina Infantry,
Parnassus Methodist Church, Marlboro Co., SC.

The Roster

of

Gettysburg's Identified

Confederate Burials

NAME	RANK	AGE	CO.	UNIT REGT.	DEATH	BATTLEFIELD or INITIAL BURIAL	FINAL INTERMENT
A							
AARON, Edward S.	PVT		G	3rd GA		Adam Butt's brick schoolhouse on Fairfield Road	Laurel Grove, Savannah, Lot 853, Grave 12, 9/24/71
ADAIR, Alexander	PVT		I	4th VA	d. July 25	Camp Letterman Cemetery	
ADAMS, Duncan L.F.	PVT	22	A	55th NC	d. Sept. 20 U.S. Gen. Hosp. Chester, PA	Chester Rural Cemetery, Chester, PA	Philadelphia National Cemetery, 1891; his left tibia and fibula are in the National Museum of Health and Medicine, Specimen #3728
ADAMS, Edwin Thomas	LT		D	8th VA	d. July 18	Jacob Schwartz's farm, in cornfield on Rock Creek, Yard D, Row 1	Box 1-S-23, Hollywood, Richmond, 6/13/72
ADAMS, Elijah	SGT	24	G	8th SC	d. July 15	Francis Bream's farm, north of tavern, near graveyard and creek	Magnolia, Charleston, Grave 44, 5/10/71
ADAMS, Harris R.	LT		G	8th SC	k. July 2	George Rose's farm, back or north of stone barn	Box 1-165, Hollywood, Richmond, 6/13/72
ADAMS, James	PVT		A	13th MS		John S. Crawford's farm, "where Basil Biggs lives;" in garden	Box 4-Y, Hollywood, Richmond, 5/17/73
ADAMS, J.T.	PVT	34	A	14th LA	d. Oct. 2	Camp Letterman, Row 7, Grave 26; "body removed by friends"	Box 1-56, Hollywood, Richmond, 6/13/72
ADERHOLT, Jacob E.	PVT	33	D	55th NC	d. July 30	Camp Letterman, Row 2, Grave 20	Oakwood, Raleigh, 10/1/71
ADKINS, John O.	PVT		E	38th VA		Francis Bream's mill; "on the hill from Bream's Mill"	Box 2-P-Currns, Hollywood, Richmond, 8/3/72, with 33 others
ADKINS, William H.	1SGT		E	53rd NC	k. July 2	Elizabeth Shultz's house, on Seminary Ridge nearby; also, J.E. Culp's field, which was in the vicinity	Oakwood, Raleigh, 10/1/71
ADKINSON, Benjamin	PVT		B	8th SC	k. July 2	George Rose's farm, back or north of stone barn	Box 1-148, Hollywood, Richmond, 6/13/72
AGEE, Alexander	PVT		D	37th VA	d. July 13	Martin Shealer's farm, in meadow next to Elizabeth Wible's	Box 3-V, Hollywood, Richmond, with 11 others, 9/10/72
AKERS, James L.	PVT	18	K	2nd MS	k. July 3		Believed by some to be buried in the Gettysburg National Cemetery, Pa. Plot D-26, as "John Aker"
ALBRIGHT, George M.G.	CPT	36	F	53rd NC	d. July 16 U.S. Gen. Hosp. Frederick, MD	None	Mt. Olivet Cemetery, Frederick, MD, Grave 204
ALDRIDGE, George L.	CPL	22	G	15th LA		W. Henry Monfort's farm; "left in enemy hands"	Box 3-M, Hollywood, Richmond, with 7 others, 9/10/72
ALEXANDER, Julius J.	LT		B	43rd NC	d. July 18	Jacob Plank's farm, back of barn, Grave 12	Box 3-P, Hollywood, Richmond, 9/10/72
ALLAN, John	ADJ	32	F&S	6th VA CAV	k. July 3 Fairfield, PA	None	His corpse was "delivered to his father in Baltimore, MD by a citizen of Fairfield for $500"
ALLEN, Albert L.	PVT		A	16th GA	d. July 13	Michael Fiscel's farm, east of house, across creek; "east side of woods;" "of Cobb's Legion"	Box 3-A, Hollywood, Richmond, 9/10/72
ALLEN, Francis Marion	LT	34	D	48th GA	k. July 2	Confederate lines, "right center;" "buried by Capt. McFadden"	

Name	Rank	Age	Co.	Unit	Death	Location	Burial
ALLEN, W. Riley	PVT		E	2nd SC	k. July 2	George Rose's farm, back of barn under cherry tree	Magnolia, Charleston, Grave 16, 5/10/71
ALLEY, Daniel S.	PVT		F	11th VA	d. July 29	Camp Letterman, Row 1, Grave 3	Box 1-54, Hollywood, Richmond, 6/13/72
ALLEY, Isaiah D.	PVT	22	F	47th NC	d. Aug. 14	Camp Letterman, Row 5, Grave 6	Oakwood, Raleigh, Grave 458, 10/1/71
AMES, Benjamin F.	CPL	28	F	3rd VA	d. July 3	Francis Bream's mill above William Myers's house by the side of the house	Box 2-P-Cums, Hollywood, Richmond, 8/3/72, with 33 others
AMICK, Draton J.	PVT	18	I	15th SC	d. July 22 Seminary Hosp. Hagerstown, MD	Probably Old Almshouse Burying Ground, Hagerstown, MD	Probably in "Rose Hill," Washington Cemetery, Hagerstown, MD
AMICK, Elijah R.	PVT	20	C	15th SC	d. Sept. 6	Camp Letterman, Row 7, Grave 18	Magnolia, Charleston, Grave 10, 5/10/71
AMOS, James M.	CPL		L	21st NC	d. July 27 Seminary Hosp. Hagerstown, MD	Probably Old Almshouse Burying Ground, Hagerstown, MD	Probably in "Rose Hill," Washington Cemetery, Hagerstown, MD
ANDERSON, James W.	PVT	28	H	47th VA	d. Oct. 3	Camp Letterman, Row 8, Grave 33	Box 1-109, Hollywood, Richmond, 6/13/72
ANDERSON, John D.G.	PVT		D	61st GA	k. July 1	Josiah Benner's farm, in meadow along fence	Laurel Grove, Savannah, Lot 853, Grave 10, 9/24/71
ANDERSON, Thomas J.	PVT	19	G	42nd MS	d. Aug. 8	Camp Letterman, Row 3, Grave 25	Box 1-43, Hollywood, Richmond, 6/13/72
ANDREWS, Henry H.	PVT		E	13th MS		John S. Crawford's homestead on Marsh Creek, north side of "Walnut Avenue"	Box 2-C-Miss, Hollywood, Richmond, 8/3/72
ANDREWS, Hezekiah L.	LTC	23	F&S	2nd NC BN	k. July 1	James J. Wills's farm, now Bender's; "first field over ridge;" "spot known by old Mr. Wills"	
◆ ANDREWS, Thomas C.	SGT		A	53rd GA	d. Sept. 20 U.S. Gen. Hosp. Chester, PA	Chester Rural Cemetery, Chester, PA	Removed to Griffin, GA
ARENT, William R.	LT	23	H	52nd NC	d. Aug. 7	Camp Letterman, Row 4, Grave 24	Oakwood, Raleigh, 10/1/71
ARMISTEAD, Lewis A.	GEN	46		Pickett's Division Longstreet's Corps	d. July 5 "in kitchen"	George Spangler's farm	St. Paul's Churchyard, Baltimore, MD
ARNOLD, David C.	PVT		B	8th AL		North of Francis Bream's stone house, in field near woods along side of Adam Butt's woods near road	Box 1-130, Hollywood, Richmond, 6/13/72
ARNOLD, Dawson W.	PVT	19	G	5th FL	d. Sept. 15	Camp Letterman, Row 8, Grave 6	Box 1-80, Hollywood, Richmond, 6/13/72; his left femur is in the collection of the National Museum of Health and Medicine, Specimen #1938
ASKEW, Joseph W.	LT	24	H	2nd NC BN	d. July 15	Jacob Plank's farm, back of barn, Grave 13	Box 3-P, Hollywood, Richmond, 9/10/72
ATKINS, Edgar S.	PVT		M	55th VA	d. July 3	Samuel Lohr's farm, opposite house, in meadow near a pear tree	Box 4-S, Hollywood, Richmond, 5/17/73
◆ ATKINS, Thomas W.	CPT		A	53rd GA		"Black Horse Tavern;" "in burying ground, center;" also, Francis Bream's farm, next to McClellan's private burial ground	"State Lot" - GA, to Hollywood, Richmond

Name	Rank	Age	Co.	Regiment	Death	Field/Farm Location	Burial Location
ATTAWAY, John Simon	PVT	19	G	1st SC	d. Aug. 10	Camp Letterman, Row 5, Grave 23	Oakwood, Raleigh, Grave 464, 10/1/71, as "S. Attorrey, Co. G, 1st NC"
AUSTIN, Marlon G.	PVT	24	D	21st VA	d. Dec. 2 West's Bldg. U.S. Gen. Hosp. Baltimore, MD	None	Loudon Park, Baltimore, Row B, Grave 84, 12/3/63
AUSTIN, Nathaniel	LT	33	E	14th SC	d. Aug. 22	Camp Letterman, Row 5, Grave 27	Magnolia, Charleston, Grave 6, 5/10/71
AUSTIN, William C.	LT	23	E	18th VA		Pennsylvania College, north of main edifice in hospital cemetery	Box 4-E, Hollywood, Richmond, 5/17/73
AUTEN, P.S.	PVT	27	A	11th NC	d.c. Aug. 1	On hill under walnut tree between Jacob Schwartz's and George Bushman's farms, Yard B, Row 2	Box 1-212, Hollywood, Richmond, 6/13/72
AVERY, Isaac Erwin	COL	34	F&S	6th NC	d. July 3	"In an oak coffin under a pine tree in a small cemetery [Public Burial Ground] near the Potomac River at Williamsport [MD]"	"Rose Hill," Washington Cemetery, Hagerstown, MD, as "Col. J.E. Ayers"
AYRE, William T.	LT	20	F	8th VA	d. July 25 U.S. Gen. Hosp. Chester, PA	Chester Rural Cemetery, Chester, PA, Grave 49	Philadelphia National Cemetery, 1891

B

Name	Rank	Age	Co.	Regiment	Death	Field/Farm Location	Burial Location
BAGWELL, Charles	PVT		F	42nd MS	d. July 6	Samuel Lohr's farm	Probably Box 4-S, Hollywood, Richmond, 5/17/73, as an unknown
BAILEY, C.A.	LT		A	10th GA	d. Aug. 12/13	Camp Letterman, Row 4, Grave 5	
BAILEY, C.A.	PVT		G	2nd GA	k./d. July 2	Adam Butt's brick schoolhouse. (Listed by Dr. Dr. John W. O'Neal as "J.W. Baley, Co. K, 22nd GA")	Laurel Grove, Savannah, Lot 853, Grave 12, 9/24/71
BAILEY, Robert W.	LT	22	H	44th VA		W. Henry Monfort's farm, under apple tree in orchard along road above house; "grave not marked"	Box 3-287, Hollywood, Richmond
BAINES, Robert G.	SGTMAJ		F&S	52nd NC	d. July 13	Jacob Schwartz's farm, in cornfield, Yard D, Row 3	Box 1-S-64, Hollywood, Richmond, 6/13/72
BAKER, E.G.	PVT	32	E	21st MS		John S. Crawford's farm "where Basil Bigg's lives;" in garden	Box 4-Y, Hollywood, Richmond, with 21 others, 5/17/73
BAKER, Elijah W.	PVT		I	56th VA	d. Aug. 7	Camp Letterman, Row 4, Grave 22	Box 1-53, Hollywood, Richmond, 6/13/72
BAKER, Henry S.	PVT	24	E	37th NC	d. Aug. 1 U.S. Gen. Hosp. Chester, PA	Chester Rural Cemetery, Chester, PA	Philadelphia National Cemetery, 1891
BAKER, Jesse J.	PVT	20	E	20th NC	d. July 3	Jacob Hankey's farm	Oakwood, Raleigh, Grave 515, 10/1/71
BAKER, Thomas W.	LT	23	D	43rd NC	d. July 26	Jacob Plank's farm, under walnut tree near the road, Grave 2; buried on south side of Lt. W. H. Gibson in Grave 1, with $364 in Confederate currency	Box 3-272, Hollywood, Richmond, 9/10/72
BALLARD, C.M.	CPT	26	C	8th GA	d. July 2	Charles B. Polley's farm, in orchard on pike; in lower part of orchard under two apple trees; "removed"	Laurel Grove, Savannah, Lot 854, Grave 13, 8/21/71

Name	Rank	Age	Co.	Regiment	Death	Original Burial Location	Reinterment
BALLARD, James H.	PVT	28	E	28th NC	d. Sept. 20 U.S. Gen. Hosp. Chester, PA	Chester Rural Cemetery, Chester, PA	Philadelphia National Cemetery, 1891
BALLARD, Thomas A.	LT	22	F	50th GA		John S. Crawford's farm on Marsh Creek, in garden	"State Lot"- GA, to Hollywood, Richmond
BALLARD, William R.	PVT	24	D	2nd SC	k. July 2	Northwest of George Rose's house, along fence near some trees north of Emmitsburg Road; "a cross the roat [road] in the thimathy field"	Magnolia, Charleston, Grave 33, 5/10/71
BANKSTON, Thomas M.	PVT		C	16th MS		In Emanuel Pitzer's orchard near George Culp's farm	Possibly in a box marked "D," to Hollywood, Richmond, 6/13/72, as an unknown
BARKER, Edward	PVT	22	A	26th NC	d. Aug. 12	Camp Letterman, Row 5, Grave 14	Oakwood, Raleigh, Grave 462, 10/1/71
BARKER, Nathan D.	PVT	29	M	22nd NC	d. Aug. 4 U.S. Gen. Hosp. Chester, PA	Chester Rural Cemetery, Chester, PA	Philadelphia National Cemetery, 1891
BARKSDALE, William	GEN	41		McLaws's Division Longstreet's Corps	d. July 3	Jacob Hummelbaugh's house on the Taneytown Road, under a cherry tree south of the lane; also listed as near Meade's Headquarters, the Lydia Leister farm; "removed"	Greenwood Cemetery, Jackson, MS, 1/9/67
BARMORE, William C.	PVT		B	7th SC	k. July 2	George Rose's farm, back or north of the stone barn	Box 1-164, Hollywood, Richmond, 6/13/72
BARNES, Smith F.	PVT	32	G	37th NC	d. July 20 or Aug. 13	On hill under a walnut tree between Jacob Schwartz's and George Bushman's farms, Yard B, Row 2	Box 1-S-2, Hollywood, Richmond, 6/13/72
BARRETT, John R.	PVT			LA Guard Artillery		Joseph Leas's farm, in northwest corner of field	Box 1-195, Hollywood, Richmond, 6/13/72
BARRETT, Thomas R.	PVT		C/H	Cobb's (GA) Legion Cavalry	d. July 2	On Hunterstown Road, under a cherry tree near Hunterstown	Laurel Grove, Savannah, Lot 854, Grave 12, 8/21/71
BARRY, Michael	PVT		E	1st MD BN		George Bushman's farm; hospital cemetery was east of house	Box 1-228, Hollywood, Richmond, 6/13/72
BARRY, William H.	PVT		G	11th AL		Michael Fiscel's farm, as "Wm. Barry, Co. C, 14th Ala."	Possibly in a box marked "A," to Hollywood, Richmond, 9/10/72, as an unknown
BARTLY, Charles	PVT		H	8th SC	k. July 2	George Rose's farm, back or north of stone barn	Box 1-147, Hollywood, Richmond, 6/13/72
BASKERVILLE, George T.	CPT	36	I	23rd NC	d. July 2	Probably Jacob Hankey's farm or vicinity	Shiloh Cemetery, Granville County, NC
BATTLE, Wesley Lewis	LT	19	D	37th NC	d. Aug. 22	Camp Letterman, Row 5, Grave 32	
BEADLES, James C.	PVT	25	King William (VA) Artillery		k. July 3	John S. Forney's farm, in a field near apple tree, or in garden	Possibly in one of six boxes marked "F," to Hollywood, Richmond, 8/3/72, as an unknown
BEAUCHAMP, Henry P.	CPL	24	E	18th MS		John S. Crawford's farm, "where Basil Biggs lives;" in garden	Box 4-Y, Hollywood, Richmond, 5/17/73
BEELER, James H.	PVT			Carpenter's (VA) Battery	k. July 2	George Wolf's farm, in field near woods; "grave leveled"	Probably in a box marked "T," to Hollywood, Richmond, 8/3/72, with 12 remains, as an unknown
BEEMAN, Christopher C.	PVT		G	3rd AR	d. July 10	John Edward Plank's farm, north side of house under walnut tree	Box 2-H, Hollywood, Richmond, 8/3/72
BELCHER, Samuel P.	LT		I	11th GA	d. July 12	John Edward Plank's farm, back of barn	Box 2-H, Hollywood, Richmond, 8/3/72

Name	Rank	Age	Co.	Regiment	Date	Location	Disposition
BELLOMY, George W.	PVT		H	57th VA	d. July 10	Jacob Schwartz's farm, in a cornfield, Yard C	Box 1-S-78, Hollywood, Richmond, 6/13/72
BENDALL, Benjamin F.	PVT	23	F	53rd VA	d. Aug. 6	Camp Letterman, Row 3, Grave 6	Box 1-57, Hollywood, Richmond, 6/13/72
BENDER, Griffin M.	PVT		H	2nd LA	d. July 6	David Stewart's farm, east of the barn; "left in hands of enemy"	Box 3-N, Hollywood, Richmond, 9/10/72
BENNETT, R.E.	PVT		K	8th AL	d. Aug. 5 "fever"	Camp Letterman, Row 3, Grave 5	Box 1-47, Hollywood, Richmond, 6/13/72
BENSHOOF, John	PVT	34	K	5th VA	d. July 6	Henry Picking's farm, in field, along fence opposite schoolhouse near road; "born near Gettysburg, PA"	Stonewall Cemetery, Winchester, VA
BERRY, W.S.	PVT		G	7th SC	d. July 25 U.S. Gen. Hosp. Chester, PA	Chester Rural Cemetery, Chester, PA	Philadelphia National Cemetery, 1891
◆ BEVERAGE, Jacob Jr.	LT	27	E	31st VA	d. July 2/3	Josiah Benner's farm, under apple tree in orchard	Box 3-275, Hollywood, Richmond, 9/10/72
BIGGERS, William E.	PVT			Troup (GA) Artillery		John S. Crawford's homestead on Marsh Creek, north side of "Walnut Avenue"	Dr. Rufus Weaver shipped remains home to his brother in Georgia in the summer of 1871.
BINNS, Charles D.	PVT	19	K	53rd VA	d. Oct. 3	Camp Letterman, Row 8, Grave 32	Box 1-84, Hollywood, Richmond, 6/13/72
BINNS, Major E.	PVT	25	K	53rd VA	d. July 23	Francis Bream's mill above William Myers's house at the side of a fence	Box 2-P-Curns, Hollywood, Richmond, 8/3/72, with 33 others
BIRD, Alfred	SGT	31	F	50th GA	k. July 2	George Rose's farm in orchard, near fence; "back of the privy" also, "in front of the house, a few yards from the Spring House"	Laurel Grove, Savannah, Lot 853, Grave 13, 9/24/71
BIRGE, James W.	PVT		C	17th MS		John S. Crawford's farm, in orchard, north of "Walnut Avenue" under apple tree	Box 2-C-Miss, Hollywood, Richmond, 8/3/72; "grave unmarked by then"
BIRMINGHAM, John	PVT	35	D	11th MS	d. July 25 DeCamp U.S. Gen. Hosp. David's Island, New York	None	Cypress Hills Cemetery, Long Island, NY, Grave 686
BISSELL, William R.	CPT		A	8th VA	d. July 16	Presbyterian Graveyard, High Street, Gettysburg, next to J.R. Young; "still marked in May 1866"	"State Lot" - GA, to Hollywood, Richmond
BLACK, John C.	PVT		I	33rd VA	d. July 15	Henry Picking's farm, in field, along fence opposite schoolhouse near road	Box 1-174, Hollywood, Richmond, 6/13/72
BLACK, John L.	PVT	25	C	48th VA	d. Aug. 11	Camp Letterman, Row 5, Grave 21	Box 1-74, Hollywood, Richmond, 6/13/72
BLACKBURN, Aurelius C.	CPT	23	K	52nd NC	d. July 1	Samuel Lohr's farm, opposite house in meadow near pear tree	Box 4-S, Hollywood, Richmond, 5/17/73
BLACKISTONE, William J.	1SGT		A	1st MD BN	d. Aug. 1 Probably Seminary Hosp. Hagerstown, MD	Possibly Old Almshouse Burying Ground, Hagerstown, MD	Probably in "Rose Hill," Washington, Cemetery, Hagerstown, MD

Name	Rank	Age	Co.	Regiment	Death	Original Burial	Final Disposition
BLACKWELDER, Charles M.	PVT	31	A	52nd NC	d. Sept. 21 U.S. Gen. Hosp. Chester, PA	Chester Rural Cemetery, Chester, PA	Philadelphia National Cemetery, 1891
BLIGH, John	PVT	22	D	2nd SC	k. July 2	Northwest of George Rose's house, along fence near some trees; "in Watt [wheat] field along the wood by the fence"	Magnolia, Charleston, Grave 31, 5/10/71
BLISS, Frederick	LT	23	B	8th GA	d. July 4 "inside farmhouse"	John Edward Plank's farm	To storage or temporary burial in Baltimore, Oct. 1863, then to Laurel Grove, Savannah, to a private family plot, on 2/9/66
BOBBITT, P.S.	PVT	20	G	47th NC	d. Aug. 20	Camp Letterman, Row 2, Grave 26	Oakwood, Raleigh, 10/1/71
BOGGAN, William W.	LT	23	H	43rd NC	d. July 2	Jacob Hankey's farm	Oakwood, Raleigh, Grave 520, 10/1/71
BOLCH, Logan	PVT		C	28th NC	d. Sept. 30 U.S. Gen. Hosp. Chester, PA	Chester Rural Cemetery, Chester, PA, Grave 214, 10/5/63	Philadelphia National Cemetery, 1891
BOND, John M.D.	CPT	25	I	53rd GA	k. July 2	George Rose's farm, in orchard near fence; "back of privy" also, "in front of the house, a few yards from the Spring House" "removed"	Laurel Grove, Savannah, Lot 853, Grave 13, 9/24/71
BONNELL, John	PVT		C	2nd FL	d. July 30	Jacob Schwartz's farm, back of barn, Grave 8	Possibly in one of seven boxes marked "S," to Richmond, Hollywood, 9/10/72, as an unknown
BOOTHE, John	PVT		E	5th TX	d. July 2	Jesse Worley's farm	Box 3-X, Hollywood, Richmond, 9/10/72
BORING, Robert McBride	PVT		K	4th GA	d. July 23	Jacob Hankey's farm	Laurel Grove, Savannah, Lot 854, Grave 13, 8/21/71
BOSS, James P.	PVT	21	H	8th VA			Union Cemetery, Leesburg, VA
BOSTIAN, Aaron	CPL	29	K	5th NC	d. Nov. 14	None	Arlington National Cemetery, Arlington, VA (In the 1880s, a group of Confederate dead was returned to Hollywood from this cemetery.)
BOSTICK, Andrew J.	PVT		H	11th AL		South of Adam Butt's house, near road	Box 1-131, Hollywood, Richmond, 6/13/72
BOSWELL, Doctor F.	PVT	18	A	13th MS	d. Oct. 7	Camp Letterman, Row 9, Grave 6	Box 1-112, Hollywood, Richmond, 6/13/72
BOSWELL, John L.C.	1SGT		E	57th VA	d. July 14	Jacob Schwartz's farm, in cornfield, Yard D, Row 3	Box 1-S-62, Hollywood, Richmond, 6/13/72, as "57th NC"
BOWDEN, William	PVT	38	G	47th NC	k. July 1	Elizabeth Shultz's house, on ridge nearby	Magnolia, Charleston, Row 3, Grave 18, 5/10/71
BOWEN, A. Cornelius	PVT		G	1st SC Rifles	d. July 8 U.S. Gen. Hosp. Chester, PA	Chester Rural Cemetery, Chester, PA	
BOWEN, John	PVT	36	B	7th VA	d. Aug. 15	Camp Letterman, Row 1, Grave 35	
BOWLES, Gibson R.	SGT	23	F	42nd VA	d. July 13 U.S. Gen. Hosp. Frederick, MD	None	Mt. Olivet Cemetery, Frederick, MD, Grave 203, 7/14/63; his skull is in the collection of the National Museum of Health and Medicine, Specimen #2494
BOWLIN, John P.	PVT	18	C	1st VA CAV		Joseph Leas's farm, northwest corner of field; also, in or adjacent to graveyard near Abe Tawney's	Box 1-196, Hollywood, Richmond, 6/13/72

Name	Rank	Age	Co.	Unit	Casualty	Original Burial	Disposition
BOWMAN, A.J.	PVT	31	E	32nd NC	d. July 15/16	Jacob Plank's farm, back of barn, Grave 11	Box 3-P, Hollywood, Richmond, 9/10/72
BOWMAN, J.T.	PVT	22	I	16th NC	d. Sept. 22 U.S. Gen. Hosp. Harrisburg, PA	None	Soldiers' Lot, Harrisburg, PA, Cemetery, Grave 134
BOX, George T.	PVT	25	A	17th MS	d. Aug. 6	Camp Letterman, Row 4, Grave 36	Box 1-27, Hollywood, Richmond, 6/13/72
BOYD, Benjamin H.	PVT		C	38th GA	d. July 28 U.S. Gen. Hosp. Frederick, MD	None	Mt. Olivet Cemetery, Frederick, MD, Grave 208
BOYD, George F.	LT	23	A	45th NC	k. July 1	"Buried on the field;" Probably on John Forney's farm	Wentworth Methodist Episcopal Cemetery, Rockingham Co., NC
◆ BOYD, John A.	PVT	23	D	13th SC	d. July 20 West's Bldg. U.S. Gen. Hosp. Baltimore, MD	None	Loudon Park, Baltimore, Row C, Grave 66, 7/20/63, as "J.A. Boyd, Co. D, 13th NC"
BRACEWELL, Wiley K.	PVT	23	G	49th GA	d. Aug. 27	Camp Letterman, Row 6, Grave 8. "I am certain he died in peace." - Chaplain Wm. B. Owen, 17th MS	Laurel Grove, Savannah, Lot 854, Grave 3
BRADLEY, George W.	LT		A	13th MS		John Trostle's farm, corner of field on south bank of Rock Creek	Box 1-238, Hollywood, Richmond, 6/13/72
BRADLEY, John M.	MAJ	36	F&S	13th MS	d. July 28 U.S. Hospital Williamsport, Maryland	Possibly in the Public Burial Ground, Williamsport, MD	Possibly Washington Cemetery, Hagerstown, MD
BRADSHAW, Hartwell H.	PVT		G	7th TN		On hill between Jacob Schwartz's and George Bushman's farms, Yard B, Row 1	Box 1-11, Hollywood, Richmond, 6/13/72
BRANCH, Jesse B.	CPL		A	61st GA	k. July 1	Josiah Benner's farm, in meadow along fence; "all removed"	Laurel Grove, Savannah, Lot 853, Grave 10, 9/24/71
BRANDON, George W.	CPL	20	C	13th NC	d. Aug. 26 U.S. Gen. Hosp. Chester, PA	Chester Rural Cemetery, Chester, PA	Philadelphia National Cemetery, 1891
BRANDON, Robert M.	CPT		D	2nd MS		Jacob Schwartz's farm; "grave still marked in July 1866"	Possibly in one of seven boxes marked "S," to Hollywood, Richmond, 9/10/72, as an unknown
BRASINGTON, George C.	LT	27	H	2nd SC	d. July 6	Francis Bream's farm, north of tavern, near graveyard and creek	Magnolia, Charleston, Grave 49, 5/10/71
BRAWNER, William T.	PVT		B	15th GA	d. July 28	Camp Letterman, Row 1, Grave 11	Laurel Grove, Savannah, Lot 854, Grave 3
BRAY, William A.	LT	29	B	2nd NC BN	d. July 1	Jacob Hankey's farm	Oakwood, Raleigh, Grave 512, 10/1/71
BRAY, William H.	LT	24	B	53rd VA	d. July 14	Jacob Schwartz's farm, in cornfield, Yard D, Row 3	Box 1-S-57, Hollywood, Richmond, 6/13/72
◆ BRENAN, Peter	MAJ	51	F&S	61st GA	k. July 1	Jacob Kime's farm, in orchard under peach tree; "removed"	Laurel Grove, Savannah, Lot 853, Grave 12, 9/24/71
BRESNAHAM, W. Mathew	PVT	24	H	1st VA	d. Aug. 1	Camp Letterman, Row 2, Grave 10	Box 1-50, Hollywood, Richmond, 6/13/72

Name	Rank	Age	Co.	Regiment	Death	Original Burial	Reburial
BREWER, Samuel J.G.	PVT		I	8th GA	d. July 5	Samuel Pitzer's farm, in orchard, under apple tree	Box 3-262, Hollywood, Richmond, 9/10/72
BREWER, William J.	PVT	19	C	47th VA	d. Aug. 30	Camp Letterman, Row 5, Grave 36	Box 1-38, Hollywood, Richmond, 6/13/72
BREWER, William L.	PVT	39	K	51st GA	d. Aug. 10	Camp Letterman, Row 4, Grave 9; "removed"	Laurel Grove, Savannah, Lot 854, Grave 3
BREWERTON, Frederick	PVT		L	21st MS	d. July 24	Jacob Schwartz's farm, behind the barn	Possibly in one of 7 boxes marked "S," to Hollywood, Richmond, 9/10/72, as an unknown
BRIAN, Doctor Jack	PVT		Chesapeake (MD) Artillery		k. July 2	Christian Benner's farm, back of Rock Creek under a large walnut tree	Loudon Park, Baltimore, c. 7/4/73
BRICE, William W.	PVT		A	6th AL	d. Oct. 4 U.S. Gen. Hosp. Harrisburg, PA	None	Soldiers' Lot, Harrisburg, PA, Cemetery, Grave 108
BRIGGS, Henry L.	PVT		C	24th VA		Jacob Schwartz's farm, in cornfield, Yard D, Row 2	Box 1-S-43, Hollywood, Richmond, 6/13/72
BRIGHT, Josiah F.	PVT	31	C	52nd VA	d. July 3	Josiah Benner's farm, under apple tree, in orchard	Box 3-276, Hollywood, Richmond, 9/10/72
BRILEY, Tilman T.	PVT	19	K	26th NC	d. Sept. 4	Camp Letterman, Row 7, Grave 7	Oakwood, Raleigh, Grave 475, 10/1/71
BRISCOE, Robert	CPL	43	F	11th NC	d. Aug. 10 U.S. Gen. Hosp. Chester, PA	Chester Rural Cemetery, Chester, PA	Philadelphia National Cemetery, 1891
BRISON, G.W.	PVT		G	11th AL		South of Adam Butt's house near road	Box 1-129, Hollywood, Richmond, 6/13/72
BRISTER, H.	PVT		I	13th MS		John S. Crawford's farm, in orchard north of "Walnut Avenue" under apple tree	Box 2-C-Miss, Hollywood, Richmond, 8/3/72; "grave unmarked by then"
◆ **BRITTAIN**, Washington	PVT	20	B	45th NC	k. July 1	Clarkson's old place, or James J. Wills's farm; left side of first railroad cut	Box 1-146, Hollywood, Richmond, 6/13/72
BROACH, J.R.	PVT		A	8th SC		George Rose's farm, back or north of stone barn	Removed after 1865 to family cemetery in Tappahannock, Essex Co., VA
◆ **BROCKENBROUGH**, Austin	CPT	21	D Staff, Gen. Joseph Davis	55th VA	d. July 2 7 PM	On Chambersburg Turnpike, about halfway between Cashtown and Gettysburg (Probably on Samuel Lohr's farm)	Laurel Grove, Savannah, Lot 854, Grave 12, 8/21/71
BROOKS, Cicero C.	LT		H Cobb's (GA) Legion Cavalry		d.c. July 2 in J.L. Grass Hotel	On Hunterstown Road under cherry tree near Hunterstown	
BROOKS, Isaac M.	PVT	30	B	47th AL	d. Sept. 27	Camp Letterman, Row 8, Grave 22	Box 1-92, Hollywood, Richmond, 6/13/72
BROOKS, Moses	SGT	28	H	16th NC	d. July 18	Jacob Schwartz's farm, in cornfield, Yard D, Row 1	Box 1-S-29, Hollywood, Richmond, 6/13/72
BROUGHTON, Benjamin	PVT	29	I	47th NC	d. Aug. 13	Samuel Lohr's farm, opposite house, in meadow, near pear tree	Box 4-S, Hollywood, Richmond, 5/17/73
BROWN, Arthur A.	PVT		D	5th FL	d. July 14	Pennsylvania College, in hospital cemetery north of main edifice	Possibly in Box 4-E, Hollywood Cemetery, with 35 remains, 27 unknown, 5/17/73

Name	Rank	Age	Regiment	Co.	Death	Original Burial Location	Final Location
BROWN, J.T.	PVT		12th SC	B	d. Aug. 15 U.S. Gen. Hosp. Chester, PA	Chester Rural Cemetery, Chester, PA	Magnolia, Charleston, Row 3, Grave 17, 5/10/71
BROWN, James A.	PVT		1st MD BN	D		Elizabeth Wible's farm, below house in fence corner; in field opposite Mrs. Wible's, near Michael Shealer's fence	Buried in, or memorial stone located in, Prospect Hill Cemetery, Front Royal, VA
BROWN, Jason J.	SGT	21	2nd NC BN	H	d. July 1	Jacob Hankey's farm	Oakwood, Raleigh, Grave 513, 10/1/71
BROWN, John	PVT		12th GA	A	d. July 10	Jacob Hankey's farm	Laurel Grove, Savannah, Lot 854, Grave 13, 8/21/71
BROWN, John W.	PVT	24	1st TX	L	d. July 10	John Edward Plank's farm, under walnut tree, north of house toward Fairfield Road and Gettysburg	Box 2-H, Hollywood, Richmond, 8/3/72
BROWN, Nathaniel	PVT		56th VA	E	d. July 11	Jacob Schwartz's farm, in cornfield on Rock Creek, Yard D, Row 1	Box 1-S-33, Hollywood, Richmond, 6/13/72
BROWN, William Jr.	PVT		11th MS	D	d. Aug. 5	None	Oakwood Cemetery, Richmond, VA, Division D, Row 26, Grave 3 (mortally wounded at Falling Waters, MD, July 10, 1863)
BROWN, William D.	CPT		Chesapeake (MD) Artillery		k. July 2	Christian Benner's farm, back of Rock Creek, under a large walnut tree	Green Mount Cemetery, Baltimore, MD, 7/31/63
BROWNLEE, William A.	LT		10th AL	H	d. July 12	Jacob Schwartz's farm, in cornfield on Rock Creek, Yard D, Row 2	Box 1-S-40, Hollywood, Richmond, 6/13/72
BRYANT, Felix M.	SGT		8th FL	F	d. July 14	Pennsylvania College, north of main edifice, in hospital cemetery	Box 4-E, Hollywood, Richmond, 5/17/73
BRYANT, George A.	PVT	37	43rd NC	C	d. July 28	Probably Jacob Hankey's farm	Oakwood, Raleigh, Grave 495, 10/1/71
BRYANT, Stephen N.	PVT	31	1st NC	K	d. July 17	George Bushman's farm; hospital cemetery was east of house	Oakwood, Raleigh, Grave 532, 10/1/71
BRYENS, George H.	PVT	18	3rd Co., Washington (LA) Artillery		d. July 3	John S. Crawford's tenant house, (Samuel Johns); "near barn in field with house;" "in woods, east of tenant house"	Box 1-65, Hollywood, Richmond, 6/13/72
BUCHANAN, Joseph D.	PVT		8th FL	G	d. July 30	Camp Letterman, Row 2, Grave 23	Box 3-V, Hollywood, Richmond, 9/10/72, with 11 remains
BUCHANAN, Samuel Jr.	PVT		37th VA	H		Martin Shealer's farm	
BUFORD, Parham Morgan	PVT	21	11th MS	G	d. Aug. 15	Camp Letterman, Row 2, Grave 26	Box 1-101, Hollywood, Richmond, 6/13/72
BURGESS, Franklin M.	PVT		15th SC	H	d. July 16	Francis Bream's farm, north of tavern, near graveyard and creek	Magnolia, Charleston, Grave 45, 5/10/71
BURGIN, John A.	LT	24	11th NC	K	k. July 3		Possibly Laurel Grove, Savannah, Lot 853, Grave 13, 9/24/71, as "Lt. J.W. Burr, Co. K, 11th Ga."
BURGWYN, Henry K. Jr.	COL	22	26th NC	F&S	d. July 1	About two miles out the Chambersburg Pike, east of a stately walnut tree, 100 yards north of road; 75 yards northeast of a medium size stone farmhouse, and across road from a large yellow barn; head toward tree; alongside W. McCreery, W. Wilson, and C. Iredell	Oakwood, Raleigh, 6/9/67
BURKE, Martin V.	PVT		22nd GA	A	d. July 11	Jacob Schwartz's farm, in cornfield, Yard D, Row 2	Box 1-S-39, Hollywood, Richmond, 6/13/72

Name	Rank	Age	Co.	Regiment	Death	Burial Location	Disposition
BURKHALTER, Isaac	CPT	32	G	50th GA	k. July 2	George Rose's farm, in orchard near fence; "in orchard near springhouse," "removed"	Laurel Grove, Savannah, Lot 853, Grave 14, 9/24/71; also, Box 4-U, Hollywood, Richmond, 5/17/73
BURKHALTER, Joseph C.	PVT	21	E	61st GA	k. July 1	Josiah Benner's farm, in meadow along fence; "all removed"	Laurel Grove, Savannah, Lot 853, Grave 10, 9/24/71
BURLY, James C.	PVT		I	12th MS	d. July 31	Camp Letterman, Row 2, Grave 19	Box 1-87, Hollywood, Richmond, 6/13/72
BURNETT, Luceillus S.	PVT	22	I	11th MS	d. July 26 U.S. Gen. Hosp. Chester, PA	Chester Rural Cemetery, Chester, PA, Grave 52	1. Glenwood Cemetery, Philadelphia 2. Possibly to Philadelphia National Cemetery, 1891
BURNEY, Theodore C.	PVT	18	G	11th MS	k. July 10 Falling Waters, Maryland	Possibly Old Almshouse Burying Ground, Hagerstown, MD	Possibly "Rose Hill," Washington Cemetery, Hagerstown, MD
BURNS, James H.	CPT	23	E	6th NC	k./d. July 1	Elizabeth Wible's farm, alone, back of the barn; "grave marked with his name"	Remains expressed to brother, C.B. Burns, 10/4/66, by Dr. John W. O'Neal
BURNS, James J.	PVT		G	42nd MS	d. Aug. 6 U.S. Gen. Hosp. Chester, PA	Chester Rural Cemetery, Chester, PA	Philadelphia National Cemetery, 1891
BURNSIDE, J. Dooly	LT	26	K	48th GA	d. July 7	Jacob Schwartz's farm, in cornfield, Yard C	Box 1-S-80, Hollywood, Richmond, ("Box Cover 4"), 6/13/72
BURROWS, Cornelius T.	SGT		H	8th FL	d. July 16	Jacob Schwartz's farm, back of barn, Grave 12	Possibly in one of seven boxes marked "S," to Hollywood, Richmond, 9/10/72, as an unknown
BURRUSS, Charles W.	CPL		G	24th VA	d. Aug. 3/15	Camp Letterman, Row 3, Grave 24	Box 1-97, Hollywood, Richmond, 6/13/72
BUTLER, George H.	PVT		G	49th VA	k./d. July 1	Josiah Benner's farm, under apple tree in orchard	Box 3-273, Hollywood, Richmond, 9/10/72
BUTLER, William C.	1SGT	26	F	2nd FL		Camp Letterman, Row 1, Grave 37	Box 1-31, Hollywood, Richmond, 6/13/72
BUTLER, William R.	CPL		H	4th GA	k. July 1	Opposite or west of Negro Church on Long Lane	
BUTTS, Frank	PVT		K	61st GA	k. July 1	Josiah Benner's farm, in meadow along fence; "all removed"	Laurel Grove, Savannah, Lot 853, Grave 10, 9/24/71
BUTTS, Walter	LT	21	F	9th VA	d. July 11	Jacob Schwartz's farm, in cornfield on Rock Creek, Yard D, Row 1	Box 1-S-34, Hollywood, Richmond, 6/13/72
BUZHARDT, Milton P.	LT	26	B	3rd SC	d. July 2	Francis Bream's farm, north of tavern near graveyard and creek	Magnolia, Charleston, Grave 52, 5/10/71

C

Name	Rank	Age	Co.	Regiment	Death	Burial Location	Disposition
CAFFEY, Hooper P.	PVT	28	H	3rd AL	d. Sept. 13	1. Camp Letterman, Row 7, Grave 34 2. Evergreen Cemetery, Gettysburg, Section E, Lot 169, "just west of Ivy Rock;" May 30, 1866, next to M. Goodson	3. To unknown spot in Evergreen Cemetery, after August 19, 1867, with M. Goodson. Also, shown as, "State Lot" - AL, Hollywood, Richmond
CAHO, William A.	LT	27	I	1st VA	d. July 31 U.S. Gen. Hosp. Chester, PA	Chester Rural Cemetery, Chester, PA, Grave 92	Returned to his home by his mother
CAIN, W.E.H.	PVT		H	62nd VA	d. July 17 Seminary Hosp. Hagerstown, MD	Probably Old Almshouse Burying Ground, Hagerstown, MD	Probably in "Rose Hill," Washington Cemetery, Hagerstown, MD

Name	Rank	Age	Co.	Regiment	Death	Burial Location	Final Disposition
CALDWELL, John	LT	18	E	33rd NC	k. July 2	Buried by W.H. Lucas on Seminary Ridge near two locust trees close to a two-story house; 7 other graves nearby; (Probably near David McMillan's house.)	
CAMAK, Thomas U.	MAJ	33	F&S	Cobb's (GA) Legion	d. July 2	John Cunningham's farm, across the creek from John S. Crawford's farm, in orchard, south side	Probably in a box marked "X," to Hollywood, Richmond, 5/17/73, with 16 others, as an unknown
CAMERON, James F.	PVT		C	11th AL	k. July 2	On road to Abraham Krise's farm in woods between Samuel Pitzer's and James Warfield's blacksmith shop, with two others	Possibly in a box marked "W," to Hollywood, Richmond, 5/17/73, as an unknown
CAMPBELL, Adolphus L.	PVT		C	28th NC	d. July 15-18	George Bushman's farm; hospital cemetery was east of house	Oakwood, Raleigh, Grave 529, 10/1/71
CAMPBELL, Elcanah M.	PVT		Blount's (VA) Battery		k. July 3	Probably near John Edward Plank's farm on Willoughby's Run; "on bluff from little house along Willoughby's Run"	Possibly in one of 11 boxes marked "H," to Hollywood, Richmond, 8/3/72, as an unknown
CAMPBELL, Joseph A.	PVT	25	K	7th NC	d. Aug. 15 U.S. Gen. Hosp. Chester, PA	Chester Rural Cemetery, Chester, PA	Philadelphia National Cemetery, 1891
CAMPBELL, Malcolm M.	PVT		D	47th AL	d. Aug. 2 U.S. Gen. Hosp. Chester, PA	Chester Rural Cemetery, Chester, PA	Philadelphia National Cemetery, 1891
CAMPBELL, Martin R.	ADJ		F&S	48th MS		Emanuel Pitzer's farm, east of house in meadow under peach tree	Box 1-214, Hollywood, Richmond, 6/13/72
CARD, Julius J.	CPL		B	12th GA	k. July 1	Almshouse field, under tree on Carlisle Rd. "on McMullin's side"	
CARICOFE, John H. Jr.	PVT		I	5th VA	d. July 10	Henry A. Picking's farm, in field, along fence, opposite schoolhouse near road; "not far from the schoolhouse and near Hunterstown Road"	Box 1-179, Hollywood, Richmond, 6/13/72, as "J.H. Kiracafe, Co. I, 33rd VA"
CARNES, James	PVT	24	H	8th GA	d. Aug. 31	Camp Letterman, Row 6, Grave 27	Laurel Grove, Savannah, Lot 854, Grave 3, 8/21/71
CARPENTER, Henry	PVT	40	I	11th NC	d. July 31 West's Bldg. U.S. Gen. Hosp. Baltimore, MD	None	Loudon Park, Baltimore, Row C, Grave 76, 7/31/63
CARPENTER, Joseph	PVT	38	G	34th NC	k. July 3		Zion Methodist Cemetery, Lincoln Co., NC
CARPENTER, William D.	SGT	34	B	23rd NC	k. July 1	Probably John Forney's farm, in field, south of house	St. Matthew's Reform Cemetery, Lincoln Co., NC
CARR, William A.	LT	22	E	5th NC	k./d. July 1	Jacob Hankey's farm	Oakwood, Raleigh, Grave 490, 10/1/71
CARROLL, George	PVT	38	H	48th VA	d. "after July 18"	W. Henry Monfort's farm	Box 3-M, Hollywood, Richmond, 9/10/72
◆ CARTER, Benjamin F.	LTC	32	F&S	4th TX	d. July 21	Methodist Cemetery, Chambersburg, PA; buried by Henry Johnson, his servant	
CARTER, Benjamin T.	PVT	35	K	13th NC	d. Aug. 29 U.S. Gen. Hosp. Chester, PA	Chester Rural Cemetery, Chester, PA	Philadelphia National Cemetery, 1891; his left knee bones are in the National Museum of Health and Medicine, Specimen #1205

Name	Rank	Age	Co.	Regiment	Death	Burial Location	Removed/Current Location
CARTER, Daniel M.	PVT	24	E	26th NC	d. July 20 Jordan Springs Hospital, Winchester, VA	None	Stonewall Cemetery, Winchester, VA
CARTER, James T.	SGT		B	5th TX	d. July 31	Camp Letterman Cemetery; "died in Federal hospital"	
CARTER, James W.	COL	32	F&S	13th MS	d. July 2	John S. Crawford's homestead on Marsh Creek, north side of "Walnut Avenue"	Box 2-241, Hollywood, Richmond, 8/3/72
CARTER, Lewis W.	PVT	27	C	52nd NC	d. July 27	On hill under walnut tree between Jacob Schwartz's and George Bushman's farms, Yard B, Row 1	Box 1-13, Hollywood, Richmond, 8/3/72
CARTER, Sidney	LT	31	A	14th SC	d. July 8	Some believed he is buried in the National Cemetery, Gettysburg, PA, in Conn. Plot A-5, as "S. Carter, Co. A, 15th CT"	
CASEY, Thomas	SGT	25	B	6th LA	d. July 30	Camp Letterman, Row 2, Grave 18	Box 1-48, Hollywood, Richmond, 6/13/72, as "Sgt. J.I. Caster, Co. D, 5th LA"
CASEY, William P.	PVT	19	Brooks (SC) Artillery		k. July 2	John S. Crawford's tenant house (Samuel Johns) near barn; also as "Crawford's barn," and "east of house in woods"	
CASON, William G.	PVT		H	57th VA	d. July 17	Jacob Schwartz's farm, in cornfield near Rock Creek, Yard D, Row 3	Box 1-S-69, Hollywood, Richmond, 6/13/72
CASSON, James H.	PVT	23	A	2nd SC	d. July 7	Francis Bream's farm, burying ground, center	Magnolia, Charleston, Grave 39, 5/10/71
CASTLEMAN, James W.	SGT	20	H	3rd AR		John Edward Plank's farm, north of house under walnut tree; "frame [stones] around grave"	Box 1-254, Hollywood, Richmond, 6/13/72
CATES, John R.	PVT		E	1st TN	d. Sept. 21 U.S. Gen. Hosp. Chester, PA	Chester Rural Cemetery, Chester, PA	Philadelphia National Cemetery, 1891
CAULEY, William C.	PVT		F	59th GA	d. Sept. 27 U.S. Gen. Hosp. Chester, PA	Chester Rural Cemetery, Chester, PA, Grave 211	Philadelphia National Cemetery, 1891
CAUSEY, Robertson C.	SGT	25	C	45th NC	d. July 21	Jacob Hankey's farm	Oakwood, Raleigh, Grave 494, 10/1/71
CHALKER, William H.	PVT	21	A	48th GA	d. July 16	Jacob Schwartz's farm, in cornfield, Yard D, Row 3	Box 1-S-72, Hollywood, Richmond, 6/13/72
CHANDLER, William S.J.	PVT		A	1st MD BN		George Bushman's farm; hospital cemetery was east of house	Box 1-226, Hollywood, Richmond, 6/13/72. Also Grave 6a, Row E, "Confederate Hill" in Loudon Park, Baltimore
CHANEY, Jacob H.	PVT	22	K	13th SC	d. Aug. 9	Camp Letterman, Row 4, Grave 5	Magnolia, Charleston, Grave 4, 5/10/71
CHAPMAN, G.W.	PVT		G	3rd GA	k. July 2	Adam Butt's schoolhouse on Fairfield Road	Laurel Grove, Savannah, Lot 853, Grave 12, 9/24/71
CHAPPELL, Rolin/Roland	PVT		E	52nd NC	d. July 23 U.S. Gen. Hosp. Chester, PA	Chester Rural Cemetery, Chester, PA	Philadelphia National Cemetery, 1891
CHEATHAM, Samuel O.	PVT		D	14th VA	d. July 17	Jacob Schwartz's farm, in cornfield on Rock Creek, Yard D, Row 1	Box 1-S-25, Hollywood, Richmond, 6/13/72

Name	Rank	Age	Co.	Regiment	Death	Original Burial	Disposition
CHEESBOROUGH, John W.	LT	25	A	Cobb's (GA) Legion Cavalry	d. July 5 in J.L. Grass Hotel	On Hunterstown Road, south of Hunterstown, under cherry tree	Laurel Grove, Savannah, Lot 854, Grave 12, 8/21/71
CHILES, John C.	PVT	19	C	14th VA	d. Aug. 9 U.S. Gen. Hosp. Chester, PA	Chester Rural Cemetery, Chester, PA, Grave 128	Philadelphia National Cemetery, 1891
◆ **CHODMAN,** James	CIV					Camp Letterman, Row 5, Grave 12	Box 2-240, Hollywood, Richmond, 8/3/72, as "James Godman, Negro"
CHRISTIE, Daniel H.	COL	31	F&S	23rd NC	d. July 17 on retreat	None	Stonewall Cemetery, Winchester, VA
CLARK, D.P.	PVT	19	A	22nd NC	d. July 22 U.S. Gen. Hosp. Chester, PA	Chester Rural Cemetery, Chester, PA	Philadelphia National Cemetery, 1891; his right femur is in the National Museum of Health and Medicine, Specimen #2313
◆ **CLARK,** Jonathan or Albert H.	PVT		F	42nd MS	k. July 1	Somewhere near the Chambersburg turnpike northwest of Gettysburg; buried with his father, Thomas Clark, and Capt. J.M. Gaston; headboard found in the 1880s	
CLARK, Samuel C.	PVT	20	D	10th AL	d.c. July 6 "in Butt's barn"	North of Francis Bream's house, in field near woods along side of Adam Butt's woods near road, south of house; buried by his brother, Jack Clark	Box 1-133, Hollywood, Richmond, 6/13/72
CLARK, Thomas G.	CPT	39	F	42nd MS	k. July 1	Somewhere near the Chambersburg turnpike northwest of Gettysburg: buried with one son, and Capt. J.M. Gaston	
CLAYBROOK, Samuel	PVT	23	H	22nd NC	d. July 27 U.S. Gen. Hosp. Chester, PA	Chester Rural Cemetery, Chester, PA	Philadelphia National Cemetery, 1891
CLEM, Michael	PVT		Carpenter's (VA) Battery		k. July 2	George Wolf's farm, in field, near woods; "along edge of Hospital Woods;" "grave obliterated"	
CLEMENTS, Thomas W.	SGT		D	8th GA	d. July 7	John Edward Plank's farm, back of barn, under locust tree toward John S. Crawford's farm	Box 2-H, Hollywood, Richmond, 8/3/72
CLIETT, E.W.	PVT		D	20th GA		John Edward Plank's farm, under large locust tree toward John S. Crawford's place and near road to Bream's Mill	Box 2-H, Hollywood, Richmond, 8/3/72, as "E.W. Clytt, Co. E, 8 Ga."
CLINK, Robert H.	PVT	24	K	5th VA	d. July 10	Henry A. Picking's farm, in field along fence opposite the schoolhouse	Stonewall Cemetery, Winchester, VA
CLYDE, Charles E.	SGT		C	Phillips (GA) Legion		On hill between Jacob Schwartz's and George Bushman's farms, under a walnut tree, Yard B, Row 2	Box 1-S-9, Hollywood, Richmond, 6/13/72
COBB, Livingston G.	PVT	36	H	45th NC	d. Aug.16	Camp Letterman, Row 2, Grave 29	Oakwood, Raleigh, 10/1/71
COBLER, John H.	PVT	36	F	45th NC	k./d. July 6	John Reed's place at the foot of South Mountain, two miles above Fairfield, near sawmill	Oakwood, Raleigh

Name	Rank	Age	Co.	Regiment	Death	Burial	Final Disposition
COCHRAN, John S.	CPT	26	D	5th FL	d. Oct. 29 West's Bldg. U.S. Gen. Hosp. Baltimore, MD	None	Loudon Park, Baltimore, Row A, Grave 43
COCHRAN, William H.	PVT	22	A	11th MS	d. July 15	Jacob Schwartz's farm	Probably in one of seven boxes marked "S," to Hollywood, Richmond, 9/10/72, as an unknown
◆ COCKE, James M.	PVT		G	4th AL	died at Williamsport, Maryland	Possibly Public Burial Ground, Hagerstown, MD	Possibly Washington Cemetery, Hagerstown, MD
COCKE, William F.	LT	26	E	18th VA		"Taken to a house;" "body never recovered"	His VA military records say he is buried in Charlotte Co., VA, cemetery unknown
CODY, Barnett H.	LT	19	G	15th AL	d. July 21	Michael Fiscel's farm, east of house, across creek	Box 3-A, Hollywood, Richmond, 9/10/72
COE, William W.	SGT	25	M	21st NC	d. Sept. 17	Camp Letterman, Row 8, Grave 16	Oakwood, Raleigh, Grave 482, 10/1/71
COFFEY, Thomas M.	PVT	28	F	26th NC	d. Aug. 12	Samuel Lohr's farm, opposite house, in meadow near pear tree	Box 4-S, Hollywood, Richmond, 5/17/73
COLEMAN, B.G.	SGT		A	19th MS		Adam Butt's farm, south of house, near road toward Francis Bream's place	Box 1-181, Hollywood, Richmond, 6/13/72
COLQUITT, James B.	PVT	33	G	6th AL		David Shriver's farm, north of house, corner of orchard	Box 1-120, Hollywood, Richmond, 6/13/72
COMPTON, James	PVT		I	8th GA	d. July 3	John Edward Plank's farm, back of barn	Box 2-H, Hollywood, Richmond, 8/3/72
CONE, Neverson	PVT	20	A	47th NC	d. Aug. 26	Camp Letterman, Row 6, Grave 9	Oakwood, Raleigh, Grave 467, 10/1/71
CONLEY, William B.	PVT		F	17th MS		John S. Crawford's farm, in orchard north of "Walnut Avenue" under apple tree	Box 2-C-Miss., Hollywood, Richmond, 8/3/72; "grave unmarked by then"
CONNELL, Ira T.	PVT	19	G	30th NC	d. July 3/4	Buried near barn along Fairfield Road about three miles from Gettysburg by Chaplain A.D. Betts, next to soldier of the 4th NC	
CONNELL, William	PVT			Moody's Co., (LA) Madison Lt. Artillery	d. Sept. 9 U.S. Gen. Hosp. Chester, PA	Chester Rural Cemetery, Chester, PA	Philadelphia National Cemetery, 1891
CONNER, John	PVT		K	5th AL	k. July 1	"James J. Wills's farm, in woods;" probably Moses McClean's farm, as James J. Wills owned it in post-war years; buried next to Jackson Kersey	Possibly in a box marked "B," to Hollywood, Richmond, 6/13/72, as an unknown
CONRAD, James D.	PVT	18	F	28th NC	d. Sept. 16	Possibly Camp Letterman Cemetery	Conrad Cemetery, Yadkin County, NC
COOK, Columbus M.	CPL	23	D	11th MS	k. July 3	Buried by his brother Wm. B. Cook "in the field where he died;" possibly on William Bliss's farm	
COOLEY, Joseph W.	PVT			Carpenter's (VA) Battery	d. July 4	David Stewart's farm, in woods near the barn, with one unknown soldier	Box 3-288, Hollywood, Richmond, 9/10/72
COOLEY, Lemuel	PVT	15	B	47th NC	d.c. July 14	Jacob Schwartz's farm, in cornfield, Yard D, Row 3	Box 1-S-61, Hollywood, Richmond, 6/13/72

Name	Rank	Age	Co.	Regiment	Death	Chester Rural Cemetery, Chester, PA	Philadelphia National Cemetery, 1891
COON, J.	PVT		H	8th AL	d. Aug. 26 U.S. Gen. Hosp. Chester, PA	Chester Rural Cemetery, Chester, PA	Box 1-202, Hollywood, Richmond, 6/13/72
COOPER, Giles H.	LT		D	24th VA	d. July 27	On hill between Jacob Schwartz's and George Bushman's farms, under a walnut tree, Yard B, Row 2	Possibly Green Mount Cemetery, Baltimore, MD
◆ COOPER, Thomas W.	LT	22	C	11th NC	k. July 1	Along Willoughby's Run, near Herr's Tavern, or near the Seminary; buried next to Lt. Edward Rhodes; "Schoolmasters removed April 26" [1866?]	
COPELAN, W.O.	PVT		I	8th GA	d. July 5	John Edward Plank's farm, back of barn	Box 2-H, Hollywood, Richmond, 8/3/72
COPELAN, William H.	CPL		K	44th GA	k. July 1	North of Almshouse, under walnut tree near graveyard	
CORMIER, Louis A.	CPT		C	6th LA	d. July 3	Elizabeth Wible's farm, back of barn	Box 3-265, Hollywood, Richmond, 9/10/72
COSBY, James R.	PVT		B	16th GA		John Cunningham's farm, across creek from John S. Crawford's, orchard, south side	Laurel Grove, Savannah, Lot 853, Grave 11
COULTER, R. Smith	PVT		E	12th GA	d. July 7	Probably on Jacob Hankey's farm	Laurel Grove, Savannah, Lot 854, Grave 13, 8/21/71
COUSINS, Masston C.	PVT		G	44th VA	d. July 2	W. Henry Monfort farm, under apple tree in orchard above the house near road	Box 3-287, Hollywood, Richmond, 9/10/72
COVIN, Oscar W.	PVT	20	K	15th SC	d. Aug. 11 U.S. Gen. Hosp. Chester, PA	Chester Rural Cemetery, Chester, PA	Magnolia, Charleston, Grave 57, 5/10/71, as "O.W. Covern."
COX, Henry C.	PVT	20	F	2nd NC BN	k. July 1	John Reed's place at the foot of South Mountain, two miles above Fairfield, near sawmill	Oakwood, Raleigh, probably Grave 545, 10/1/71
◆ COX, Samuel N.	PVT		I	10th GA		John Edward Plank's farm	Possibly Box 2-H, Hollywood, Richmond, 8/3/72, as "S.C., Ga."
COXWELL, William Gray	PVT		F	48th GA	d. July 2	Jacob Schwartz's farm, in cornfield, Yard C	Box 1-S-79, Hollywood, Richmond, 6/13/72
CRAIG, William S.	PVT		G	42nd VA	d. July 13	George Bushman's farm; hospital cemetery was east of house	Box 1-229, Hollywood, Richmond, 6/13/72
CRAIN, Jesse	PVT	23	A	32nd NC	d. July 3	Jacob Hankey's farm	Oakwood, Raleigh, Grave 505, 10/1/71
CRAWFORD, Robert N.	PVT		B	11th AL		South of Adam Butt's farmhouse, near road in woods	Box 1-122, Hollywood, Richmond, 6/13/72
CRAWFORD, William C.	LT	25	G	17th MS			Possibly to Oakwood, Raleigh, NC, 10/1/71, as "Lt. C.W.C., Co. F, 14th NC"
◆ CREECY, William Pryor	PVT		4th Co., Washington (LA) Artillery			Near John S. Crawford's stone tenant house "where Basil Biggs lives"	Possibly Box 4-Y, to Hollywood, Richmond, 5/17/73, as an unknown
CREWS, Joshua J.	PVT		K	8th FL		Jacob Schwartz's farm, back of barn, Grave 1	Possibly in one of seven boxes marked "S" to Hollywood, Richmond, 9/10/72, as an unknown
CROMER, William P.	CPT	26	D	13th SC	k. July 1	Along or west of Seminary Ridge, or in southwest corner of Seminary Woods	Box 3-U, Hollywood, Richmond, 9/10/72, with 14 other remains of A.P. Hill's Corps

Name	Rank	Age	Co.	Unit	Death	Notes	Burial
CROW, Berry	PVT	32	F	6th AL	d. Sept. 12	Camp Letterman, Row 7, Grave 33	Box 1-83, Hollywood, Richmond, 6/13/72
CRUMP, Willis J.	PVT		K	13th MS	d. July 4	John S. Crawford's farm, "where Basil Biggs lives;" in garden	Box 4-Y, Hollywood, Richmond, with 21 others, 5/17/73
CRUTCHFIELD, Joseph R.	SGT		D	2nd GA BN	d. July 27	On hill under walnut tree between Jacob Schwartz's and George Bushman's farms, Yard B, Row 2	Box 1-6, Hollywood, Richmond, 6/13/72
CULBERTSON, Young J., Jr.	SGT		C	3rd SC BN	k. July 2	George Rose's farm, west of stone barn, under large cherry tree; "deep grave with board cover, with 6 others"	Magnolia, Charleston, Grave 24, 5/10/71
CULLER, Henry L.	CPL	23	E	1st SC CAV	d.c. July 8-10	Probably Jacob Schwartz's farm	Columbia, SC
CULP, John Wesley	PVT	24	B	2nd VA	k. July 3	Near Culp's Hill, "where he fell," under a crooked tree; grave well marked by Ben Pendleton, 2nd VA; "He sleeps there now." – Maj. H.K. Douglas	If his body was not moved by friends or family, he was possibly shipped to Hollywood, Richmond, as an unknown, in one of 19 boxes marked "E," 9/10/73, with 189 remains; or, in one of three boxes marked "H," 5/17/73
CULVER, Everard	PVT		K	15th GA	k. July 2	Buried "on battlefield by enemy;" "noble, gallant, and good"	Town cemetery in Culverton, Hancock County, GA
CUMMINGS, C.C.	PVT		K	8th AL	k. July 3	North of Francis Bream's farmhouse, in field near woods along side of Adam Butt's woods near road, south of house	Box 1-128, Hollywood, Richmond, 6/13/72
CUNNINGHAM, Joseph P.	CPT	29	G	2nd SC	k. July 2	George Rose's farm, north of house inside of fence on south side of Emmitsburg Road, "under an apple tree near the meadow stream;" in field next to Joseph Sherfy's orchard, close to fence	Magnolia, Charleston, Grave 30, 5/10/71
CURRIN, Hampton	PVT	37	K	55th NC	d. July 29 Seminary Hosp. Hagerstown, MD	Probably Old Almshouse Burying Ground, Hagerstown, MD	Probably in "Rose Hill," Washington Cemetery, Hagerstown, MD
CUSHING, Robert H.	1SGT	28	C	1st MD BN	k. July 3		Stonewall Cemetery, Winchester, VA
CUSICK, Frederick	PVT			Chesapeake (MD) Artillery	k. July 2	Christian Benner's place, back of Rock Creek under a large walnut tree	Loudon Park, Baltimore, 7/4/73
D							
DAILEY, Franklin O.	LT	31	A	11th MS	k. July 3		He has a stone in Hollywood Cemetery, Richmond, VA
DALEY, John	CPL		G	14th LA	d. July 18	Henry W. Monfort's farm	Box 3-M, Hollywood, Richmond, 9/10/72, with 46 others
◆ DALTON, Lemuel	PVT		D	29th VA	k. c. July 3	West of David McMillan's house in woods; "close by Gen. Pickett's line. Name cut on Hickory tree"	Box 1-216, Hollywood, Richmond, 6/13/72, as "L. Dallen, Va."
DANCE, James A.	PVT		B	3rd GA	k. July 2	Adam Butt's farm or schoolhouse off Fairfield Road	
DANIEL, James M.	LT	27	E	7th SC	k. July 2	On road to Abraham Krise's near Pitzer Schoolhouse in the field near fence under wild cherry tree; "corner of Shefferer's farm near Pitzer Schoolhouse;" buried close to C.V. Hammond and J.M. Stricker. (His brother, William L., was also killed.)	Probably "State Lot" - SC to Hollywood, Richmond
DANIEL, John P.	CPL	26	H	11th VA	d. July 28	Francis Bream's mill above William Myers's house at the side of a fence	Box 2-P-Curns, Hollywood, Richmond, 8/3/72, with 33 others

Name	Rank	Age	Co.	Regiment	Death	Original Burial	Final Burial
DANIEL, William J.	PVT	22	H	3rd NC	d. July 22 West's Bldg. U.S. Gen. Hosp. Baltimore, MD	None	Loudon Park, Baltimore, Row D, Grave 51, 7/23/63
DANIEL, William L.	LT	30	I	2nd SC	k. July 2	George Rose's farm, "on the gravl walk in the woods." Said to have been buried by his servant, "Bob," which was untrue. His last words were, "Tell my father that I died doing my duty." (His brother, James M., was also killed at Gettysburg.)	If not removed by his family, then possibly to Magnolia, Charleston, Common Grave 28, 5/10/71, as "Sgt. E. W. Eure (or Ewie), Co. H, 15th S.C.V."; his corpse is the third from the left in the photo on the back cover of this book.
◆ DANLEY, Henry	PVT	31	K	47th NC	d. Aug. 5	Camp Letterman, Row 3, Grave 9	Oakwood, Raleigh, 10/1/71
DAVENPORT, Henry	CPT		E	42nd MS	d. July 17	Jacob Schwartz's farm, Yard D, Row 1	Box 1-S-24, Hollywood, Richmond, 6/13/72
DAVENPORT, Theophilus R.	SGT	20	C	11th MS	d. July 10	Samuel Lohr's farm	Possibly in a box marked 4-S to Hollywood, Richmond, 5/17/73, as an unknown
DAVERS, Anthony	PVT		E	2nd NC BN	d. July 7	Jacob Plank's farm, back of barn, Grave 3; "grave ploughed over"	Box 3-284, Hollywood, Richmond, 9/10/72
DAVIS, Archibald J.	PVT	24	K	32nd NC	d. July 3	Jacob Hankey's farm	Oakwood, Raleigh, Grave 503, 10/1/71
DAVIS, Hamilton	PVT	31	K	52nd NC	d.c. July 13	Samuel Lohr's farm, opposite house in meadow near pear tree	Box 4-S, Hollywood, Richmond, with 44 others, 5/17/73
DAVIS, Jacob N.	PVT		A	1st MD BN		"Removed from Gettysburg battlefield in 1874"	Loudon Park, Baltimore, Row E, Grave 34
DAVIS, James T.	CPT		D	12th AL	k. July 1	John S. Forney's farm; also "west of Samuel Cobean's house in woods along Poor House fence;" "a brave, good man"	Possibly in one of six boxes marked "F," to Hollywood, Richmond, 8/3/72, as an unknown
DAVIS, John F.	SGT		I	11th GA	k. July 2	South of George Rose's house, edge of woods; also, "in the woods beyond where Bird & Bond were buried;" (Capt. Bond, 53rd GA and Sgt. Bird, 50th GA)	Laurel Grove, Savannah, Lot 853, Grave 13, 9/24/71
DAVIS, Joseph	PVT		E	8th VA	d. July 11	Jacob Schwartz's farm, in cornfield on Rock Creek, Yard D, Row 2	Box 1-S-36, Hollywood, Richmond, 6/13/72
DAVIS, Joseph W.	PVT		I	13th MS		John S. Crawford's farm, in orchard north of "Walnut Avenue" under apple tree	Box 2-C-Miss, Hollywood, Richmond, 8/3/72; "grave unmarked by then"
DAVIS, Philip	PVT	25	I	14th VA	d. July 24	Jacob Schwartz's farm, back of barn	Possibly in one of seven boxes marked "S," to Hollywood, Richmond, 9/10/72, as an unknown
DAVIS, W.P.	PVT		K	2nd LA	d. July 2	George Wolf's farm, under an oak tree, near a fence, near the gatehouse on York Road; "killed in the ranks near Gettysburg"	Box 2-253, Hollywood, Richmond, 8/3/72
DAVIS, William J.	PVT		E	48th GA	k. July 2	Adam Butt's brick schoolhouse, Fairfield Road	Laurel Grove, Savannah, Lot 853, Grave 12, 9/24/71
DAVIS, Winborn C.	SGT	22	F	1st NC		Martin Shealer's farm, in meadow next to Elizabeth Wible's, under little apple tree	Box 3-V, Hollywood, Richmond, 9/10/72
DAWSON, Leroy T.	PVT		C	24th VA	d. July 21	On hill between Jacob Schwartz's and George Bushman's farms, Yard B, Row 2, under a walnut tree	Box 1-10, Hollywood, Richmond, 6/13/72
DAWSON, William P.	SGT	28	K	52nd NC	k. July 1	Samuel Lohr's farm, opposite house in meadow near pear tree	Box 4-S, Hollywood, Richmond, 5/17/73

Name	Rank	Age	Co.	Regiment	Date	Location	Burial
DEAL, Lewis	PVT		H	8th AL		West side of Adam Butt's house at the road in corner of woods	Box 1-141, Hollywood, Richmond, 6/13/72
DEAN, Charles N.	PVT		K	3rd GA	k. July 2	Adam Butt's brick schoolhouse, Fairfield Road	Laurel Grove, Savannah, Lot 353, Grave 12, 9/24/71
DEARMAN, William F.	PVT	25	I	16th NC	d. Oct. 13	Camp Letterman, Row 9, Grave 8	Oakwood, Raleigh, Grave 486, 10/1/71
DEATON, T.J.	PVT		A	2nd GA BN	k. July 2	Adam Butt's farm or schoolhouse, possibly "south of house"	
DEEMS, Theodore D.	LT	19	G	5th NC		Jacob Hankey's farm. (Two weeks after the battle, Rev. Dr. Deems was with the army inquiring about his wounded son.)	If not returned home by his family to Wilson, NC, then possibly in one of eight boxes marked "N," to Hollywood, Richmond, 8/3/72, as an unknown
DEES, Clement Allen	PVT	29	B	43rd NC	d. Sept. 1	Camp Letterman, Row 6, Grave 30	Oakwood, Raleigh, Grave 471, 10/1/71
DEGGS, C.W.	PVT		A	5th TX	d. July 2	John Edward Plank's farm, under tree, right and front of house toward Fairfield Road and Gettysburg; "north side of Plank's under walnut tree"	Probably Box 2-H, Hollywood, Richmond, 8/3/72, as "M.E. Diggs, Co. F, 8th GA"
DEMENT, Albert L.	1SGT	29	F	47th NC	d. July 23	On hill under a walnut tree between Jacob Schwartz's and George Bushman's farms, Yard B, Row 1	Box 1-12, Hollywood, Richmond, 6/13/72
DEMPSTER, John	PVT	42	E	4th NC CAV	k. July 4 "in a skirmish on 4th by Gen. Kilpatrick making charge on wagon train"	At Gatehouse above Monterey Springs; "South Mountain," "removed"	Oakwood, Raleigh, probably Grave 546, 10/1/71
DENNIS, Samuel	PVT		G	49th VA		Josiah Benner's farm on Harrisburg Road, under apple tree in orchard	Box 3-274, Hollywood, Richmond, 9/10/72
DENTON, John T.	PVT	30	D	56th VA	d. Aug. 1	Camp Letterman, Row 2, Grave 4	Box 1-52, Hollywood, Richmond, 6/13/72
DERRICK, Frederick E.	PVT	24	I	15th SC	d. Aug. 22	Camp Letterman, Row 5, Grave 31	Magnolia, Charleston, Grave 7, 5/10/71
DERRICK, George M.	PVT	18	H	13th SC	d. July 18/24	Chester Rural Cemetery, Chester, PA	Magnolia, Charleston, Grave 59, 5/10/71
DeSAUSSURE, William D.	COL	43	F&S	15th SC	k. July 2	Francis Bream's farm, in the old McClellan family cemetery or burying ground, center	First Presbyterian Church Cemetery, Columbia, SC
DICKSON, Joseph C.	PVT		K	15th GA	k. July 3	John Edward Plank's farm, under large locust tree toward John S. Crawford's and near road to Bream's Mill; also, "back of barn"	Box 2-H, Hollywood, Richmond, 8/3/72
DICKSON, Samuel W.G.	PVT	22	C	8th SC	k. July 2	George Rose's farm, north or back of stone barn	Box 1-153, Hollywood, Richmond, 6/13/72
DINKLE, Enos	SGT		H	7th VA CAV		Flohr's Church Cemetery, Cashtown, PA	Box 4-291, Hollywood, Richmond, 5/17/73, also Stonewall Cemetery, Winchester, VA
DIXON, Benjamin Franklin	SGT	24	B	7th LA	d. Oct. 16	Camp Letterman, Row 9, Grave 1	
◆ DIXON, John E. "Dixie"	PVT		K	3rd GA	k. July 2	South of Emanuel Pitzer's house in edge of woods; buried and marked by James S. Parr and others of the 3rd GA	Possibly in a box marked "D," to Hollywood, Richmond, 6/13/72, as an unknown

Name	Rank	Age	Co.	Regiment	Death	Burial Location	Disposition
DOBSON, John O.	PVT	19	A	2nd NC	d. Sept. 3	Camp Letterman, Row 7, Grave 4	Oakwood, Raleigh, Grave 474, 10/1/71
DONLY, William J.	PVT		E	11th MS		Samuel Lohr's farm, north side of woods	Box 3-L, Hollywood, Richmond, 9/10/72
DORSEY, Joel	PVT		E	53rd GA	k. July 3	George Rose's farm, "on the gravl walk in the woods"	Possibly in one of 15 boxes marked "L," to Hollywood, Richmond, 8/3/72, as an unknown
DOUGHERTY, Daniel	CPL			Chesapeake (MD) Artillery	k. July 2	Below Christian Benner's farm in orchard opposite a stone house [Daniel Lady's]; also, under a large walnut tree back of Rock Creek	Loudon Park, Baltimore, 7/4/73 (?)
DOWDY, James H.	PVT		E	18th VA	d. July 16	Jacob Schwartz's farm, in cornfield on Rock Creek, Yard D, Row 3	Box 1-S-75, Hollywood, Richmond, 6/13/72
DOWNER, David C.	PVT		G	61st GA	k. July 1	Probably on Josiah Benner's farm, in meadow along fence	Possibly to Laurel Grove, Savannah, Lot 853, Grave 10, 9/24/71, as "T. Dausne, Co. G, 61st GA"
DREAN, John F.	PVT	26	A	53rd VA	d. Nov. 4 "Last death at Camp Letterman"	Camp Letterman, Row 9, Grave 13	Box 1-99, Hollywood, Richmond, 6/13/72
DRISCOLL, Larkin R.	PVT		I	56th VA	d. July 28 U.S. Gen. Hosp. Chester, PA	Chester Rural Cemetery, Chester, PA, Grave 63	Philadelphia National Cemetery, 1891
DUBOSE, John E.	SGT		C	5th AL		Jacob Hankey's farm	Probably in one of eight boxes marked "N," to Hollywood, Richmond, 8/3/72, as an unknown
DUCKETT, Joseph N.	LT	28	H	2nd NC BN	d. July 7	Jacob Plank's farm, back or east of barn, Grave 2; "grave ploughed over"	Box 3-283, Hollywood, Richmond, 9/10/72
DUDDING, James O.	PVT	22	C	28th VA	d. Sept. 13	Camp Letterman, Row 7, Grave 30	Box 1-115, Hollywood, Richmond, 6/13/72
DUKE, Archibald Y.	PVT		C	17th MS		John S. Crawford's homestead on Marsh Creek, north side of "Walnut Avenue"	Box 2-C-Miss, Hollywood, Richmond, 8/3/72
DULANEY, Jeremiah	PVT		C	1st MD BN		Elizabeth Wible's farm, near Hunterstown Road; "still marked in 1866"	Probably in Box 3-Y, Hollywood, Richmond, 9/10/72, with 12 remains, as an unknown
DUNCAN, William Frank	PVT	27	C	13th MS	d. Sept. 27	Camp Letterman, Row 8, Grave 19	Box 1-102, Hollywood, Richmond, 6/13/72
DUNDERDALE, John A.F.	PVT	23	K	9th VA	d. July 21	Francis Bream's Mineral Mills, in woods across Marsh Creek from mill; "nicely buried & a rude marker"	
DUNGAN, Thomas W.	PVT	26	D	48th VA	d. July 2	Daniel Lady's farm on Hanover Road below Christian Benner's; buried back of the barn; "still marked in 1866"	Box 4-298, Hollywood, Richmond, 5/17/73
DUNSTON, James Henry	PVT	25	D	14th VA	d. Sept. 12	Camp Letterman, Row 7, Grave 35	Box 1-78, Hollywood, Richmond, 6/13/72
DUNWODY, Henry Macon	MAJ	37	F&S	51st GA	k. July 2	George Rose's farm, "on the gravl walk in the woods"	Probably in one of 15 boxes marked "L," to Hollywood, Richmond, 8/3/72, as an unknown
DYESS, Reuben M.	PVT		A	Sumter (GA) Artillery BN	k. July 3	Ephraim Wisler's farm, in woods toward creek near Jacob Lott's; left of Wisler's	Laurel Grove, Savannah, Lot 854, Grave 13, 8/21/71

E

Name	Rank	Age	Co.	Regiment	Death	Location	Disposition
EADY, John T.	PVT	23	G	15th SC	d.c. July 2	Francis Bream's farm, in burying ground, center	Magnolia, Charleston, Grave 40, 5/10/71
◆ EARLY, H.F.	PVT		D	11th GA	k. July 2	George Rose's farm, somewhere near or in the meadow by the orchard, as "E. Early, Co. F, 11th Ga."	Probably in one of 15 boxes marked "L," to Hollywood, Richmond, 8/3/72, as an unknown
EASLEY, Frederick B.	PVT	27	E	14th VA		Along Jacob Schwartz's farm lane, under walnut tree near creek	Probably in one of seven boxes marked "S," to Hollywood, Richmond, 9/10/72, as an unknown
EASTERLING, Josiah K.	PVT	20	G	8th SC	k. July 2	George Rose's farm, back or north of stone barn	Box 1-159, Hollywood, Richmond, 6/13/72
EASTHAM, George C.	CPT		I	33rd VA		Henry A. Picking's farm	Box 1-64, Hollywood, Richmond, 6/13/72
◆ EASTRIDGE, John	PVT		B	48th VA		Camp Letterman, Row 1, Grave 4	Probably in one of 11 boxes marked "H," to Hollywood, Richmond, 8/3/72, as an unknown
ECHOLS, J.H.	LT		H	8th GA	d.c. July 2	John Edward Plank's farm, under large locust tree toward John S. Crawford's and near road to Bream's Mill; also, "back of barn"	Box 2-H, Hollywood, Richmond, 8/3/72
EDGE, S.C.	PVT		D	8th GA	d. July 21	John Edward Plank's farm, under large locust tree toward John S. Crawford's place and near road to Bream's Mill; also, "back of barn"	Loudon Park, Baltimore, Row D, Grave 57, 8/3/63
EDWARDS, Allen R.	PVT	23	K	26th NC	d. Aug. 1 West's Bldg. U.S. Gen. Hosp. Baltimore, MD	None	Box 1-76, Hollywood, Richmond, 6/13/72
EDWARDS, David S.	PVT	24	D	1st VA	d. Sept. 11	Camp Letterman, Row 7, Grave 28	Probably in "Rose Hill," Washington Cemetery, Hagerstown, MD
EDWARDS, J.J.	PVT	20	E	55th NC	d. Aug. 9 Seminary Hosp. Hagerstown, MD	Probably Old Almshouse Burying Ground, Hagerstown, MD	Philadelphia National Cemetery, 1891
EDWARDS, James D.	PVT		C	57th VA	d. July 25 U.S. Gen. Hosp. Chester, PA	Chester Rural Cemetery, Chester, PA, Grave 76	Box 1-S-16, Hollywood, Richmond, 6/13/72
ELINGTON, William P.	PVT	25	E	26th NC	d. July 21	On hill under walnut tree between Jacob Schwartz's and George Bushman's farms, Yard B, Row 2	Box 1-S-51, Hollywood, Richmond, 6/13/72
ELLETT, Lemuel Overton	CPL	19	I	1st VA	d. July 12	Jacob Schwartz's farm, in cornfield on Rock Creek, Yard D	Box 2-246, Hollywood, Richmond, 8/3/72
ELLIS, John Thomas	LTC	36	F&S	19th VA	k. July 3	John F. Curren's farm, southeast of house in orchard, under apple tree	Box 2-H, Hollywood, Richmond, 8/3/72
ELMORE, Thomas A.	PVT		A	7th GA	d. July 7	John Edward Plank's farm, back of barn	Laurel Grove, Savannah, Lot 853 Grave 11, 9/24/71
ELROD, W.B.	PVT		G	16th GA	d. "after July 3"	John Cunningham's farm, across creek from John S. Crawford's, cemetery was in the orchard, south side	

Name	Rank	Age	Co.	Regiment	Death	Burial Location	Disposition
EMERSON, John R.	LT	24	E	26th NC	d. Aug. 11 DeCamp Hosp. David's Island, New York	None. "I have had his body embalmed and it is vaulted in N.Y. City" – Lt. O.A. Hanner, 26th NC	Grave #773, Cypress Hill Cemetery, Brooklyn, NY
ENNIS, B.T.	PVT		E	14th AL	d. July 26	Jacob Schwartz's farm, back of barn, Grave 4	Possibly in one of seven boxes marked "S," to Hollywood, Richmond, 9/10/72, as an unknown
EPPS, William D.	PVT	31	B	53rd NC	d. July 4	Jacob Hankey's farm	Oakwood, Raleigh, Grave 510, 10/1/71
ESTES, Richard B.	PVT	31	H	45th NC	d. July 23	Jacob Hankey's farm	Oakwood, Raleigh, Grave 491, 10/1/71
EURE, James R.	PVT	23	C	52nd NC	d. Sept. 20 U.S. Gen. Hosp. Chester, PA	Chester Rural Cemetery, Chester, PA	Philadelphia National Cemetery, 1891

F

Name	Rank	Age	Co.	Regiment	Death	Burial Location	Disposition
FARMER, Absalom	PVT	22	G	57th NC	d. July 26	Jacob Schwartz's farm, behind barn, Grave 2	Possibly in one of seven boxes marked "S," to Hollywood, Richmond, 9/10/72, as an unknown
FARMER, Adoniram J.	PVT	20	F	11th MS		Samuel Lohr's farm, in woods, north side	Box 3-L, Hollywood, Richmond, 9/10/72
FARMER, Chesley M.	PVT		H	14th VA	d. July 10	On Widow [Jonathan] Young's farm; also, "Samuel Durboraw's farm, formerly Baubalitz," next to J.R. Gibson	Philadelphia National Cemetery, 1891; his left knee bones are at the National Museum of Health and Medicine, Specimen #1204
FARRAR, Andrew W.	LT		H	8th GA	d. July 21 U.S. Gen. Hosp. Chester, PA	Chester Rural Cemetery, Chester, PA	
FARSON, Stephen	PVT	36	H	1st VA	d. Aug. 29	Southwest corner of Seminary Woods	Box 4-U, Hollywood, Richmond, 5/17/73
FEATHERSTON, Daniel A.	LT	27	F	11th MS	k. July 3	John Horting's farm; "near the garden fence;" under a cherry tree	Probably Box 4-A, Hollywood, Richmond, 5/17/73, with 11 others; also, as "State Lot" - MS, Hollywood, Richmond
FELDER, William E.	PVT	20	D	2nd SC	k. July 2	Northwest of George Rose's farmhouse, along fence near some trees; "in Watt [wheat] field along the wood by the fence."	Magnolia, Charleston, Grave 32, 5/10/71
FERRELL, S. Dave	PVT		G	4th TX	k. July 2	John Edward Plank's farm	In 1912, his brother, R.W. Ferrell, stated, "My father had [S.D.'s] body brought back to Mississippi and reinterred by the side of our mother near Holly Springs."
FIELDS, F.L.	PVT		C	4th TX	k. July 2	John Edward Plank's farm, under walnut tree north of house toward Fairfield Road and Gettysburg	Box 2-H, Hollywood, Richmond, 8/3/72
FILGER, Daniel	PVT		D	44th VA	d. July 4	George Bushman's farm; cemetery was east of house	Box 1-220, Hollywood, Richmond, 6/13/72
FISER, James H.	PVT		C	14th TN	d. Aug. 2	Camp Letterman, Row 3, Grave 19	
FLETCHER, Henry Y.	PVT		K	14th VA	d. July 13	George Bushman's farm; cemetery was east of house	Box 1-103, Hollywood, Richmond, 6/13/72
FLETCHER, J.M.	LT		G	12th AL		David Shriver's farm, north of house, corner of orchard	Box 1-125, Hollywood, Richmond, 6/13/72, as "Lt. J.M. Flemming, Co. G, 12th AL"

Name	Rank	Age	Co.	Regiment	Death	Battlefield Location	Disposition
FLOWERS, W.H.	CPL		C	4th NC CAV	d. July 5	At Gatehouse above Monterey Springs; "South Mountain," "removed"	Oakwood, Raleigh, Grave 548, 10/1/71
FONTENOT, Horthere	PVT	19	F	8th LA	d. July 10	Under apple tree in northeast corner of orchard on William Douglas farm or lot, five miles out on the Fairfield Road and just east of Lower Marsh Creek Church; "left wounded in Pa."	Box 1-197, Hollywood, Richmond, 6/13/72
FOOSHE, James A.	PVT		A	3rd SC BN	d. July 2	George Rose's farm, west of barn, under a large cherry tree; "deep grave with board cover with 6 others"	Magnolia, Charleston, Common Grave 24, 5/10/71
FORBES, Wyatt A.	PVT	20	E	55th NC	d. Aug. 11 U.S. Gen. Hosp. Chester, PA	Chester Rural Cemetery, Chester, PA	Philadelphia National Cemetery, 1891; his left tibia and fibula are in the National Museum of Health and Medicine, Specimen #2992
FORD, Edward M.	CPT	43	A	50th GA	k. July 2	George Rose's farm, in orchard near fence; "in orchard near springhouse"	Laurel Grove, Savannah, Lot 853, Grave 13, 9/24/71
FORD, William	PVT	25	B	7th LA	d. Aug. 29	Camp Letterman, Row 5, Grave 35	Box 1-26, Hollywood, Richmond, 6/13/72
FORREST, Samuel P.	CPL	21	K	28th NC	d. Sept. 14	Camp Letterman, Row 8, Grave 10	Oakwood, Raleigh, Grave 479, 10/1/71
FORRESTER, Joel	PVT		K	4th TX	k. July 2	John Edward Plank's farm, under walnut tree north of house toward Fairfield Road and Gettysburg	Box 2-H, Hollywood, Richmond, 8/3/72
FORRESTER, S.B.	PVT		I	24th GA	d. Aug. 11	Camp Letterman, Row 4, Grave 18	Laurel Grove, Savannah, Lot 854, Grave 3
◆ FOSTER, Horace H.	PVT		G	18th VA	d. July 17	Jacob Schwartz's farm, in cornfield on Rock Creek, Yard D, Row 1	Box 1-S-26, Hollywood, Richmond, 6/13/72
FOWLER, Everett	PVT	21	G	47th NC	d. July 3	Samuel Lohr's farm, opposite house in meadow near or under a pear tree	Box 4-S, Hollywood, Richmond, 5/17/73, as "A.B.F., 47th NC"
FRANKLIN, George W.	PVT	19	E	50th GA	d. Aug. 10	Camp Letterman Cemetery	Possibly to Laurel Grove, Savannah, Lot 853, Grave 13, 9/24/71, as "E.F., 50th Ga."
FRANKS, Rufus B.	PVT		I	4th AL		John Edward Plank's farm under large locust tree toward John S. Crawford's place and near road to Bream's Mill; also, "back of barn"	Box 2-H, Hollywood, Richmond, 8/3/72
FRASER, John Couper	CPT	35(?)		Pulaski (GA) Artillery		John S. Crawford's farm, Marsh Creek, under tree from mansion to tenant house	Possibly in Box 2-C-Miss, Hollywood, Richmond, 8/3/72, as an unknown. A stone in Laurel Grove, Savannah, states, "In memory of …," "He died for his country."
FRAZOR, Francis M.	PVT		E	7th TN		Samuel Lohr's farm, opposite house in meadow near pear tree	Box 4-S, Hollywood, Richmond, 5/17/73
FREEMAN, John C.	PVT	23	E	6th NC	d. Aug. 20	Camp Letterman, Row 5, Grave 25	Oakwood, Raleigh, Grave 465, 10/1/71
FREEMAN, William	CPL		I	2nd MS		On a hill between Jacob Schwartz's and George Bushman's farms, Yard B, Row 2	Box 1-S-4, Hollywood, Richmond, 6/13/72
FRENCH, Edward	PVT		I	8th FL		Pennsylvania College; hospital cemetery was north of main edifice	Probably one of three boxes marked "E," to Hollywood, Richmond, 5/17/73, as an unknown
FRENCH, Junius Butler	ADJ	25	F&S	23rd NC	d. July 2	Jacob Hankey's farm	Possibly in one of eight boxes marked "N," to Hollywood, Richmond, 8/3/72, as an unknown

Name	Rank	Age	Co.	Regiment	Death	Burial	Final Burial
FRERET, Jules	PVT	26	2nd Co., Washington (LA) Artillery		d. Aug. 4 11 a.m. "in hospital"	None	Mount St. Mary's, Grotto Cemetery, Emmitsburg, MD, near Campbell Byrne; "an old playmate"
FRICK, John D.	PVT	19	C	1st SC Rifles	d. Sept. 10 U.S. Gen. Hosp. Baltimore, MD	None	Loudon Park, Baltimore, Row A, Grave 41
FRIDLEY, John H.	PVT		K	28th VA	d. Aug. 3 U.S. Gen. Hosp. Chester, PA	Chester Rural Cemetery, Chester, PA, Grave 114	Philadelphia National Cemetery, 1891
FRINK, John	CPT		F	5th FL	d.c. July 7	Pennsylvania College; hospital cemetery was north of main edifice	Possibly Box 4-E, Hollywood, Richmond, 5/17/73, with 35 remains, 27 unknown
FULENWIDER, Andrew C.	PVT	37	E	34th NC		Lutheran Theological Seminary, behind Dr. Charles B. Krauth's house	Box 4-K, Hollywood, Richmond, 5/17/73
FULKS, James M.	PVT	20	G	19th VA	d. Aug. 6	Camp Letterman, Row 3, Grave 7	
FULLER, Adolphus A.	LT		B	3rd SC BN	d. July 16	Francis Bream's farm, north of tavern, near graveyard and creek; also, "in burying ground, center"	Magnolia, Charleston, Grave 38, 5/10/71
FULLER, Edward P.	PVT		B	3rd SC BN		Francis Bream's burying ground, center, or "near burial ground"	Magnolia, Charleston, Grave 35, 5/10/71
FULMER, W.E.C.	PVT	20	F	3rd SC BN	d. Aug. 14	Camp Letterman, Row 1, Grave 34	Magnolia, Charleston, Grave 1, 5/10/71

G

Name	Rank	Age	Co.	Regiment	Death	Burial	Final Burial
GADDY, Elisha D.	PVT	24	K	26th NC	d. July 8	Jacob Schwartz's farm, in cornfield, Yard D, Row 2	Box 1-S-44, Hollywood, Richmond, 6/13/72
GADSDEN, Thomas S.	PVT	22	I	2nd SC	d. July 3	George Rose's farm, "on the gravl walk in the woods," his captain said he died fighting, "as coolly and bravely as usual"	Magnolia, Charleston, Common Grave 28, 5/10/71; his corpse is the first on the left in the photo on the back cover of this book.
GAFF, Dempsey	PVT		H	10th GA	k. July 2	George Rose's farm, in the meadow by the orchard	Laurel Grove, Savannah, Lot 853, Grave 14, 9/24/71
GAGE, Jeremiah Sanders	PVT	23	A	11th MS	d. July 3	John Horting's farm, near Willoughby's Run; his last words were to his mother: "I died like a man."	Supposedly to Hollywood, Richmond, and possibly in a box marked "A," 5/17/73, as an unknown
GAILLARD, Thomas E.	SGT	23	I	2nd SC	d. Oct. 12	Camp Letterman, Row 2, Grave 5	Magnolia, Charleston, Grave 1, 5/10/71
GAMBLE, George H.	1SGT		F	31st GA	k. July 1	North of Almshouse farm under walnut tree near graveyard; on hill back of Almshouse burial ground	
GAMMONS, John R.	PVT	16	D	43rd NC	k. July 1	Jacob Plank's farm, under walnut tree near road, Grave 1	Box 3-268, Hollywood, Richmond, 9/10/72
GARRATT, Esau	PVT	20	G	11th NC	d. July 11 Seminary Hosp. Hagerstown, MD	Probably Old Almshouse Burying Ground, Hagerstown, MD	Probably in "Rose Hill," Washington Cemetery, Hagerstown, MD
GARRETT, C.P.	PVT	24	I	2nd LA	d. Aug. 31	Camp Letterman, Row 6, Grave 28	Box 1-24, Hollywood, Richmond, 6/13/72

Name	Rank	Age	Co.	Regiment	Status	Location	Reburial
GARRETT, Henry B.	PVT	19	G	26th NC	k. July 1		Rock Creek Methodist Protestant Cemetery, Alamance Co., NC
GARRISON, Edward J.	LT	23	F	3rd NC	k. July 2		Rock Creek Methodist Protestant Cemetery, Randolph Co., NC
GASKINS, William H.	SGT	20	K	8th VA	d. Nov. 5	Camp Letterman, Row 9, Grave 14	
GASTON, James M.	CPT		G	42nd MS	k. July 1	Somewhere near or along the Chambersburg turnpike northwest of Gettysburg; next to Capt. Thomas Clark and son headboard found in the 1880s, "on the old McPherson Farm"	
GAY, Galbert G.	PVT	26	F	43rd NC		Jacob Hankey's farm	Oakwood, Raleigh, Grave 502, 10/1/71
GEE, Leonidas J.	SGT		B	56th VA	d. July 17	Jacob Schwartz's farm, in cornfield on Rock Creek, Yard D, Row 2	Box 1-S-47, Hollywood, Richmond, 6/13/72
GEE, Theodore W.	PVT		I	21st MS	d. Aug. 2	Camp Letterman, Row 2, Grave 1	Box 1-62, Hollywood, Richmond, 6/13/72
GEIGER, George Henry	CPT	37	K, Staff, Gen. J.L. Kemper	2nd VA CAV	d. July 17	Possibly Jacob Schwartz's farm	Grace Episcopal Church, "Albermarle Co., VA"
GEOGHEGAN, T.Q.	PVT	18	D	19th MS		Camp Letterman, Row 3, Grave 28	Box 1-66, Hollywood, Richmond, 6/13/72
GERINGER, Henry	PVT	23	K	47th NC		Samuel Lohr's farm, opposite house in meadow and near pear tree	Box 4-S, Hollywood, Richmond, 5/17/73, with 44 others
GERINGER, John H.	PVT	34	H	1st NC	d. July 28	Camp Letterman, Row 1, Grave 15 (from fence)	Oakwood, Raleigh, 10/1/71
GIBSON, Hardy V.	LT		B	13th AL		South of Emanuel Pitzer's farm in edge of woods near Zachariah Myers's buildings; in woods in front of breastworks southeast of Pitzer's; ½ mile north of Henry Spangler's, in center of woods	Possibly in a box marked "Y," to Hollywood, Richmond, 8/3/72, as an unknown, or in a box marked "D," 6/13/72, as an unknown
GIBSON, Henry T.	PVT	27	H	56th VA	d. Aug. 19 West's Bldg. U.S. Gen. Hosp. Baltimore, MD	None	Loudon Park, Baltimore, Row A, Grave 40, 8/20/63
GIBSON, Joachim	SGT	30	I	7th LA	k. July 2	John Crist's farm	
GIBSON, John R.	PVT		G	22nd GA	d. July 14/15	Widow [Jonathan] Young's farm north of Two Taverns, PA; also, west of Samuel Durboraw's farm, next to C.M. Farmer	Box 3-267, Hollywood, Richmond, 9/10/72
GIBSON, St. Pierre	LT		D	4th VA CAV	k. June 29 Westminster, Maryland	1. Union Churchyard, Westminster, MD 2. Ascension Episcopal Churchyard, 8/13/63	To a Culpepper, VA, cemetery by his brother, Colonel J.C. Gibson, 49th VA
GIBSON, William H.	LT	24	C	33rd NC	k. July 3	Jacob Plank's farm, under walnut tree near Fairfield Road, next to Lt. T.W. Baker, 43rd NC	Box 3-268, Hollywood, Richmond, 9/10/72, as "Gibson, unknown"
GILBERT, Charles Lee	PVT		C	27th VA	d. July 10	Henry A. Picking's farm, in field, along fence, opposite schoolhouse near road. (Musket found with remains.)	Box 1-178, Hollywood, Richmond, 6/13/72
GILBERT, George W.	CPL		I	11th GA	k. July 2	South of George Rose's house, edge of woods	Laurel Grove, Savannah, Lot 853, Grave 13, 9/24/71

Name	Rank	Age	Co.	Unit	Death	Initial Burial	Disposition
GILBERT, James M.	PVT	18	E	52nd VA	d. July 5	Christian Byers's farm, Fairfield Road, with 23 others not marked	Oakwood, Raleigh, Grave 521, 10/1/71, as "J.M. Gilbert, NC"
GILBERT, William	PVT	28	D	23rd NC	d. Aug. 5	Camp Letterman, Row 1, Grave 38 (from fence)	Oakwood, Raleigh, 10/1/71
GILES, Jackson B.	PVT	19	C	9th GA Courier, Gen. G. Anderson	d. July 2	Probably John Edward Plank's farm; his final words were, "Tell them I died for my country."	Possibly in one of 11 boxes marked "H," to Hollywood, Richmond, 8/3/72, as an unknown
GILES, Richard E.	PVT		C	1st VA	d. Aug. 21 DeCamp U.S. Gen. Hosp. David's Island, New York	None	Cypress Hills Cemetery, Long Island, NY, Grave 815
GILL, James C.	SGT MAJ	19	F&S	18th VA	d. July 11	Jacob Schwartz's farm, in cornfield on Rock Creek, Yard D, Row 2	Box 1-S-37, Hollywood, Richmond, 6/13/72
GILLESPIE, Richard	PVT		F	Phillip's (GA) Legion		David Stewart's farm, east of the barn	Box 3-N, Hollywood, Richmond, 9/10/72, as "Gillespie, Va."
GILREATH, Lawrence P.	PVT	23	B	2nd SC	d. Oct. 2	Camp Letterman Cemetery	Springwood Cemetery, Greenville, SC
GLADDEN, John T.	PVT	27	C	55th NC	k. July 1		Pleasant Grove Baptist Cemetery; Shelby, Cleveland County, NC
GLADNEY, Amos J.	PVT	17	E	15th SC	d. July 3	George Rose's farm, "in the woods," his headboard was present but no grave - Ambrose M. Emory	Possibly in one of 15 boxes marked "L," to Hollywood, Richmond, 8/3/72, as an unknown
GLASS, Sanford W.	CPT		E	53rd GA	d. July 5	John S. Crawford's farm on Marsh Creek	"State Lot" - GA, Hollywood, Richmond
GLASSCO, Andrew J.	PVT	24	H	21st NC	d. Sept. 18	Camp Letterman, Row 9, Grave 10	Oakwood, Raleigh, Grave 487, 10/1/71
GLASSELL, James S.	PVT	36	I	11th VA	d. July 5	Jacob Schwartz's farm	Possibly in one of seven boxes marked "S," to Hollywood, Richmond, 9/10/72, as an unknown
GLENDY, Robert J.L.	LT	23	C	4th VA	d. July 23	Jacob Brinkerhoff's farm on Hanover Road	Oakwood, Raleigh, 10/1/71
GLENN, H. Coslett	PVT	23	C	6th NC	d. July 4	Elizabeth Wible's farm	Possibly in one of seven boxes marked "S," to Hollywood, Richmond, 9/10/72, as an unknown
GOETCHIUS, John M.	PVT		A	2nd GA BN		Jacob Schwartz's farm, back of barn; "removed"	Box 3-X, Hollywood, Richmond, 9/10/72
GOLDSTICKER, John A.	PVT		A	4th TX	d.c. July 2	Jesse Worley's farm, west of Two Taverns, Pa.	
GOOD, Albert H.	LT	20	I	7th VA	d. Aug. 29 DeCamp U.S. Gen. Hosp. David's Island, New York	None	Brady's Receiving Tomb, 2nd Ave., New York, NY
GOOD, Marcus L.	PVT	26	G	16th NC	d. Aug. 20 U.S. Gen. Hosp. Chester, PA	Chester Rural Cemetery, Chester, PA	Philadelphia National Cemetery, 1891
GOODRUM, William J.	PVT	18	A	11th NC	d. July 23 U.S. Gen. Hosp. Chester, PA	Chester Rural Cemetery, Chester, PA	Philadelphia National Cemetery, 1891

Name	Rank	Age	Co.	Regiment	Death	Burial	Disposition
GOODSON, John H.	PVT	28	B	18th NC	d. July 14	Jacob Schwartz's farm, in cornfield, Yard D, Row 3	Box 1-S-65, Hollywood, Richmond, 6/13/72
GOODSON, Matthew	SGT	35	A	52nd NC	d. July 12	1. Jacob Schwartz's farm, in cornfield on Rock Creek, Yard D, Row 2 2. Jan. 29, 1866, Evergreen Cemetery, Gettysburg, Sec. E, Lot 169, "just west of Ivy Rock," with H.P. Caffey	3. After Aug. 19, 1867, he was reinterred to an unknown spot in Evergreen Cemetery, with H.P. Caffey; also, listed in Box 1-S-49, Hollywood, Richmond; in addition, he has a memorial stone in Old Presbyterian Cemetery, Evergreen, Concord Co., NC
GOODWIN, Frank G.	PVT	19	B	8th GA	d. July 21 West's Bldg. U.S. Gen. Hosp. Baltimore, MD	None	Loudon Park, Baltimore, Row C, Grave 70, 7/21/63
GOODWIN, Robert W.	PVT	21	A	11th MS	d. Dec. 30 West's Bldg. U.S. Gen. Hosp. Baltimore, MD	None	Loudon Park, Baltimore, "Confederate Hill," Row A, Grave 44
GORDON, James D.	PVT		G	8th GA	k. July 3	John Edward Plank's farm	Possibly to Locust Grove, Savannah, Lot 853, Grave 11, as "J.D. Gore, GA"
GORLEY, Andrew William	PVT		G	12th GA	d. July 15	Jacob Hankey's farm	Possibly in one of eight boxes marked "N," to Hollywood, Richmond, 8/3/72, as an unknown
GOSS, William W.	LT	20	E	19th VA	d. July 17	"In the yard of the school building in Gettysburg"	Mt. Olivet Cemetery, Frederick, MD, Grave 202
GOSSETT, Henry	PVT		D	53rd NC	d. July 6/7 U.S. Gen. Hosp. Frederick, MD	None	Box 3-285, Hollywood, Richmond, 9/10/72
GOULD, James L.	SGT		G	4th TX		Jesse Worley's farm, next to Pvt. W. Sensebaugh, and five others not marked	Possibly in one of five boxes marked "F," to Hollywood, Richmond, 9/10/72, as an unknown
GOULDMAN, John J.	PVT		E	55th VA	k. July 1	North of Emanuel Harman's house from west of Gatehouse; "the east side of Willoughby's Run had the other graves"	
GRADY, Preston F.	PVT			Blount's (VA) Battery	d. U.S. Gen. Hospital Harrisburg, PA	None	Soldiers' Lot, Harrisburg, PA Cemetery, Grave 107
GRAHAM, John C.	PVT	30	F	4th TX	d. Aug. 29	Camp Letterman, Row 6, Grave 17	Box 1-116, Hollywood, Richmond, 6/13/72
GRANNISS, Edward J.	LT		B	2nd GA BN	d. July 7	"Under a pear tree, near a house, a short distance north of the 11th Corps hospital, [George Spangler's farm], on east side of Taneytown road;" "Buried side-by-side with Lt. Col. James Huston, 82nd NY. The graves are neatly prepared. Both killed July 2." "Elliott's Map" shows him east, southeast of Sarah Patterson's farmhouse	
GRANT, Willis B.	PVT	22	I	2nd MS	d. July 11	Jacob Schwartz's farm, in cornfield, Yard D, Row 2	Box 1-S-38, Hollywood, Richmond, 6/13/72
GRAVES, Hardy	PVT	25	C	6th AL	d. July 25	Camp Letterman, Row 1, Grave 18	Box 1-30, Hollywood, Richmond, 6/13/72

Name	Rank	Age	Co.	Unit	Death	Field Burial / Circumstance	Reinterment / Disposition
◆ GRAVES, Thomas J.	SGT	32	I	21st GA	d. July 22 Probably Seminary Hosp. Hagerstown, MD	Possibly in Old Almshouse Burying Ground, Hagerstown, MD	Possibly in "Rose Hill," Washington Cemetery, Hagerstown, MD
GRAY, Samuel Wiley	CPT	21	D	57th NC	k. July 2	To the right or south of Menchey's Spring at the foot of East Cemetery Hill; possibly buried by a "Capt. C.H. Hawkins, USA"	His father, Robert Gray, with the help of Dr. O'Neal, removed his body Nov. 13-16, 1865 to Winston, NC
GRAY, Thomas W.	PVT	32	K	38th VA	d. Oct. 4	Camp Letterman, Row 8, Grave 35	Box 1-98, Hollywood, Richmond, 6/13/72
GRAY, William G.	1SGT	28	C	3rd VA	d. Oct. 7	Camp Letterman, Row 9, Grave 5	Box 1-77, Hollywood, Richmond, 6/13/72
GREEN, David H.	PVT	37	D	55th NC	d.c. July 1		Double Springs Baptist Cemetery, Cleveland Co., NC
GREEN, Drury A.	PVT	26	D	55th NC	d. Aug. 19	Camp Letterman, Row 1, Grave 33 (from fence)	Oakwood, Raleigh, 10/1/71
GREEN, Eli T.	PVT	23	E	14th VA	d. Aug. 15	Camp Letterman, possibly in U.S. section	Some believe him to be buried in the National Cemetery, Gettysburg, PA, PA Plot D-30, as "E.T. Green, 14th PA"
GREEN, John T.	CPT	27	I	8th VA	k. July 3		Glenwood Cemetery, Washington, D.C.; "He offered up his life as a sacrifice."
GREEN, Thomas	PVT	22	G	48th VA	d. July 12	George Bushman's farm; "buried Gettysburg"	Cemetery in Washington County, VA
GREENE, John H.	PVT		G	4th TX		Jesse Worley's farm	Box 3-X, Hollywood, Richmond, 9/10/72
GREER, Augustus S.	PVT	22	F	11th MS	d. July 30 U.S. Gen. Hosp. Chester, PA	Chester Rural Cemetery, Chester, PA, Grave 80	Philadelphia National Cemetery, 1891
GREGORY, William R.	CPL	22	G	3rd GA	d.c. July 2	Adam Butt's brick schoolhouse	Laurel Grove, Savannah, Lot 853, Grave 12, 9/24/71
GRIFFIN, John	PVT	30	B	26th NC	d. July 20	On hill under walnut tree between Jacob Schwartz's and George Bushman's farms, Yard B, Row 2	Box 1-S-6, Hollywood, Richmond, 6/13/72
GRIFFIN, William A.	PVT	24	D	37th NC	d. July 21	On hill under walnut tree between Jacob Schwartz's and George Bushman's farms, Yard B, Row 2	Box 1-S-15, Hollywood, Richmond, 6/13/72
GRIFFITH, James A.	LT	22	G	14th NC	k. July 1	John S. Forney's farm, at foot of garden	Oakwood, Raleigh, 10/1/71
GRIGGS, Lewis	PVT	22	K	43rd NC	d. July 23 U.S. Gen. Hosp. Frederick, MD	None	Mt. Olivet Cemetery, Frederick, MD, Grave 205; also "Rose Hill," Washington Cemetery, Hagerstown, MD
GUERRY, Thomas L.	PVT	17	B	Sumter (GA) Artillery BN	k. July 3	Ephraim Wisler's place, in woods toward creek, near Jacob Lott's; "right of Wisler's"	Laurel Grove, Savannah, Lot 854, Grave 13
GUNN, Radford G.	PVT		A	17th MS	d. July 27	John S. Crawford's homestead on Marsh Creek; silver nameplate was on headboard; it read: "OH. God preserve his body for friends"	Box 2-245, Hollywood, Richmond, 8/3/72
GUSMAN, Leon P.	CPL	21	A	8th LA	d. July 2	George Spangler's farm	Dr. O'Neal was in contact with a Sarah Barker, 388 19th St., Washington, D.C. about his remains; no further information available

Name	Rank	Age	Co.	Regiment	Death	Location	Burial
GUY, Leander	PVT	29	A	7th NC	d. July 3	White Church on the Baltimore Pike, in cemetery, grave next to Edgar Hammond, 1st MD BN	Box 2-244, Hollywood, Richmond, 8/3/72, as "Gates, 7NC"
GUY, Robert F.	LT	23	B	3rd VA	d. July 4	Francis Bream's mill, "on the hill from Bream's Mill," as "Lt. B.F.A., Co. B, 3rd Va"	Box 2-P-Curns, Hollywood, Richmond, 8/3/72, with 33 others

H

Name	Rank	Age	Co.	Regiment	Death	Location	Burial
HAGANS, James W.	PVT	24	B	33rd NC	d. July 23 U.S. Gen. Hosp. Chester, PA	Chester Rural Cemetery, Chester, PA	Philadelphia National Cemetery, 1891
HAGER, Sidney H.	PVT	20	K	23rd NC	d. Sept. 18	Camp Letterman, Row 8, Grave 15	Oakwood, Raleigh, Grave 481, 10/1/71
HAGGARD, S.L.	PVT		F	5th AL	k. July 1	Moses McClean's farm, south along the lane in cherry thicket	Box 1-188, Hollywood, Richmond, 6/13/72, as "S.L.H., Co. F, 5th Alabama"
HALBERT, Henry P.	CPT	24	E	11th MS	d. Aug. 9	Samuel Lohr's farm, north side of woods	Box 3-269, Hollywood, Richmond, 9/10/72
HALL, Dennis	PVT		I	8th AL		West side of Adam Butt's house at the road in corner of woods	Box 1-121, Hollywood, Richmond, 6/13/72
HALL, Henry	SGT	20	H	18th NC	d. July 22	On hill under walnut tree between Jacob Schwartz's and George Bushman's farms, Yard B, Row 1	Box 1-19, Hollywood, Richmond, 6/13/72
HALL, R.M.	PVT		F	17th MS		Southwest corner of Seminary Woods	Box 4-U, Hollywood, Richmond, 5/17/73
HALL, William L.J.	LT	18	F	48th GA	d. July 2 (?)	Jacob Schwartz's farm, back of barn, Grave 10	Possibly in one of seven boxes marked "S," to Hollywood, Richmond, 9/10/72, as an unknown
HALLOWELL, J.H.	PVT	20	H	13th MS		John Crawford's farm on Marsh Creek, in orchard north of the "Walnut Avenue" under apple tree	Box 2-C-Miss, Hollywood, Richmond, 8/3/72; "grave unmarked by then"
HALLOWELL, Joshua C.	SGT	33		Parker's (VA) Battery	d. July 20 Probably Seminary Hosp., Hagerstown, MD	Possibly Old Almshouse Burying Ground, Hagerstown, MD; "removed by his wife"	Hollywood, Richmond, Section E, Lot 71, 11/22/65
HAMBRICK, Abner P.	PVT		F	22nd GA	d. July 9	Jacob Schwartz's farm, in cornfield, Yard C; "a little board with I on it," and, "died July 9, 1863"	Box 1-S-77, Hollywood, Richmond, 6/13/72
HAMBY, Andrew J.	PVT		G	42nd MS		On hill under walnut tree between Jacob Schwartz's and George Bushman's farms, Yard B, Row 1	Box 1-7, Hollywood, Richmond, 6/13/72
HAMILTON, Francis P.	PVT	22	H	11th MS	d. July 5	John Horting's farm, "near the garden fence" under walnut tree, in southeast corner of garden	Box 4-A, Hollywood, Richmond, 5/17/73, with 12 remains, 5 named
HAMILTON, Miles R.	PVT	30	E	32nd NC	d. July 2	Jacob Hankey's farm	Oakwood, Raleigh, Grave 504, 10/1/71
HAMILTON, Newton J.	PVT		E	14th TN		Samuel Lohr's farm, opposite the house in meadow near pear tree	Box 4-S, Hollywood, Richmond, 5/17/73, as "N.J. Hamnor, E, 17th Tenn."
HAMMOND, Christian V.	PVT		B	1st SC Rifles	d. July 3	New county road at handboard between Samuel Pitzer's farm and John Sachs's place; in field on road to Abraham Krise's farm; buried near Lt. J.M. Daniel under wild cherry tree	Probably "State Lot" - SC, to Hollywood, Richmond

Name	Rank	Age	Co.	Regiment	Casualty	Burial Location	Final Disposition
HAMMOND, Edgar	PVT		C	1st MD BN		White Church, Baltimore Pike, in graveyard next to Leander Guy, 7th NC	Box 2-243, Hollywood, Richmond, 8/3/72
HAMMOND, William	PVT	31	B	52nd NC	d. July 22 Jordan Springs Hospital, Winchester, VA	None	Stonewall Cemetery, Winchester, VA
HAMPTON, Thomas	PVT	24	H	8th SC	d. July 3	Francis Bream's farm and tavern, in orchard; "in apple orchard at Black Horse Tavern"	Magnolia, Charleston, Grave 27, 5/10/71
HANCE, James Washington	LTC	35	F&S	53rd GA	k. July 2	George Rose's farm, possibly "on the gravl walk in the woods"	Remains expressed to father in Laurens Court House, S.C., Summer, 1871, by Dr. Rufus B. Weaver
HANCOCK, Benjamin L.	CPT		H	2nd GA	k. July 2	John Slyder's farm under a cherry tree; possibly back of house near Col. J.A. Jones	Box 3-262, Hollywood, Richmond, 9/10/72
HANCOCK, John H.	PVT		D	52nd NC	k. July 1	East of Dr. Samuel E. Hall's stone house in woods near county road, with J.D. Leaman, 52nd NC	Oakwood, Raleigh, 10/1/71
HANIGAN, T.	PVT		A	Phillips (GA) Legion Cavalry		Jacob Brinkerhoff's farm, along Hanover Road	Laurel Grove, Savannah, Lot 854, Grave 12, 8/21/71, as "G. Hangman, GA Cavalry"
HARDESTY, Richard	PVT			Chesapeake (MD) Artillery	d. July 2	Possibly at Christian Benner's farm, back of Rock Creek under a large walnut tree	Loudon Park, Baltimore, Row E, Grave 45
HARDGROVE, John	PVT		A	55th VA	d. July 1	Samuel Lohr's farm, opposite house, in meadow, near pear tree	Box 4-S, Hollywood, Richmond, 5/17/73
HARDMAN, Burton L.	PVT		K	13th AL	k. July 2	Samuel Lohr's farm, opposite house, in meadow, near pear tree	Box 4-S, Hollywood, Richmond, 5/17/73
HARDWICK, William E.G.	LT	27	F	10th AL	d. July 16 U.S. Gen. Hosp. Chester, PA	Chester Rural Cemetery, Chester, PA	Philadelphia National Cemetery, 1891
HARDWICK, William H.	LT		K	15th GA	d. July 25	John Edward Plank's farm	Laurel Grove, Savannah, Lot 853, Grave 11, 9/24/71
HARDY, John R.	PVT		I	28th VA	d. July 3	Pennsylvania College, north of main edifice in hospital cemetery	Box 4-E, Hollywood, Richmond, with 34 other remains, 5/17/73, as "J.E. Hay, Co. F, 28th Va."
HARDY, N.P.	PVT		H	14th AL		North of Francis Bream's tavern in field near woods, along side of Adam Butt's woods near road; Adam Butt's farm, south of house near road in woods	Box 1-127, Hollywood, Richmond, 6/13/72
HARDY, William F.	PVT	21	F	11th MS	d. July 20	On hill between Jacob Schwartz's and George Bushman's farms, Yard B, Row 2	Box 1-208, Hollywood, Richmond, 6/13/72
HARLING, Thomas	CPL		I	7th SC	k. July 2	George Rose's farm, back or north of the barn	Box 1-154, Hollywood, Richmond, 6/13/72, as "I. Thurling, 7th SC"
HARMON, Samuel	CPL	27	I	13th SC	d. July 28 U.S. Gen. Hosp. Chester, PA	Chester Rural Cemetery, Chester, PA	Magnolia, Charleston, Grave 61, 5/10/71
HARNEY, Frank M.	LT	25	F	14th NC	d. July 2	David Shriver's farm, probably north of house, corner of orchard	Oakwood, Raleigh, Grave 525, 10/1/71

Name	Rank	Age	Co.	Regiment	Date	Location/Notes	Burial
HARRELL, John J.	PVT		A	59th GA	d. July 7	John Edward Plank's farm, under large locust tree toward John S. Crawford's near road to Bream's Mill; also, "back of barn"	Box 2-H, Hollywood, Richmond, 8/3/72
HARRELL, John W.	SGT	25	B	26th AL	d. July 3	George Bushman's farm; hospital cemetery was east of house.	Box 1-232, Hollywood, Richmond, 6/13/72
HARRELL, Leonard B.	SGT	18	F	8th SC	d. July 3	Francis Bream's farm, McClellan's old burying ground, center	Possibly in one of two boxes marked "B," to Hollywood, Richmond, 8/3/72, as an unknown
HARRIS, James L.	PVT		F	56th VA	d. July 16	Jacob Schwartz's farm, in cornfield on Rock Creek, Yard D, Row 3	Box 1-S-73, Hollywood, Richmond, 6/13/72
HARRIS, Samuel	PVT	28	F	45th NC	d. July 15	George Bushman's farm; hospital cemetery was east of his stone house	Oakwood, Raleigh, Grave 530, 10/1/71, as "S. Harris, G, 55th NC"
HARRIS, Thomas N.	PVT		H	18th NC	d. Aug. 16 U.S. Gen. Hosp. Chester, PA	Chester Rural Cemetery, Chester, PA	Philadelphia National Cemetery, 1891
HARRIS, William C.	PVT	23	I	55th NC	d. July 19 Jordan Springs Hospital, Winchester, VA	None	Stonewall Cemetery, Winchester, VA
HARRIS, W.T.	PVT		F	7th VA	k. July 2	John F. Curren's farm; "in garden"	Box 2-250, Hollywood, Richmond, 8/3/72
HARRIS, William Terrell	LTC	33	F&S	2nd GA	k. July 2	Charles B. Polley's farm, in orchard; also, "near white oak tree, tree marked 'A,' grave has no mark;" "removed"	Linwood Cemetery, Columbus, GA
HARRISON, Bradford	PVT		G	4th GA	k. July 1	At Almshouse farm under walnut tree near graveyard north of Almshouse; "on McMullin's side"	
HARRISON, George W.	PVT		I	11th GA	d. July 20	John Edward Plank's farm, under a large locust tree toward John S. Crawford's place and near road to Bream's Mill; also, "back of barn"	Box 2-H, Hollywood, Richmond, 8/3/72
HARTSFIELD, John A.	PVT		H	17th MS		John S. Crawford's homestead on Marsh Creek, north side of "Walnut Avenue"	Box 2-C-Miss, Hollywood, Richmond, 8/3/72
HARVEY, Edward B.	LT	35	H	18th VA	d. Aug. 6/18	Camp Letterman, Row 3, Grave 13	Box 1-45, Hollywood, Richmond, 6/13/72
HARVEY, Stephen R.	PVT	30	D	18th VA	d. July 28	Camp Letterman, Row 1, Grave 10	Box 1-63, Hollywood, Richmond, 6/13/72
HASKELL, William T.	CPT	26	A	1st SC	k. July 2	Possibly near Long Lane, south of Gettysburg. Removed by friends and ex-Confederates after the war	Trinity Episcopal Church, Abbeville, SC
HATLEY, Alfred	PVT	28	I	52nd NC	d. July 17	Jacob Schwartz's farm, in cornfield, Yard D, Row 2	Box 1-S-46, Hollywood, Richmond, 6/13/72
HATLEY, Daniel A.	PVT	19	K	28th NC	d. July 24	On hill under walnut tree between Jacob Schwartz's and George Bushman's farms, Yard B, Row 1	Box 1-14, Hollywood, Richmond, 6/13/72, as "Co. K, 21st NC"
HAWKINS, Charles	PVT		Woolfolk's (VA) Battery		k. July 3	In front of Nicholas Codori's house on the Confederate line northeast of Joseph Sherfy's farmhouse near edge of woods; "along Rebel artillery line, edge of woods in front of Codori's place;" "buried next to J.R. Terrell"	Possibly in one of 21 boxes marked "P," to Hollywood, Richmond, 8/3/72, as one of 225 unknowns

Name	Rank	Age	Co.	Regiment	Death	Burial Location	Disposition
HAYDEN, George	CPL		B	1st MD BN	d. Sept. 23	Camp Letterman Cemetery, possibly in U.S. section	Some believe him to be buried in the National Cemetery, Gettysburg, PA, as "George Hayden, Co. D, 1st Ind. Cav."
HAYDEN, Joseph S.	PVT	23	E	13th GA	d. Aug. 30	Camp Letterman, Row 6, Grave 25	Laurel Grove, Savannah, Lot 854, Grave 3
HAYNES, John H.	PVT		B	8th AL		North of Francis Bream's tavern in field near woods; along side of Adam Butt's woods, near road, south of house	Box 1-137, Hollywood, Richmond, 6/13/72
HAYS, Shelton	PVT	25	B	26th NC	d. July 19 Jordan Springs Hospital, Winchester, VA	None	Stonewall Cemetery, Winchester, VA, Grave 27, NC Section
HAYS, Thomas	PVT			Bachman's (SC) Battery	k. July 2	John S. Crawford's farm, near barn, at Samuel John's tenant house	Magnolia, Charleston, Grave 54, 5/10/71, as "T. Hays, Rhett's (SC) Battery"
HAYS, Ulissus A.	PVT		K	13th MS		John S. Crawford's farm, Marsh Creek, in orchard north of "Walnut Avenue" under apple tree	Box 2-C-Miss, Hollywood, Richmond, 8/3/72; "grave unmarked by then"
HEAD, William H.	PVT		K	12th SC	d. July 2	Seminary Ridge, Elizabeth F. Schultz's, in orchard near the house	Box 3-270, Hollywood, Richmond, 9/10/72
HEARN, Joseph L.	PVT		C	35th GA	d. July 5		Laurel Grove, Savannah, Lot 853, Grave 12, 9/24/71
HEATON, Elijah H.	PVT	22	G	52nd VA	d. Aug. 9	Camp Letterman, Row 4, Grave 11	Box 1-107, Hollywood, Richmond, 6/13/72
HEDGES, Owen T.	PVT	47	D	2nd VA	d. July 9/11	Henry A. Picking's farm, in field, along fence opposite schoolhouse	Hedgesville Cemetery, Hedgesville, WV
HEGGIE, Mathew E.	CPL		F	8th GA	d. July 2	John Edward Plank's farm	"State Lot" - GA, to Hollywood, Richmond
HENDRICKS, Jesse S.	PVT		C	12th SC	d. July 29 U.S. Gen. Hosp. Chester, PA	Chester Rural Cemetery, Chester, PA	Magnolia, Charleston, Grave 56, 5/10/71
♦ HENKLE, Michael P.	LT	38	K	25th VA		Back of Rock Creek, in orchard below Christian Benner's, and opposite Daniel Lady's stone house, as "Lt. P.M.H., Co. A," with two men of the Chesapeake (MD) Battery	Possibly in a box marked "V," to Hollywood, Richmond, 5/17/73, as an unknown
HENRY, Charles	CPL		E	7th VA CAV	d. July 5	Benjamin A. Marshall's farm, north of Fairfield, PA	Box 4-W, Hollywood, Richmond, with 11 others, 5/17/73
HENRY, Z.P.	PVT		D	5th TX	d. July 11 Hagerstown or Williamsport Hospital	None	Possibly Washington Cemetery, Hagerstown, MD
HERNDON, Jacob W.	PVT	19	C Gen. J.B. Hood's courier	4th TX	k. July 2	Carried back and buried at or near John Edward Plank's farm under a locust tree toward John S. Crawford's farm, and near road to Bream's Mill; also, "back of barn"	Possibly in one of 11 boxes marked "H," to Hollywood, Richmond, 8/3/72, as an unknown
HERRING, N.B.	PVT		I	7th VA	d. July 27	Jacob Schwartz's farm, back of barn, Grave 6	Possibly in one of seven boxes marked "S," to Hollywood, Richmond, 9/10/72, as an unknown

Name	Rank	Age	Co.	Regiment	Death	Location	Notes
HICKS, William F.	LT	28	B	14th TN	d. Aug. 10 U.S. Gen. Hosp. Chester, PA	Chester Rural Cemetery, Chester, PA	Philadelphia National Cemetery, 1891; his left tibia and fibula are in the National Museum of Health and Medicine, Specimen #0509
HILL, Asoph	CPT		F	7th TN	d. July 8	Jacob Schwartz's farm, in cornfield, Yard D, Row 2	Probably "State Lot" – TN, to Hollywood, Richmond
HILL, Nicholas	CPL		A	3rd SC BN		Francis Bream's farm, north of tavern near graveyard by the creek	Magnolia, Charleston, Grave 53, 5/10/71
HILLHOUSE, Barton N.	PVT	27	F	5th FL	d.c. July 4	Pennsylvania College, hospital cemetery was north of main edifice	Possibly in Box 4-E, Hollywood, Richmond, 5/17/73, with 35 remains, 27 unknown
◆ HINDMAN, N. Bony	PVT		A	13th MS	d. Aug. 14	Camp Letterman, Row 1, Grave 31	Box 1-36, Hollywood, Richmond, 6/13/72, as "N.B. Hyndman"
HINES, Thomas J.	PVT	32	D	1st MD BN		Camp Letterman Cemetery	There is some evidence the family may have later claimed his remains
HINSON, Marion R.	LT	33	H	2nd SC	d. July 3	Francis Bream's farm, back of the tavern lot	Possibly in one of two boxes marked "B," to Hollywood, Richmond, 8/3/72, as an unknown
HITE, John P.	PVT	22	H	33rd VA	d. July 5	Henry Picking's farm, in a field along fence opposite the schoolhouse by road; gold plate and teeth found in upper jaw	Box 1-170, Hollywood, Richmond, 6/13/72
HITT, Paskill A.	PVT		G	7th VA	d. July 27 U.S. Gen. Hosp. Chester, PA	Chester Rural Cemetery, Chester, PA, Grave 70	Philadelphia National Cemetery, 1891
HOCKMAN, Whiting F.	PVT	23	F	10th VA	d. July 15	George Bushman's farm; hospital cemetery was east of the house	Box 1-221, Hollywood, Richmond, 6/13/72
HODGES, David	PVT		F	41st VA		John Edward Plank's farm in orchard under apple tree; "on Weigle's Mill Rd. 2 ½ miles northwest of Gettysburg"	Possibly Box 1-180, Hollywood, Richmond, 6/13/72, as "Jasper Hodges, Co. F, 41st Miss."
HODGES, James	PVT		A	3rd GA	k. July 2	Near Adam Butt's brick schoolhouse	Laurel Grove, Savannah, Lot 853, Grave 12, 9/24/71
HODGES, James G.	COL	33	F&S	14th VA	k. July 3	According to Dr. John O'Neal, "Col. Hodges (of Portsmouth), was killed…in the charge on the Breastworks. Some embalmer is likely to have the body." "J.G. Frey hunted the ground but failed to find."	If not recovered by the family, he could have been sent to Hollywood, Richmond as an unknown in one of 21 boxes marked "P," 8/3/72
HODGES, John F.	PVT	22	D	9th LA	d. July 4	William Douglas's farm or lot, Fairfield Road, northeast corner of orchard under apple tree	Box 1-198, Hollywood, Richmond, 6/13/72
HODGES, Thomas M.	CPL		G	10th AL		North of Francis Bream's house in field near woods, along side of Adam Butt's woods near road; also, "Adam Butt's, south of house"	Box 1-139, Hollywood, Richmond, 6/13/72
HODGES, William C.C.	LT	28	B	7th SC	k. July 2	George Rose's farm, back or north of stone barn	Box 1-168, Hollywood, Richmond, 6/13/72
HOGE, Andrew J.	CPL	20	E	4th VA			"Supposed to be in Hollywood Cemetery. Identified by papers and a photo in pockets."
HOLLAND, William B.	PVT		A	42nd MS	d. July 4	Emanuel Pitzer's place, back of Zachariah Myers's lot and above the garden; also, back of Elizabeth Shultz's house	Possibly in a box marked "D," to Hollywood, Richmond, 6/13/72, as an unknown

Name	Rank	Age	Co.	Regiment	Death	Original Burial	Reinterment
HOLMES, James L.	PVT		I	5th TX	d. July 5	John Edward Plank's farm, north of house under walnut tree	Box 2-H, Hollywood, Richmond, 8/3/72
HOLMES, Rufus	PVT	25	F	47th NC	d. July 17	Jacob Schwartz's farm, in cornfield, Yard D, Row 2	Box 1-S-45, Hollywood, Richmond, 6/13/72, as "B. Holmes, Co. F, 57th NC"
HORNE, William B.	PVT	34	H	43rd NC	d. Aug. 18	Camp Letterman, Row 3, Grave 27	Oakwood, Raleigh, 10/1/71
HORTON, W.C.	PVT	33	H	2nd SC	d. July 5	Francis Bream's farm, back of tavern lot	Possibly in one of two boxes marked "B," to Hollywood, Richmond, 8/3/72, as an unknown
HOUGH, Joseph A.	PVT		E	9th GA	d. July 9	John Edward Plank's farm, back of barn, "under locust tree, toward John S. Crawford's"	Box 2-H, Hollywood, Richmond, 8/3/72
HOUSE, James P.	PVT	25	C	47th NC	d. July 20	On hill under walnut tree between Jacob Schwartz's and George Bushman's farms, Yard B, Row 2	Box 1-S-7, Hollywood, Richmond, 6/13/72
HOUSTON, David G. Jr.	CPT	25	D	11th VA	d. July 4 "in Curren's barn"	John F. Curren's farm, on sandy hill along Fairfield Road; also, "upon the roadside," and "on the hill from Bream's Mill"	Green Mount Cemetery, McCrea Family plot, Baltimore, MD, 7/18/64
HOWARD, Alfred B.	PVT	19	E	26th NC	k. July 1	Frederick Herr's farm, under large tree, in field west of E.A. Rhodes's grave near Willoughby's Run; possibly removed by "Schoolmasters" April 26 [1866?]	Possibly to Green Mount Cemetery, Baltimore, MD
HOWARD, Thomas W.	PVT	37	G	28th NC	d. July 19	On hill under walnut tree between Jacob Schwartz's and George Bushman's farms, Yard B, Row 2; "grave still marked in July 1866"	Box 1-207, Hollywood, Richmond, 6/13/72
HOWARD, William H.	PVT	36	K	55th NC	d. July 22	On hill under walnut tree between Jacob Schwartz's and George Bushman's farms, Yard B, Row 1	Box 1-20, Hollywood, Richmond, 6/13/72
HOWELL, Thomas J.	PVT		E	3rd GA	k. July 2	South of Emanuel Pitzer's farmhouse, in edge of woods; "grave still marked in 1866"	Possibly in a box marked "D," to Hollywood, Richmond, 6/13/72, as an unknown
HOWZE, George Adrian	LT		D	42nd MS	k. July 1	Samuel Lohr's farm, next to grave of R.S. Phillips, 42nd MS; buried by his servant; "graves well marked"	Probably Box 4-S, Hollywood, Richmond, 5/17/73, as an unknown
HOWZE, Thomas	PVT		C	Cobb's (GA) Legion Cavalry	d. July 2	On Hunterstown Road under cherry tree near Hunterstown; buried in a "rude coffin" by his servant	Laurel Grove, Savannah, Lot 854, Grave 12, 8/21/71
HUBBARD, Thomas J.	PVT		B	7th TN	d. Aug. 3 West's Bldg. U.S. Gen. Hosp. Baltimore, MD	None	Loudon Park, Baltimore, Row C, Grave 78, 8/3/63
HUBBARD, W.P.	PVT		G	18th GA		John Cunningham's farm, on south side of orchard	Box 4-297, Hollywood, Richmond, 5/17/73
HUCKABY, Leander	PVT	22	E	11th MS	d. Aug. 7	Camp Letterman, Row 3, Grave 4	Box 1-67, Hollywood, Richmond, 6/13/72
HUFFMAN, Adison C.	PVT	22	A	18th MS	d. Sept. 5	Camp Letterman, Row 7, Grave 2	Box 1-108, Hollywood, Richmond, 6/13/72
HUFFMAN, Jeremiah	PVT	28	C	28th NC	d. Sept. 20	Camp Letterman, Row 9, Grave 12	Oakwood, Raleigh, Grave 488, 10/1/71
HUGHES, Joseph H.	PVT	23	A	28th VA	d. July 31	Camp Letterman, Row 1, Grave 6	Box 1-89, Hollywood, Richmond, 6/13/72

Name	Rank	Age	Co.	Regiment	Death	Location	Disposition
HULEN, Thomas B.	PVT		F	48th GA	d. July 14	Jacob Schwartz's farm, in cornfield, Yard D, Row 3	Box 1-S-63, Hollywood, Richmond, 6/13/72
HULSEY, Henry	PVT		G	11th GA	d. July 26 DeCamp U.S. Gen. Hosp. David's Island New York	None	Probably Cypress Hills Cemetery, Long Island, NY
HUMPHREYS, Charles L.	CPL		E	2nd MS	d. July 15	Somewhere along the Chambersburg turnpike, likely northwest of the "railroad cut," poorly buried by Union soldiers	
HUNDLEY, Richard H.	PVT			Johnson's (VA) Battery	k. July 1 (?)	East end of Emanual Pitzer's woods; also, west of David McMillan's house in woods to rear; "board nailed to oak tree"	Box 3-282, Hollywood, Richmond, 9/10/72
HUNLEY, Claiborne	PVT	43	A	45th NC	d. July 17	George Bushman's farm; hospital cemetery was east of house	Oakwood, Raleigh, Grave 531, 10/1/71, as "C.P. Handley, Co. A, 45th NC"
HUNTER, James F.	PVT	24	C	37th NC	d. July 23 U.S. Gen. Hosp. Chester, PA	Chester Rural Cemetery, Chester, PA	Philadelphia National Cemetery, 1891
HUSON, John C.	PVT	22	F	1st NC	k. July 2	Martin Shealer's farm, in meadow next to Elizabeth Wible's	Box 3-V, Hollywood, Richmond, 9/10/72
HUSS, Joseph H.	SGT	21	E	34th NC	d. July 3	Martin Shealer's farm, in meadow next to Elizabeth Wible's	Possibly in one of two boxes marked "3-V," to Hollywood, Richmond, 9/10/72, as an unknown
HUTCHINS, Andrew J.	PVT	30	C	6th NC	k. July 1	Elizabeth Wible's farm; "still marked in 1866"	Probably in Box 3-Y, to Hollywood, Richmond, 9/10/72, as an unknown
HUTCHINSON, James B.	PVT	22	B	42nd VA	d. Aug. 17	Camp Letterman, Row 4, Grave 28	Box 1-41, Hollywood, Richmond, 6/13/72
INGRAM, John	PVT	24	K	15th AL	d. July 13	Camp Letterman, Row 1, Grave 30	Box 1-55, Hollywood, Richmond, 6/13/72
INMAN, Benjamin	PVT		H	5th FL	d. July 21	Pennsylvania College, hospital cemetery was north of main edifice out toward Adam Doersom's farm	Possibly Box 4-E, Hollywood, Richmond, 5/17/73, with 35 remains, 27 unknown
IREDELL, Campbell T.	CPT	27	C	47th NC	d. July 1	About two miles out the Chambersburg Pike, east of a stately walnut tree, 100 yards north of road; 75 yards northeast of a medium size stone farmhouse, and across road from a large yellow barn; alongside H. Burgwyn, W. McCreery and W. Wilson.	City Cemetery, Raleigh, NC
ISBELL, Walter D.	SGT	27	C	2nd SC	d. July 16	North of Francis Bream's tavern, by the graveyard near the creek	Magnolia, Charleston, Grave 36, 5/10/71
ISELEY, Lewis C.	PVT	17	F	6th NC	d. July 16	Christian Byers's farm, Fairfield Road, with 23 others, not marked	Oakwood, Raleigh, Grave 489, 10/1/71
ISOM, Dudley A.	PVT	26	G	11th MS		John Horting's farm, near garden fence, under walnut tree in southeast corner of garden; "a fine soldier…with a proud spirit"	Box 4-A, Hollywood, Richmond, 5/17/73, with 12 remains, 5 known

Name	Rank	Age	Co.	Regiment	Death	Location	Final Disposition
IVEY, William P.	PVT		A	8th AL		West side of Adam Butt's house at the road in corner of woods	Box 1-132, Hollywood, Richmond, 6/13/72

J

Name	Rank	Age	Co.	Regiment	Death	Location	Final Disposition
JACKSON, Andrew	PVT		G	5th TX	d. July 23	In the area of Michael Fiscel's farm, near road along fence under apple tree	Probably in "Box 3-A," to Hollywood, Richmond, 9/10/72, as an unknown
JACKSON, Benjamin E.	PVT	30	D	8th VA	k. July 3		Union Cemetery, Leesburg, VA
JACKSON, Lewis	PVT		A	38th VA	d. Aug. 1 U.S. Gen. Hosp. Chester, PA	Chester Rural Cemetery, Chester, PA, Grave 100	Philadelphia National Cemetery, 1891
JACOBS, Bailey S.	CPT	27	D	49th VA	d. July 16 Winchester, Virginia	None	"Maple Grove," Shumate farm, Bayard, Warren Co., VA
JAMISON, George H.	PVT	32	B	8th LA	k. July 1	North of brickyard, Harrisburg Road; back of Jacob Codori's [John S. Crawford's] brick house toward Almshouse along fence; (Henry L. Baugher's lot); under wild cherry tree, northeast border of Gettysburg, near Almshouse	Box 3-266, Hollywood, Richmond, 9/10/72
JARMAN, Elijah C.	PVT	19	K	26th NC	d. Aug. 1	Samuel Lohr's farm, opposite house, in meadow near pear tree	Box 4-S, Hollywood, Richmond, 5/17/73
JEFFERSON, James T.	PVT		E	57th VA	d. Aug. 16	Jacob Schwartz's farm, in cornfield, Yard D, Row 3	Box 1-S-59, Hollywood, Richmond, 6/13/72, as "Jefferson, 58th Va," also, as "Unknown"
JENNINGS, James	SGT	30	I	18th VA	d. July 16	Jacob Schwartz's farm, back of barn	Possibly in one of seven boxes marked "S," to Hollywood, Richmond, 9/10/72, as an unknown
JENNINGS, John A.	PVT	26	B	2nd SC	k. July 2	George Rose's farm, back of stone barn	Box 1-166, Hollywood, Richmond, 6/13/72
JENNINGS, Thomas	PVT		G	11th VA	d. July 18	Jacob Schwartz's farm, back of barn, probably Grave 15	Possibly in one of seven boxes marked "S," to Hollywood, Richmond, 9/10/72, as an unknown
JESSEE, Jefferson B.	PVT		C	37th VA	d. July 4	George Bushman's farm; hospital cemetery was east of house	Box 1-231, Hollywood, Richmond, 6/13/72
JINKINS, William S.	SGT	34	G	7th NC	d. July 3	Peter Frey's farm, in orchard, south of house and west of road; his death was witnessed by Lt. Abner Small, 16th ME. "I'm cold; so cold. Won't you cover me up?"	
JOHNSON, Daniel M.	PVT	26	I	13th AL	d. Sept. 11	Camp Letterman, Row 7, Grave 32	Box 1-79, Hollywood, Richmond, 6/13/72
JOHNSON, Edwin T.	PVT	19	I	8th GA	d. Sept. 7	Camp Letterman, Row 7, Grave 19	Laurel Grove, Savannah, Lot 854, Grave 3, 8/21/71
JOHNSON, John L.	LT		F	14th VA	d. July 3	Francis Bream's mill, "on the hill from Bream's Mill," above William Myers's house	Box 2-P-Currs, Hollywood, Richmond, 8/3/72, with 33 others
JOHNSON, John R.	PVT	26	H	47th NC	d. July 30	On hill under walnut tree between Jacob Schwartz's and George Bushman's farms, Yard B, Row 2	Box 1-209, Hollywood, Richmond, 6/13/72
JOHNSON, John T.	PVT	20	K	11th MS	d. Aug. 4	Possibly in the Camp Letterman Cemetery, U.S. Section	Some believe he is buried in the National Cemetery, Gettysburg, PA, in Mass. Plot C-1, as "J.L. Johnson, Co. K, 11th Mass Inf."

Name	Rank	Age	Co.	Unit	Death	Original Location	Reinterment
JOHNSON, Thomas	PVT	38	I	42nd MS	d. Aug. 14	Camp Letterman, Row 1, Grave 30	Box 1-90, Hollywood, Richmond, 6/13/72
JOHNSON, William C.	PVT		K	7th TN		On hill between Jacob Schwartz's and George Bushman's farms, Yard B, Row 1	Box 1-210, Hollywood, Richmond, 6/13/72
JOHNSTON, H.C.	PVT		F	48th MS		John Edward Plank's farm, near C. Dougherty's, in orchard, under apple tree	Box 1-182, Hollywood, Richmond, with two other soldiers unknown, 6/13/72
JOHNSTON, Joseph Jr.	CPT		B	47th AL	d. July 19	Jacob Schwartz's farm, back of barn, Grave 11	Possibly in one of seven boxes marked "S," to Hollywood, Richmond, 9/10/72, as an unknown
JOLLY, Wesley	PVT	26	I	32nd NC	d. Aug. 15	Camp Letterman, Row 1, Grave 39 (from fence)	Oakwood, Raleigh, 10/1/71
JONES, Charles M.	CPT	25	H	49th GA		Michael Crist's farm	Possibly in one of six boxes marked "F," to Hollywood, Richmond, 8/3/72, as an unknown
JONES, Floyd K.	PVT		I	3rd AL	k. July 1	John S. Forney's farm, in a field under an apple tree	Interred in a church cemetery near his home in Louisa Court House, VA, near his brother who was killed at Cold Harbor
JONES, Francis Pendleton	LT	21	D	13th VA Staff, Gen. J.M. Jones	d. Sept. 2	None. Died at his home	
JONES, Henry N.	LT		I	1st TX		John Edward Plank's farm, north side of house under walnut tree	Box 2-H, Hollywood, Richmond, 8/3/72
JONES, Isaac N.	PVT	21	E	45th NC	d. July 4	Jacob Hankey's farm	Oakwood, Raleigh, Grave 500, 10/1/71
JONES, John Augustus	COL	43	F&S	20th GA	k. July 2	John Slyder's farm, 150 yards from house under a cherry tree, with Capt. B.L. Hancock; "Confederate Officer of apparent rank and refinement, back of barn"	c. Dec. 10, 1866, the remains of Col. Jones were lost overboard at sea. On board was Leonard Jones, a son, who had recovered his skeleton near Gettysburg; memorial marker in Linwood Cemetery, Columbus, GA
JONES, John O.	PVT		I	11th VA	d. July 15	Jacob Schwartz's farm, Yard D, Row 3, in cornfield on Rock Creek; "removed"	Box 1-S-56, Hollywood, Richmond, 6/13/72, with 110 others
JONES, John Thomas	PVT	24	E	11th MS	d. July 15	Jacob Schwartz's farm, in cornfield, Yard D, Row 1, on Rock Creek	Box 1-S-30, Hollywood, Richmond, 6/13/72
JONES, Lineous	PVT	26	C	11th VA	d. July 8	Francis Bream's mill, above William Myers's house, at side of fence	Box 2-P-Curns, Hollywood, Richmond, 8/3/72, with 33 others
JONES, Lucien S.	1SGT	21	F	19th VA	d. July 4	Francis Bream's mill, above William Myers's house, at side of fence	Box 2-P-Curns, Hollywood, Richmond, 8/3/72, with 33 others
JONES, Thomas S.	PVT		H	1st SC	d. Aug. 10	Camp Letterman, Row 5, Grave 16	Magnolia, Charleston, Grave 5, 5/10/71, as "Sgt. H.S. Jones, 7th SC"
JONES, Walter L.	PVT	20	I	26th NC		South of Adam Butt's stone house, near road in woods	Chapel of Rest Cemetery, Caldwell County, NC
JONES, William	PVT		E	11th AL			Box 1-126, Hollywood, Richmond, 6/13/72
JONES, William P.	PVT		D	2nd GA BN	d. July 20	On hill between Jacob Schwartz's and George Bushman's farms, Yard B, Row 2, under a walnut tree	Possibly in a "State Lot" to Hollywood, Richmond
JORDAN, Benjamin O	PVT		A	21st VA		George Bushman's farm; hospital cemetery was east of house	Box 1-223, Hollywood, Richmond, 6/13/72

Name	Rank	Age	Co.	Regiment	Death	Burial Location	Disposition
JORDAN, John C.	PVT	25	G	15th AL		Michael Fiscel's farm; hospital cemetery was east of house across a stream	Probably in Box 3-A, to Hollywood, Richmond, 9/10/72, as an unknown
JORDAN, John Chappell	PVT	21	F	3rd VA	d. July 12	Francis Bream's mill above William Myers's house, by the side of a fence	Box 2-P-Currns, Hollywood, Richmond, 8/3/72, with 33 others
JORDAN, Leroy	PVT		F	3rd GA	d. Aug. 10 U.S. Gen. Hosp. Chester, PA	Chester Rural Cemetery, Chester, PA	Philadelphia National Cemetery, 1891
JOYCE, Festy	PVT			Letcher Light (VA) Artillery		Michael Crist's farm, under big oak tree	
JOYNER, Eli	PVT	23	A	47th NC	d. July 6/10	Isaac Rife's farm, in Cashtown, PA, possibly under a chestnut tree	Oakwood, Raleigh, Grave 466, 10/1/71

K

Name	Rank	Age	Co.	Regiment	Death	Burial Location	Disposition
KARR, James M.	PVT		A	21st GA	k. July 2	Jacob Hankey's farm	Laurel Grove, Savannah, Lot 854, Grave 13, 8/21/71, as "James Carr, Co. A, 21st Ga."
KEARNS, Isaac N.	LT	29	H	38th NC	d. July 24	On hill under walnut tree between Jacob Schwartz's and George Bushman's farms, Yard B, Row 1	Box 1-5, Hollywood, Richmond, 6/13/72
KEARSE, Francis	LTC	26	F&S	50th GA	k. July 2	George Rose's farm, in orchard, near fence; also, "near the spring house"	Laurel Grove, Savannah, Lot 853, Grave 14, 9/24/71
KEEL, William M.	SGT		I	42nd MS		On hill under walnut tree between Jacob Schwartz's and George Bushman's farms, Yard B, Row 2	Box 1-8, Hollywood, Richmond, 6/13/72
KEITH, Anderson C.	PVT	29	I	3rd NC	d. Aug. 1	Camp Letterman, Row 2, Grave 17	Oakwood, Raleigh, 10/1/71
KELLIS, Josiah	PVT		E	27th NC		On hill under walnut tree between Jacob Schwartz's and George Bushman's farms, Yard B, Row 1	Box 1-2, Hollywood, Richmond, 6/13/72
KELLY, Gersham P.	SGT		B	10th AL	"died in Adam Butt's barn"	North of Francis Bream's farm in field along side of Adam Butt's woods near road; Adam Butt's, south of house; buried by his brother	Box 1-136, Hollywood, Richmond, 6/13/72
KELLY, Richard	PVT		I	6th LA	d. July 12/24 Hospital, Williamsport, Maryland	Possibly in the Catholic Church or Public Burial Ground, Williamsport, MD. (He was wounded July 8.)	If moved to a second location, it was probably to "Rose Hill," Washington Cemetery, Hagerstown, MD
KELLY, Thomas J.	LT		B	3rd NC	d. July 9	Martin Shealer's farm, in the meadow under little apple tree	Box 3-264, Hollywood, Richmond, 9/10/72, also listed as Box 3-V
KENNEDY, W.D.	PVT	22	A	2nd FL	d. July 12	Pennsylvania College, north of main edifice in hospital cemetery	Box 4-E, Hollywood, Richmond, 5/17/73, with 35 remains, 27 unknown
KERSEY, Jackson	PVT		D	6th AL	k. July 1	"James J. Wills's farm in woods;" probably Moses McClean's farm as J.J. Wills owned it in post-war years; buried next to John Conner	

Name	Rank	Age	Co.	Regiment	Death	First Burial	Reinterment
KEY, Hugh	PVT		C	17th GA	d. July 5 or Aug. 5	John Edward Plank's farm	"State Lot" – GA, to Hollywood, Richmond
KILGORE, Andrew J.	CPL	20	E	8th FL	d. Sept. 27	Camp Letterman, Row 7, Grave 30	Box 1-114, Hollywood, Richmond, 6/13/72
KINCAID, James M.	CPT	26	G	52nd NC	d. Aug. 27	Camp Letterman, Row 6, Grave 14	Oakwood, Raleigh, 10/1/71
KING, Daniel S.	PVT		A	17th MS		John S. Crawford's farm, "where Basil Biggs lives;" in garden	Box 4-Y, Hollywood, Richmond, 5/17/73
KING, James M.D.	CPT		K	9th GA	d. Nov. 4 Johnson's Island Prison, Ohio	None	Johnson's Island Prison Cemetery, OH, Grave 96
KING, William A.	CPL	22	K	8th GA		John Edward Plank's farm under a large locust tree toward John S. Crawford's, and near road to Bream's Mill; also, "back of barn"	Box 2-H, Hollywood, Richmond, 8/3/72
KIRKMAN, Henry C. B.	PVT	19	G	26th NC	d. Sept. 1	Camp Letterman, Row 6, Grave 34	Oakwood, Raleigh, Grave 472, 10/1/71
KNABKE, Benjamin	1SGT		D	18th MS		John Trostle's farm, south bank of Rock Creek near woods, northeast corner of field; buried in one grave with Daniel Madden, 21st MS	Box 2-257, Hollywood, Richmond, 8/3/72
KNOTT, Minion F.	PVT	23	F	1st MD BN	d. Aug. 24	Camp Letterman Cemetery, possibly in U.S. section	Some believe he is buried in the National Cemetery, Gettysburg, PA, in Md. Plot C-4, as "M.F. Knott, 1st MD"
◆ KOINER, Christian H.	PVT	20	E	1st VA CAV	d.c. Aug. 30 Ft. Delaware U.S. Mil. Prison	None	National Cemetery, Firm's Point, NJ
KOON, Walter W.	PVT	26	I	15th SC	d. July 10	Francis Bream's farm, behind the house, in McClellan's old burying ground, center	Magnolia, Charleston, Grave 37, 5/10/71
KYLE, James Jr.	PVT	19	C	11th MS	d. July 16	Samuel Lohr's farm	Probably in a box marked 4-S to Hollywood, Richmond, 5/17/73, as an unknown

L

Name	Rank	Age	Co.	Regiment	Death	First Burial	Reinterment
LACKEY, William H.	PVT	25	I	4th VA		George Bushman's farm; hospital cemetery was east of house	Box 1-230, Hollywood, Richmond, 6/13/72
LACKMAN, E.	PVT		D	5th TX	d. July 16	Jacob Schwartz's farm, back of barn, Grave 13, as "E. Lockman, Co. D, 5th Fla"	Probably in one of seven boxes marked "S," to Hollywood, Richmond, 9/10/72, as an unknown
LAGUE, Aristide	PVT	20	F	8th LA		John Crist's farm, near gum tree	None
LANCASTER, William T.	CPL	24	F	3rd VA	d. Aug. 11 West's Bldg. U.S. Gen. Hosp. Baltimore, MD	None	Loudon Park, Baltimore, Row D, Grave 61, 8/11/63
LAND, William B.	PVT	23	K	55th NC	k. July 3	John Horting's farm on Willoughby's Run, under walnut tree, southeast corner of garden	Box 4-A, Hollywood, Richmond, 5/17/73

Name	Rank	Age	Co.	Unit	Death	Burial Note	Final Location
LANE, John T.	CPT	30	G	4th GA	d. July 25 U.S. Gen. Hosp. Frederick, MD	None	Mt. Olivet Cemetery, Frederick, MD, Grave 206
LANEY, William B.	PVT	22	B	26th NC	d. July 10	Samuel Lohr's farm, opposite house, in meadow, near pear tree	Box 4-S, Hollywood, Richmond, 5/17/73
LANGFORD, John	CPL	36	E	60th GA	d. Aug. 10 U.S. Gen. Hosp. Frederick, MD	None	Mt. Olivet Cemetery, Grave 212, Frederick, MD; his left femur is in the National Museum of Health and Medicine, Specimen #2202
LANGFORD, Pickens B.	LT	21	E	3rd SC	k. July 2	George Rose's farm, "on the gravl walk in the woods"	Magnolia, Charleston, Common Grave 28, 5/10/71
LANIER, Hosea W.	CPL	24	A	38th NC	d. Aug. 13 U.S. Gen. Hosp. Chester, PA	Chester Rural Cemetery, Chester, PA	Philadelphia National Cemetery, 1891
LANTZ, Joseph T. V.	CPL			Taylor's (VA) Battery	k. July 2	Near handboard along county road from Samuel Pitzer's schoolhouse toward John Sachs; his final words to a friend were: "You can do me no good; I am killed."	
LASSITER, Ezekiel	PVT	29	H	38th NC		George Bushman's farm; hospital cemetery was east of house	Box 1-224, Hollywood, Richmond, 6/13/72
LATIMER, Joseph W.	MAJ	19		Andrews's Artillery BN	d. Aug. 1 "Mrs. Warren's House"	None	"Mrs. [Harriet] Warren's plot," in cemetery at Harrisonburg, VA. Grave marker at site.
LATTIMER, John W.	PVT	24	G	9th VA	d. Sept. 18	Camp Letterman, Row 8, Grave 9	Probably "State 'Lot'" - VA, to Hollywood, Richmond
LAUGHLIN, John	PVT		K	15th GA	k. July 3	John Edward Plank's farm, under large locust tree toward John S. Crawford's, and near road to Bream's Mill	Box 2-H, Hollywood, Richmond, 8/3/72
LAUGHLIN, Thomas	PVT	20	H	29th VA	d. July 30	Camp Letterman, Row 2, Grave 21	Box 1-61, Hollywood, Richmond, 6/13/72
LAW, Josiah H.	PVT		B	4th GA	k. July 1	David Blocher's farm, under a tree near house with Col. Winn and others; "still marked in 1866"	Remains sent to a brother in Ga. by Dr. Weaver during the summer of 1871. Probably in "Box-5" to Savannah with Capt. Leonard, Cols. Wasden and Winn, and 5 other Georgians
LAWRENCE, G.A.	PVT	31	G	24th GA	d. Aug. 19	Camp Letterman, Row 1, Grave 39	Laurel Grove, Savannah, Lot 854, Grave 3, 8/21/71
LAWSON, Spencer	PVT	41	E	22nd GA	d. Sept. 6 West's Bldg. U.S. Gen. Hosp. Baltimore, MD	None	Loudon Park, Baltimore, Row B, Grave 79, 9/6/63
LAYMAN, William	PVT	27		2nd Co., Washington (LA) Artillery	d. July 18	John S. Crawford's tenant house, (Samuel Johns) near barn in field with house; "in woods, east of tenant house"	
LEAMAN, James D.	PVT	36	D	52nd NC	d.c. July 10	East of Dr. Samuel E. Hall's house in woods near county road; buried next to John Hancock, 52nd NC	Oakwood, Raleigh, 10/1/71
LEDFORD, Samuel	PVT	35	D	55th NC	k. July 1	Possibly James J. Wills's farm, Chambersburg Road	Poplar Springs Cemetery, Cleveland Co., NC

Name	Rank	Age	Co.	Regiment	Death	Location	Disposition
LEE, Berry B.	CPL	35	D	47th NC	d. Aug. 4 U.S. Gen. Hosp. Chester, PA	Chester Rural Cemetery, Chester, PA	Philadelphia National Cemetery, 1891
LEE, Elisha L.	PVT	26	K	11th MS	d. July 10	Samuel Lohr's farm, north side of woods	Box 3-L, Hollywood, Richmond, 9/10/72
LEE, Richard H.	PVT		I	57th VA	d. July 15	Jacob Schwartz's farm, in cornfield on Rock Creek, Yard D, Row 3	Box 1-S-67, Hollywood, Richmond, 6/13/72, with others in 13 boxes
LEE, William	CPT	28	E	4th AL	d. July 3	John Edward Plank's farm, at foot of garden near road; the garden fence runs over the grave	Probably in one of 11 boxes marked "H," to Hollywood, Richmond, 8/3/72, as an unknown
LEFTWICH, William W.	CPT	23	F	4th AL	d. July 3	John Edward Plank's farm, back of barn	Box 2-H, Hollywood, Richmond, 8/3/72
LEIGH, Benjamin Watkins	MAJ	32	Staff, Gen. E. Johnson		k. July 3 11 a.m.	Back or east of Culp's Hill, near U.S. 2nd Division, 12th Corps' burial ground; grave marked by Rev. J.R. Warner of Gettysburg in August/September, 1863	His remains supposedly were removed to Baltimore, MD, then to Shockoe Cemetery, Richmond, VA in 1866; a stone in the Gettysburg National Cemetery is marked "B.W. Laigh"
LEITZEY, David M.	LT		H	13th SC	d. July 2	Probably Samuel Lohr's farm or Andrew Heintzelman's farm/tavern area	Possibly in one of four boxes marked "4-S," 5/17/73, or one of eight boxes marked "3-H," 9/10/72, to Hollywood, Richmond, as an unknown
LENHARDT, Cameron L.	PVT	20	I	11th NC	d. July 30	George Spangler's farm, "with 6 graves unmarked"	
LEONARD, Jeff W.	CPT		D	22nd GA	k. July 2	Nicholas Codori's farm, west of barn, with 10 others	Remains sent to Georgia by Dr. Weaver during the summer of 1871; probably in "Box-5" to Savannah with Pvt. Law, Cols. Wasden and Winn, and five other Georgians
LESLEY, James N.	PVT	24	C	2nd MS	d. Oct. 5	Camp Letterman, Row 9, Grave 2	Box 1-91, Hollywood, Richmond, 6/13/72
LESLIE, William A.	PVT		A	8th VA	k. July 3	Arnold Grove Cemetery, Loudon Co, VA; his brother, Thomas, 8th VA, is buried nearby	
LeTELLIER, William B.	LT	23	E	19th VA	d. Aug. 11 U.S. Gen. Hosp. Chester, PA	Chester Rural Cemetery, Chester, PA, Grave 137	Philadelphia National Cemetery, 1891
LEWIE, Emanuel W.	SGT	19	C	15th SC	k. July 2	George Rose's farm, "on the gravl walk in the woods"	Magnolia, Charleston, Common Grave 28, 5/10/71
LEWIS, Miles W.	PVT		D	22nd GA	d. July 22	George Bushman's farm; cemetery was east of the house	Laurel Grove, Savannah, Lot 854, Grave 12, 8/21/71
LEWIS, W.F.	PVT	21	B	28th NC	d. July 17	Jacob Schwartz's farm, in cornfield, Yard D, Row 1	Box 1-S-28, Hollywood, Richmond, 6/13/72
LEWIS, William M.	PVT		D	17th GA	d. July 19	John Edward Plank's farm	Laurel Grove, Savannah, Lot 853, Grave 11, 9/24/71
LIGHT, Charles M.	PVT		F	38th VA	d. July 30 DeCamp U.S. Gen. Hosp. David's Island, New York	None	Cypress Hill Cemetery, Long Island, NY, Grave 710
LIGHT, George W.	PVT	28	H	14th VA	d. July 10 West's Bldg. Gen. Hosp., Baltimore, MD	None	Loudon Park, Baltimore, Row C, Grave 64, 7/10/63

Name	Rank	Age	Co.	Regiment	Death	Location	Burial
LILE, William H.	PVT	24	I	11th MS	d. Aug. 1	On hill under a walnut tree between Jacob Schwartz's and George Bushman's farms, Yard B, Row 2	Box 1-205, Hollywood, Richmond, 6/13/72
LINDAMOOD, James	PVT		B	7th VA CAV	d. July 7	Benjamin A. Marshall's farm, north of Fairfield, PA	Box 4-W, Hollywood, Richmond, with 11 others, 5/17/73
LINDSEY, James A.	SGT		I	3rd GA	d. July 24	Jacob Schwartz's farm, back of barn	Possibly in one of seven boxes marked "S," to Hollywood, Richmond, 9/10/72, as an unknown
LISTENBEE, Isaac W.	PVT	21	G	11th MS	d. "August 1863"	None; "A faithful soldier, modest, unassuming, but always ready for duty"	Probably in a cemetery in Winchester, VA; mortally wounded, Falling Waters, July 14 1863
LITTLE, Ellis P.	PVT	26	D	37th NC	d. July 23	On hill under a walnut tree between Jacob Schwartz's and George Bushman's farms, Yard B, Row 1	Box 1-17, Hollywood, Richmond, 6/13/72
LITTLETON, Elisha A.	PVT	25	G	3rd NC	d. July 2	Martin Shealer's farm, under a little apple tree; in same grave as J.T. Williams, 3rd NC	Box 3-V, Hollywood, Richmond, 9/10/72
LITTRELL, Murray M.	CPL	23	A	47th VA	d. July 3	John Herbst's woods, back or west of Lutheran Seminary; buried next to Lewis Williams, Co. A, 47th VA	Possibly in Box 3-U or 3-T, to Hollywood, Richmond, 9/10/72, as an unknown or, Box 4-U, to Hollywood, Richmond, 5/17/73, as an unknown
LIVINGSTON, Lewis A.	CPT	29	F	8th AL		Camp Letterman Cemetery	
LOCKETT, S.S.	PVT		E	5th TX	d. July 6	Michael Fiscel's farm, east side of woods	Probably Box 3-A, Hollywood, Richmond, 9/10/72, as an unknown
LOMAX, William G.	PVT	22	F	2nd SC	k. July 2	George Rose's meadow, in or near a peach orchard	Magnolia, Charleston, Grave 22, 5/10/71
◆ LONG, John E.	PVT		G	42nd MS	k. July 1	"Clarkson's old place;" probably James J. Wills's farm north of the Chambersburg Road, as "J. Long, 42nd Miss."	
LOONEY, Richmond D.	PVT		C	10th AL		Pennsylvania College; hospital burial ground, north side of main edifice, with 27 unknowns	Box 4-E, Hollywood, Richmond, 5/17/73
◆ LOTT, John Bolivar	PVT	19	H	7th SC	k. July 2	George Rose's farm, possibly "on the gravl walk in the woods"	Probably in one of 15 boxes marked "L," to Hollywood, Richmond, 8/3/72, as an unknown
LOUGHRIDGE, James B.	CPL	23		Parker's (VA) Battery		John S. Crawford's tenant house where Samuel Johns lives; east of house near Pvt. Patrick McNeil; both names "cut into a crude pine board"	
LOVE, Joseph A.	PVT		E	7th TN	d.c. July 15	Jacob Schwartz's farm, in cornfield, Yard D, Row 3	Box 1-S-70, Hollywood, Richmond, 6/13/72
◆ LOVE, Joseph E.	PVT	31	A	5th TX	d. Aug. 22 West's Bldg. U.S. Hosp. Baltimore, MD	None	Loudon Park, Baltimore, on "Confederate Hill," Row B, Grave 77, 8/23/63; the lower two-thirds of his right humerus and upper third of radius and ulna were once in the National Museum of Health and Medicine, Specimen #1592
LOVE, Rutledge McDuffie	PVT	24	G	2nd SC	k. July 2	George Rose's farm, back of barn, under a cherry tree	Magnolia, Charleston, Grave 12, 5/10/71
LOVE, Thomas R.	CPT		B	8th FL	d. July 10	Jacob Schwartz's farm, back of barn	Possibly in one of seven boxes marked "S," to Hollywood, Richmond, 9/10/72, as an unknown
LOVELADY, Noah H.	PVT		K	11th AL		South of Adam Butt's stone house near road in woods	Box 1-123, Hollywood, Richmond, 6/13/72

Name	Rank	Age	Co.	Regiment	Death	Original Burial	Final/Reburial
LOWDER, Jacob W.	PVT	22	B	20th NC	d. July 10	Jacob Hankey's farm	Oakwood, Raleigh, Grave 517, 10/1/71
LOWRIE, James B.	LT	25	H	11th NC	k. July 1	Willoughby's Run, near Herr's Tavern or near Seminary; "Schoolmasters removed April 26, [1866?]"	Possibly to Green Mount Cemetery, Baltimore, MD, with A.B. Howard and others
LUMMAS, William D.	PVT	22	B	53rd GA		John S. Crawford's farm on Marsh Creek; "a mason"	"State Lot" - GA, to Hollywood, Richmond
LUMPKIN, Samuel P.	COL	29	F&S	44th GA	d. Sept. 18 Seminary Hosp. Hagerstown, Maryland	Old Presbyterian Burying Ground, South Potomac Street, Hagerstown; buried with Corp. T.W. Metcalf, Co. A, Jeff Davis Legion; myrtle planted over grave	Washington Cemetery, Hagerstown, MD, 5/8/1913; (marker placed in 1914)
LUTHER, Franklin	CPL	23	B	52nd NC	d. Sept. 14	Camp Letterman, Row 8, Grave 2	Oakwood, Raleigh, Grave 477, 10/1/71
LUTZ, Wade D.	LT	19	A	22nd NC	d. Aug. 9 U.S. Gen. Hosp. Chester, PA	Chester Rural Cemetery, Chester, PA	Philadelphia National Cemetery, 1891
LYDAY, T.L.	PVT		B	9th GA	k. July 2	John Edward Plank's farm, under a large locust tree toward John S. Crawford's and near road to Bream's Mill; also, "back of barn"	Box 2-H, Hollywood, Richmond, 8/3/72
LYNCH, J. Pinkney	PVT		F	13th GA	k. July 1	Near or in the Almshouse Burying Ground or Cemetery	
LYNCH, John S.	PVT		I	3rd AL	d. Aug. 1	Camp Letterman, Row 2, Grave 16	Box 1-33, Hollywood, Richmond, 6/13/72, as "Sgt. John J. Ainch"

M

Name	Rank	Age	Co.	Regiment	Death	Original Burial	Final/Reburial
McCAIN, John C.	CPT	32	I	52nd NC	k. July 1	Samuel Lohr's farm, opposite house in meadow under pear tree	Box 4-S, Hollywood, Richmond, 5/17/73, with 44 others,
McCALL, Martin C.	CPL	20	K	8th SC	k. July 2	George Rose's farm, north or back of stone barn	Box 1-144, Hollywood, Richmond, 6/13/72
McCARTHY, W.C.	PVT		B	4th TX	d. July 20	Jacob Schwartz's farm, back of barn	Possibly in one of seven boxes marked "S," to Hollywood, Richmond, 9/10/72, as an unknown
McCARTY, Thomas	PVT	40	I	8th LA	d. July 2	George Spangler's farm; hospital cemetery was east of house	None
McCASKILL, Daniel	PVT	24	H	26th NC	d. Nov. 17 West's Bldg. U.S. Gen. Hosp. Baltimore, MD	None	Loudon Park, Baltimore, Row B, Grave 81
McCLURE, S.L.	PVT		H	23rd NC	d. July 5	Probably Jacob Hankey's farm	Possibly in one of eight boxes marked "N," to Hollywood, Richmond, 8/3/72, as an unknown
McCORMICK, John	PVT		H	38th VA	d. July 23	On hill between Jacob Schwartz's and George Bushman's farms, under walnut tree, Yard B, Row 2	Box 1-211, Hollywood, Richmond, 6/13/72
McCOWAN, William C.	PVT		B	2nd MS		Jacob Schwartz's farm, in cornfield, Yard D, Row 3	Box 1-S, Hollywood, Richmond, 6/13/72
McCOWEN, Benjamin B.	LT		K	53rd GA	k. July 2	George Rose's farm, west of barn, under large cherry tree; "grave deep, with board cover with 6 others"	Magnolia, Charleston, Grave 24, 5/10/71, as "Lt. M.B. McGowan, Co. K, 3rd SC"

Name	Rank	Age	Co.	Unit	Death	Burial Location	Final Disposition
McCOY, John F.	PVT	32	C	37th NC			Hopewell Cemetery, Mecklenburg Co., NC
McCRACKEN, R. Hayne	PVT	24	D	13th SC	d. Aug. 4 U.S. Gen. Hosp. Chester, PA	Chester Rural Cemetery, Chester, PA	Magnolia, Charleston, Row 2, Grave 16, *5/10/71*
McCRARY, Alexander A.	PVT		E	9th GA	d. July 5	John Edward Plank's farm, back of barn, "under locust tree toward John S. Crawford's"	Box 2-H, Hollywood, Richmond, *8/3/72*
McCREA, William H.	PVT			Blount's (VA) Battery		William Felix's farm, in the woods, by the road, near the House; on left side of country road toward Samuel Pitzer's	Box 2-256, Hollywood, Richmond, *8/3/72*
McCREERY, William W.	CPT	26		Staff, Gen. James J. Pettigrew	d.c. July 1	About two miles out the Chambersburg Pike, east of a stately walnut tree, 100 yards north of road; 75 yards northeast of a medium size stone farmhouse, and across road from a large yellow barn; alongside H. Burgwyn, C. Iredell and W. Wilson.	Oakwood, Raleigh, Grave 533, *10/1/71*
McCRIMMON, Farquhar	LT		H	20th GA	k. July 2	John Slyder's farm, back of barn, front of row	
McCULLAR, Jesse C.	PVT		F	9th GA	k. July 2	John Edward Plank's farm, under large locust tree toward John S. Crawford's place, and near road to Bream's Mill	Box 2-H, Hollywood, Richmond, *8/3/72*
◆ **McCULLOUGH**, John T.	SGT		A	3rd GA	d. July 27 "fever"	Camp Letterman Cemetery	
McCURLEY, Joseph	PVT	26	A	2nd LA	d. July 28	Camp Letterman, Row 1, Grave 16	Box 1-40, Hollywood, Richmond, *6/13/72*
McCURRY, William L.	SGT		D	7th SC	k. July 2	George Rose's farm, north or back of stone barn	Box 1-143, Hollywood, Richmond, *6/13/72*
McDADE, John H.	LT		G	11th NC	k. July 1	On Willoughby's Run, probably near Herr's Tavern; buried next to N.B. Tenney and E.A. Rhodes	Possibly to Green Mount Cemetery, Baltimore, MD, with several others
McDANIEL, David E.	PVT		K	24th VA	d. July 31 DeCamp U.S. Gen. Hosp. David's Island, New York	None	Cypress Hill Cemetery, Long Island, NY, Grave 707
McDOWELL, George M.	CPT	24	F	2nd SC	k. July 3	Francis Bream's farm, north of tavern, near graveyard by the Creek; his last words were, "Tell my Mother, I die with sword drawn….and have no fear of death."	Magnolia, Charleston, Grave 51, *5/10/71*
McDUFFIE, Daniel Q.	SGT		I	8th SC	d.c. July 2	Francis Bream's tavern, in apple orchard	Magnolia, Charleston, Grave 26, *5/10/71*
McDUFFIE, Norman L.	CPT		F	18th MS	d. July 2	John Crawford's farm, "where Basil Biggs lives;" in garden	Box 4-Y, Hollywood, Richmond, *5/17/73*
McELROY, James H.	PVT	25	A	1st LA	d. July 2	W. Henry Monfort's farm, first brick house on left, from York Pike	Box 3-M, Hollywood, Richmond, *9/10/72*
McGEE, Franklin M.	PVT	22	I	32nd NC	d.c. July 11	Jacob Hankey's farm	Oakwood, Raleigh, Grave 497, *10/1/71*, as "F.M. May, Co. I, 3rd NC"
McGEE, William B.	PVT		C	17th MS		John S. Crawford's homestead on Marsh Creek, north side of "Walnut Avenue"	Box 2-C-Miss, Hollywood, Richmond, *8/3/72*

Name	Rank	Age	Co.	Regiment	Death	Burial Location	Disposition
McGINNIS, James L.B.	PVT	18	H	28th NC	d. Sept. 5 U.S. Gen. Hosp. Chester, PA	Chester Rural Cemetery, Chester, PA	Philadelphia National Cemetery, 1891; his left knee bones are in the National Museum of Health and Medicine, Specimen #1063
McGINNIS, John W.	1SGT		E	53rd GA	d. July 27	Lutheran Theological Seminary, in woods	Possibly in Box 4-X, or Box 4-U, 5/17/73, to Hollywood, Richmond, as an unknown, or Box 3-T, 9/10/72, to Hollywood, Richmond, as an unknown
♦ McGLEMRE, John W.	PVT	27	K	12th VA	d. Aug. 5 Probably Seminary Hosp. Hagerstown, MD	Possibly Old Almshouse Burying Ground, Hagerstown, MD	Probably in "Rose Hill," Washington Cemetery, Hagerstown, MD
McGRADY, Jacob	PVT	29	K	37th NC	d. July 14	Peter Conover's farm; "all removed"	Oakwood, Raleigh, Grave 542, 10/1/71
McGUIRE, Benjamin H.	LT		D	22nd VA BN		Samuel Lohr's farm	Probably in one of four boxes marked "S," to Hollywood, Richmond, 5/17/73, as an unknown
McHENRY, Alkana	PVT	25	B	11th MS	d. Aug. 23 DeCamp U.S. Gen. Hosp. David's Island New York	None	Cypress Hills Cemetery, Long Island, New York, Grave 820
♦ McHONE, Micajah	PVT		C	24th VA	d. July 4	John Trostle's farm, south bank of Rock Creek in northeast corner of field, 40 yards east of graves of Ben Knabke and Daniel Madden	Box 2-251, Hollywood, Richmond, 8/3/72
McINTOSH, Alexander	CPL		G	8th SC	k. July 2	George Rose's farm, back or north of stone barn	Box 1-149, Hollywood, Richmond, 6/13/72
McINTOSH, Thomas R.	PVT			Garden's (SC) Battery	d. July 4	John Edward Plank's farm	"State Lot" - GA, to Hollywood, Richmond, as "T.R. McIntosh, Co. C, Georgia"
McINTURFF, Franklin	PVT		B	33rd VA	d. July 12	George Bushman's farm; hospital cemetery was east of house	Box 1-122, Hollywood, Richmond, 6/13/72
McKEE, Levi T.	PVT		G	42nd MS	d. Aug. 13 Probably U.S. Gen. Hosp., Frederick, MD	None	Mt. Olivet Cemetery, Frederick, MD, Grave 213
McKIE, Thomas Fondren	PVT	17	A	11th MS	d. July 4	Samuel Lohr's farm	Probably in one of four boxes marked "S," to Hollywood, Richmond, 5/17/73, as an unknown
McKINNEY, David	SGT	21	B	2nd NC BN	d. July 1	Jacob Hankey's farm	Oakwood, Raleigh, Grave 511, 10/1/71
McKINNEY, Moses J.	1SGT	26	E	6th NC	d. July 2-6	Elizabeth Wible's farm	Oakwood, Raleigh, 10/1/71
McLAURIN, R. Lewis	CPL		A	18th MS		John S. Crawford's farm, near William Felix's place along road on left side going to Samuel Pitzer's; under a walnut or locust tree out in the field; under a walnut tree at bend of road on Marsh Creek	Box 1-236, Hollywood, Richmond, 6/13/72
McLEAN, J.P.F.	SGT		A	9th AL		North of Adam Butt's house under a cherry tree	Box 1-118, Hollywood, Richmond, 6/13/72

Name	Rank	Age	Co.	Regiment	Death	Original Burial	Disposition / Reinterment
McLEOD, Donald Mc.	MAJ	41	F&S	8th SC	d. July 5 on retreat	Buried on J.W. George's farm, on road to New Franklin, from Fairfield, a few miles southeast of Chambersburg, PA	Jacob Hoke says McLeod's wife's brother recovered the remains on April 20, 1866, and took them home to Parnassus Methodist Church Yard, Marborough Co., SC.
McLEOD, William L.	CPT	21 (commanding regiment)	C	38th GA (c. 8 PM)	d. July 1	Jacob Kime's farm, upper end of orchard under apple tree; buried by his slave, Moses; "a tall man - removed;" remains recovered from Gettysburg by a family member and Moses in 1865.	His remains lay in his mother's parlor for 7 years. Reinterred in the family cemetery, Swainsboro, Emanuel Co., Georgia in 1872
McLUCAS, Hugh	SGT	22	K	8th SC	k. July 2	George Rose's farm, north or back of stone barn; the graves of 40 or 50 others, all unmarked, were nearby	Box 1-145, Hollywood, Richmond, 6/13/72
McMAKIN, John B.	CPL		A	13th MS		On hill between Jacob Schwartz's and George Bushman's farms, Yard B, Row 2	Box 1-199, Hollywood, Richmond, 6/13/72
McNAIR, James L.	PVT		C	31st GA	d. July 25 Probably U.S. Gen. Hosp., Frederick, MD	None	Mt. Olivet Cemetery, Frederick, MD, Grave 207
McNEIL, Patrick	PVT	36		Parker's (VA) Battery	d. July 3	John S. Crawford's tenant house where Samuel Johns lives; east of house, near Cpl. J.B. Loughridge; both names "cut into a crude pine board"	
McPHERSON, Angus M.	PVT	25	K	8th SC	k. July 2	George Rose's farm, north or back of stone barn	Box 1-150, Hollywood, Richmond, 6/13/72
McPHERSON, Malcolm	PVT	27	K	8th SC	k. July 2	George Rose's farm, back or north of stone barn	Box 1-157, Hollywood, Richmond, 6/13/72, as "M. McP, 8th SC"
McPHERSON, Norvel J.	PVT	31	A	42nd MS		On hill between Jacob Schwartz's and George Bushman's farms, Yard B, Row 2, under walnut tree	Box 1-S-17, Hollywood, Richmond, 6/13/72
McRAE, Montford Stokes	SGT MAJ	26	F&S	26th NC	d. Aug. 2	Camp Letterman, Row 2, Grave 6	
McWILLIAMS, David W.	PVT	34	B	17th MS	d. Sept. 10	Camp Letterman, Row 7, Grave 31	Box 1-94, Hollywood, Richmond, 6/13/72
MACKEY, Thomas	PVT		D	10th AL		North of Francis Bream's farmhouse, in field near woods along side of Adam Butt's woods, near road, south of house	Box 1-135, Hollywood, Richmond, 6/13/72
MADDEN, Daniel	SGT		C	21st MS		John Trostle's farm, south bank of Rock Creek near woods; northeast corner of Trostle's field; buried in one grave with Sgt. Ben Knabke, 18th MS	Box 2-257, Hollywood, Richmond, 8/3/72
◆ MAGRUDER, John Bowie	COL	23	F&S	57th VA	d. July 5	George Bushman's farm, or on ground near or on the Jacob Schwartz farm; returned to Richmond, VA in Oct. 1863, in a "metallic coffin" by Epsilon Alpha fraternity of the University of Virginia	Reinterred at Maplewood Cemetery, Charlottesville, VA
MAGRUDER, William T.	CPT	37		Staff, Gen. J. Davis	d. July 13	Peter Conover's farm	Body possibly recovered by his wife, Mary C. Magruder, of Baltimore
MAHORNER, Harris	PVT	19	F	11th MS	d. July 27	On hill between Jacob Schwartz's and George Bushman's farms, Yard B, Row 2	Box 1-206, Hollywood, Richmond, 6/13/72

Name	Rank	Age	Co.	Regiment	Casualty	Original Burial	Final Disposition
MALLOY, John Thomas	PVT	21	E	45th NC	d. Aug. 12	Camp Letterman, Row 5, Grave 9	Oakwood, Raleigh, 10/1/71
MALONE, Matthew J.	LT	24	D	5th NC	k. July 1	John S. Forney's farm	Possibly in one of six boxes marked "F," to Hollywood, Richmond, 8/3/72, as an unknown
MANLEY, James M.	LT	28	G	1st TN	d. Aug. 6	Camp Letterman, Row 3, Grave 12	Box 1-68, Hollywood, Richmond, 6/13/72
MANNING, Richard or Samuel H.	PVT		K	4th AL	d.c. July 3	Francis Bream's farm, north, in field near woods along side of Adam Butt's woods near road; also, "Adam Butt's farm, south"	Box 1-142, Hollywood, Richmond, with several others as "F.G. Manning, Co. H, 4th Ala."
MARCOM, William B.	PVT	36	E	47th NC	d.c. July 3	On hill under walnut tree between Jacob Schwartz's and George Bushman's farms, Yard B, Row 1	Box 1-22, Hollywood, Richmond, 6/13/72
MARKLEY, Charles A.	PVT	22	B	2nd SC	k. July 2	George Rose's farm, back or north of stone barn	Box 1-169, Hollywood, Richmond, 6/13/72
MARKS, Thomas E.	PVT		B	53rd NC	d. July 24	On hill under walnut tree between Jacob Schwartz's and George Bushman's farms, Yard B, Row 1	Box 1-16, Hollywood, Richmond, 6/13/72
MARLEY, John	PVT	28	K	53rd NC	d. Sept. 25	Camp Letterman, Row 8, Grave 24	Oakwood, Raleigh, Grave 483, 10/1/71
MARSHALL, Lauister L.	SGT	23	E	53rd NC	k. July 2/3	Elizabeth Shultz's house on Seminary Ridge, nearby, or, J.E. Culp's field near Gettysburg	Oakwood, Raleigh, 10/1/71
MARSHBOURN, Joseph J.	CPL	23	A	55th NC	d. July 14	Jacob Schwartz's farm, in cornfield, Yard D, Row 3	Box 1-S-66, Hollywood, Richmond, 6/13/72, as "J.J. Marshall, 55th NC"
MARTIN, A.J.	PVT		K	9th AL		North of Adam Butt's house under a cherry tree	Box 1-124, Hollywood, Richmond, 6/13/72
MARTIN, Andrew	CPL			Brooks (SC) Artillery	k. July 3	John S. Crawford's tenant farm, (Samuel Johns), east of barn	
MARTIN, James B.	CPL	24	C	14th VA	d. July 10	George Bushman's farm; hospital cemetery was east of house	
MARTIN, James F.	PVT	35	K	2nd SC	d. Aug. 6	Camp Letterman, Row 3, Grave 14	Box 1-106, Hollywood, Richmond, 6/13/72
MARTIN, John B.	PVT	28	H	26th NC	d. Aug. 1 Jordan Springs Hospital Winchester, VA	None	Stonewall Cemetery, Winchester, VA
MASON, Joseph L.	PVT	19	I	17th MS	d. Aug. 12	Camp Letterman, Row 5, Grave 13	Box 1-37, Hollywood, Richmond, 6/13/72
MASON, Miles	PVT	34	G	5th NC	d. July 19	Jacob Hankey's farm	Oakwood, Raleigh, Grave 519, 10/1/71
MASSEY, Jacob W.	PVT	22	A	4th NC	d. Sept. 3	Camp Letterman, Row 7, Grave 3	Oakwood, Raleigh, Grave 473, 10/1/71
MATHIS, W.H.	CPL		I	7th SC	k. July 2	George Rose's farm, back or north of the stone barn	Box 1-163, Hollywood, Richmond, 6/13/72
◆ MATHIS, William W.	PVT		B	8th GA		John Edward Plank's farm, back of barn	Box 2-H, Hollywood, Richmond, 8/3/72
MATTHEWS, Andrew J.	PVT	21	C	28th VA	d. July 23	On hill under walnut tree between Jacob Schwartz's and George Bushman's farms, Yard B, Row 2	Box 1-15, Hollywood, Richmond, 6/13/72
MATTHEWS, Archibald P.	CPL	22	B	11th MS	d. July 17 Seminary Hosp. Hagerstown, MD	Probably in Old Almshouse Burying Ground, Hagerstown, MD	Probably to "Rose Hill," Washington Cemetery, Hagerstown, MD (mortally wounded at Falling Waters, MD, July 10, 1863)

Name	Rank	Age	Co.	Regiment	Date	Burial location	Disposition
MAUPIN, James R.	PVT	30		2nd Co., Richmond (VA) Howitzers	k. July 3	Buried "where he fell" next to H.T. Pendleton, on Seminary Ridge on or near Elizabeth Shultz's lot	Reinterred to a "cemetery In Washington City," to be relocated in family burial ground at the University of VA
MAYEUX, Octave	PVT		E	2nd LA	d. Aug. 10 U.S. Gen. Hosp. Chester, PA	Chester Rural Cemetery, Chester, PA	Philadelphia National Cemetery, 1891
MAYNARD, John H.	SGT	26	K	6th NC	d. July 4	Elizabeth Wible's farm	Oakwood, Raleigh, 10/1/71
MAYNOR, Laban F.	PVT		F	6th AL		John Horting's farm, Fairfield Road	Possibly in Box 4-A, Hollywood, Richmond, 5/17/73, as an unknown
MAYS, John C.	SGT		G	1st SC	k. July 3	David McMillan's farm, in apple orchard along Seminary Ridge near C.S. fortifications	Magnolia, Charleston, Grave 17, 5/10/71
MEACHAM, R. W.	LT		B	13th GA	k. July 1	On the southwest edge of Blocher's Hill, on the David Blocher farm; also, Almshouse "burial ground"	
MEADOR, Jesse L.	PVT		A	57th VA	d. July 9	Francis Bream's mill; "on the hill from Bream's Mill," above William Myers's house	Box 2-P-Curns, Hollywood, Richmond, 8/3/72, with 33 others
MEADOWS, John W.	PVT		G	61st GA	k. July 1	"Buried Gettysburg" Probably on Josiah Benner's farm in meadow along fence	Laurel Grove, Savannah, Lot 853, Grave 10, 9/24/71, as "T. Madders"
MEDLIN, Thomas L.	PVT		E	47th NC		Possibly Jacob Schwartz's farm	Oakwood, Raleigh, Grave 460, 10/1/71, as "Thomas Mellon, Co. E, 45th NC"
MEDLIN, William C.	PVT	27	E	47th NC	d. July 16	Jacob Schwartz's farm, in cornfield, Yard D, Row 3	Box 1-S-76, Hollywood, Richmond, 6/13/72
MEECE, J.P.	PVT		K	5th TX		John Edward Plank's farm, north of house under walnut tree; right and front of house toward Fairfield Road and Gettysburg	Box 2-H, Hollywood, Richmond, 8/3/72
MERCER, Oliver Evans	CPT	22	G	20th NC	k. July 1	Possibly John Forney's farm, or Jacob Hankey's farm; his mother made inquiries to Dr. John O'Neal on Aug. 16, 1866 with intent to move remains	Mercer Farm, New Hanover Co., NC. He was, "a brave, noble boy in the full bloom of youth…"
MEREDITH, Wilson C.	PVT	20	D	18th VA		Isaac Diehl's farm along Rock Creek near Baltimore Pike, to the rear of the barn	Box 3-290, Hollywood, Richmond, 9/10/72, as "Meredith, 18th Va"
MERRIMAN, John E.	CPL			Blount's (VA) Battery	d. July 3	John S. Crawford's farm, back of John Sachs's place, corner of woods under a white oak tree near the fence	Probably in one of two boxes marked "2-C-Miss," to Hollywood, Richmond, 8/3/72, as an unknown
MICKLE, William N.	LT	20	K	37th NC	k. July 3	A comrade believed he was in an unmarked grave about 30 yards west of the apex of the "Angle" on Peter Frey's farm along Cemetery Ridge	Probably in one of 21 boxes marked "P," to Hollywood, Richmond, 8/3/72, as an unknown
MIDKIFF, E.P.	PVT		G	4th TX		John Edward Plank's farm, under walnut tree north of house toward Fairfield Road and Gettysburg	Box 2-H, Hollywood, Richmond, 8/3/72
◆ MILAN, James C.	SGTMAJ		F&S	60th GA	d. July 3	George Culp's farm near Willoughby's Run	Box 4-294, Hollywood, Richmond, 5/17/73, as "Milan, Ala"
MILES, Septimus C.	PVT	27	I	2nd SC	k. July 2	George Rose's farm, "on the gravl walk in the woods;" his captain said a headboard was made for Miles, but before he could be buried they had to retreat; it was noted he was, "the life of the company"	Magnolia, Charleston, Common Grave 28, 5/10/71; his corpse is second from the left in the photo on the back cover of this book.

Name	Rank	Age	Co.	Regiment	Death	Gettysburg Burial Location	Final Disposition
MILLAM, James E.	1SGT		G	53rd VA	d. Aug. 6 U.S. Gen. Hosp. Chester, PA	Chester Rural Cemetery, Chester, PA, Grave 123	Philadelphia National Cemetery, 1891
MILLER, Alexander	MAJ	30	F&S	21st NC	d. Aug. 2	On hill between Jacob Schwartz's and George Bushman's farms, Yard B, Row 2, under walnut tree	Box 1-204, Hollywood, Richmond, 6/13/72
MILLER, Hugh Reid	COL	51	F&S	42nd MS	d. July 19 "at a house in Gettysburg"	None. Embalmed and boxed in a metallic coffin, and taken to Baltimore by his son Edwin, from a private residence in Gettysburg.	First Presbyterian Church, Richmond, VA, 7/29/63
MILLER, James B.	LT	27	A	18th VA	d. Aug. 5 U.S. Gen. Hosp. Chester, PA	Chester Rural Cemetery, Chester, PA	Philadelphia National Cemetery, 1891
MILLER, Joel	PVT		M	7th SC	d. July 8	Francis Bream's farm, north of tavern, near graveyard and creek	Magnolia, Charleston, Grave 48, 5/10/71
MILLER, John T.	PVT	21	E	45th NC	d. July 20	Jacob Hankey's farm	Oakwood, Raleigh, Grave 493, 10/1/71
MILLER, Joseph M.	PVT	32	A	52nd NC	d. July 9/21	On hill between Jacob Schwartz's and George Bushman's farms, Yard B, Row 2, under walnut tree	Box 1-S-10, Hollywood, Richmond, 6/13/72, as "A. Miller"
MILLER, William P.	PVT		B	3rd SC BN	k. July 2	George Rose's farm, west of barn, under large cherry tree "grave deep, with board cover with 6 others"	Magnolia, Charleston, Grave 24, 5/10/71
◆ MILLER, William T.	CPL	24	G	1st VA		"On hill from Bream's Mill," first grave toward John Currens's house	Possibly Box 2-249, Hollywood, Richmond, 8/3/72, as "John Miller, Va."
MILLS, Edmund J.	PVT	22	I	2nd SC	k. July 2	George Rose's farm, "on the gravl walk in the woods;" said to be "a gallant soldier, free from all vices"	Magnolia, Charleston, Common Grave 28, 5/10/71; his corpse is the fourth from the left in the photo on the back cover of this book.
◆ MILLS, John	PVT		G	9th GA	d.c. Dec. 2	John Edward Plank's farm	Laurel Grove, Savannah, Lot 853, Grave 11, 9/24/71
MIMMS, John R.	PVT	23	E	11th MS	d. Mar. 12, 1864 West's Bldg. U.S. Gen. Hosp. Baltimore, MD	None	Loudon Park, Baltimore, Grave A-19, 3/13/64; pieces of his left ilium are in the National Museum of Health and Medicine
MIMMS, Thomas P.	LT	27	E	11th MS	d. July 9/13	Peter Conover's farm, edge of woods, south of house	Box 3-277, Hollywood, Richmond, 9/10/72
MINTZ, Peter L.	CPL	32	D	16th NC	k. July 3	Henry Culp's farm, in orchard under apple tree	Box 4-292, Hollywood, Richmond, 5/17/73, as "P. M., Co. G, NC"
MITCHEL, William L.	PVT	17	D	1st VA	k. July 3	Nicholas Codori farm, "on the banks [or near the foundation] of a small cabin, near a brick house;" marked with a cracked board and piece of paper	Probably in one of 21 boxes marked "P," to Hollywood, Richmond, 8/3/72, as an unknown
MITCHELL, Goodrich	LT		C	49th VA		Near William E. Myers's house at Bream's Mill	
MITCHELL, Jacob	PVT	23	D	1st TN		Samuel Lohr's farm, opposite house, in meadow, near pear tree	Box 4-S, Hollywood, Richmond, 5/17/73
MITCHELL, Thomas J.	PVT	26	G	32nd NC	d. July 8	Jacob Hankey's farm	Oakwood, Raleigh, Grave 498, 10/1/71
MOBLEY, W.A.J.	PVT		G	13th GA	k. July 1 (?)	"Buried Gettysburg" Probably on Josiah Benner's farm, in meadow along fence.	Laurel Grove, Savannah, Lot 853, Grave 10, 9/24/71, as "A.J. Mallore, Co. G, 13th Ga"

Name	Rank	Age	Co.	Regiment	Death	Location	Disposition
MOCK, J.D.	PVT		E	14th SC	d. July 29 U.S. Gen. Hosp. Chester, PA	Chester Rural Cemetery, Chester, PA	Magnolia, Charleston, Grave 55, 5/10/71
MOCK, Lewis	PVT	22	G	2nd NC BN		Jacob Plank's farm, back of barn, Grave 7; "10 graves out of 20, ploughed over"	Box 3-P, Hollywood, Richmond, 9/10/72, with four others
MOFFAT, H.D.	PVT	17	H	8th AL	d. Sept. 19	Camp Letterman, Row 7, Grave 18	Box 1-117, Hollywood, Richmond, 6/13/72
MONCRIEF, David H.	SGT		K	3rd GA	d. July 12	Adam Butt's brick schoolhouse on the Fairfield Road	Laurel Grove, Savannah, Lot 853, Grave 12, 9/24/71
MONEY, Frank	SGT		G	8th VA		"Leg shot off, supposed to be dead"	Possibly "State Lot" - VA, to Hollywood, Richmond
MONTGOMERY, Green B.W.	LT	27	F	3rd SC BN	d. July 3	Francis Bream's farm, north of tavern, near graveyard and creek; also, "Burying ground," center	Probably in one of two boxes marked "B," to Hollywood, Richmond, 8/3/72, as an unknown
MOODY, John W.	PVT		I	8th GA	d. July 6	John Edward Plank's farm	"State Lot" - GA, to Hollywood, Richmond
MOODY, William H.	LT		A	2nd MS		George Spangler's farm	
MOORE, Charles	PVT		F	13th MS		John Crawford's farm, in orchard, north of "Walnut Avenue," under apple tree	Box 2-C-Miss, Hollywood, Richmond, 8/3/72; "grave unmarked by then"
MOORE, George W.	PVT	21	F	6th NC	d. July 4	Christian Byers's farm, Fairfield Rd., with 23 others, not marked	Oakwood, Raleigh, Grave 506, 10/1/71
◆ **MOORE, Henry M.**	CPL		G	14th VA	d. Aug. 17	Camp Letterman, Row 2, Grave 34	Box 1-104, Hollywood, Richmond, 6/13/72
MOORE, James M.	PVT		G	11th VA	d. July 19	Jacob Schwartz's farm, back of barn	Possibly in one of seven boxes marked "S," to Hollywood, Richmond, 9/10/72, as an unknown
MOORE, Jamison H.	CPT	25	H	11th MS	d. July 4-5	Samuel Lohr's farm, in woods on north side; Moore's father was still searching for his remains in the 1880s, and contacted Dr. Weaver in 1887	Box 3-259, Hollywood, Richmond, 9/10/72; also, possibly reinterred in Moore Cemetery, Houlka, MS
MOORE, John R.	LT	28	D	48th VA	d. July 2	W. Henry Monfort's farm, Hunterstown Road	Box 3-M, Hollywood, Richmond, 9/10/72, as "Moore, Va."
MOORE, Lewis M.	LT		E	17th MS	d. Aug. 2	Camp Letterman, Row 2, Grave 9	Box 1-70, Hollywood, Richmond, 6/13/72
MOORE, P.M.	SGT		E	1st MD BN		George Bushman's farm; hospital cemetery was east of house	
MOORE, Samuel B.	PVT	26		King William (VA) Artillery	k. July 1	John S. Forney's farm	Possibly in one of six boxes marked "F," to Hollywood, Richmond, 8/3/72, as an unknown
MOORE, William	PVT	29	H	34th NC	d. Dec. 19 U.S. Gen. Hosp. Harrisburg, PA	None	Soldiers' Lot, Harrisburg, PA Cemetery, Grave 58
MOORE, William Brice	SGT		G	18th VA CAV	k. June 29	Buried near McConnellsburg, PA, "where he had fallen," by the side of the road on the Mercersburg Pike, "just inside Daniel Fore's meadow alongside the pike," next to T.A. Shelton	The United Daughters of the Confederacy placed a marker near the site in 1929

Name	Rank	Age	Co.	Regiment	Casualty	Original Burial	Final Disposition
MOORER, Jacob F.	CPT	32	K	2nd SC	d. July 27 Probably Seminary Hosp. Hagerstown, MD	Possibly Old Almshouse Burying Ground, Hagerstown, MD	Probably in "Rose Hill," Washington Cemetery, Hagerstown, MD
MOORHEAD, James H.	LT		H	11th AL		South of Adam Butt's house, near road; "Butt's woods"	Box 1-140, Hollywood, Richmond, 6/13/72
MOOSE, Edmund	LT	30	D	28th NC	d. Sept. 27 U.S. Gen. Hosp. Chester, PA	Chester Rural Cemetery, Chester, PA	Philadelphia National Cemetery, 1891
MORGAN, John W. S.	SGT		K	35th GA	k. July 2	David McMillan's farm, east of the house, close by General Pickett's line	Box 1-215, Hollywood, Richmond, 6/13/72
MORGAN, Samuel	PVT		F	24th GA	d. July 8 or 18 Seminary Hosp. Hagerstown, MD	Old Almshouse Burying Ground, Hagerstown, MD	Probably in "Rose Hill," Washington Cemetery, Hagerstown, MD
MORRIS, John	LT	25		Ordnance Train Pegram's ART BN	k. July 1	Ephraim Wisler's blacksmith shop, under apple tree, near northeast corner of barn	Box 1-234, Hollywood, Richmond, 6/13/72
MORRISON, John A.	PVT		A	6th NC	k. July 1	John S. Forney's farm	Possibly in one of six boxes marked "F," to Hollywood, Richmond, 8/3/72, as an unknown
MORROW, Elijah G.	CPT	31	G	28th NC	d. July 19	On hill under walnut tree between Jacob Schwartz's and George Bushman's farms, Yard B, Row 2	Box 1-S-1, Hollywood, Richmond, 6/13/72; possibly reinterred in Old Chapel Hill Cemetery, NC
MORTON, Allan	CPL	21		1st Co., Richmond (VA) Howitzers	k. July 2/3	Abraham Trostle's farm; near Joseph Sherfy's, along lane to Abraham Trostle's	"Recovered in 1867"
MORTON, James W.	PVT		E	18th VA	d. July 23	On hill between Jacob Schwartz's and George Bushman's farms under walnut tree, Yard B, Row 2	Box 1-18, Hollywood, Richmond, 6/13/72, as "J.W. Marston, 18th Va."
MOUNGER, John C.	LTC	50	F&S	9th GA	k. July 2	Ephraim Wisler's blacksmith shop, "in the family plot or cemetery" near Jacob Lott's; "grave in excellent order"	Laurel Grove, Savannah, Lot 853, Grave 14, 9/24/71
MOXLEY, James H.	PVT		I	7th TN	d. July 16 Jordan Springs Hospital Winchester, VA	None	Stonewall Cemetery, Winchester, VA
MULLEN, Andrew J.	PVT	20	H	27th VA	d. July 12	Henry Picking's farm, in field along fence opposite schoolhouse near Hunterstown Road	Box 1-177, Hollywood, Richmond, 6/13/72
MUNN, David D.	SGTMAJ		F&S	17th GA	d. July 7	John Edward Plank's farm under a large locust tree toward John Crawford's farm, and near road to Bream's Mill; also, "back of barn"	Probably in one of 11 boxes marked "H," to Hollywood, Richmond, 8/3/72, as an unknown
MURPHY, Enoch E.	PVT		E	15th SC	d. Sept 2 DeCamp U.S. Gen. Hosp. David's Island, New York	None	Probably Cypress Hills Cemetery, Long Island, NY

Name	Rank	Age	Co.	Unit	Death	Location	Final Disposition
MURRAY, John W.	LT		E	4th VA CAV	k. June 29 Westminster, Maryland	Union Churchyard, Westminster, Maryland	Ascension Episcopal Churchyard, 8/13/63
MURRAY, William H.	CPT	24	A	1st MD BN	k. July 3		To Christ Church Cemetery, Owensville, MD; a memorial marker is on "Confederate Hill," Loudon Park Cemetery, Baltimore, MD
MYERS, George M.	LT	24	H	8th SC	k. July 2	George Rose's farm, north or back of stone barn	Box 1-156, Hollywood, Richmond, 6/13/72
MYERS, Jacob W.	PVT	19	B	28th VA		On the hill between Jacob Schwartz's and George Bushman's farms, under walnut tree, Yard B, Row 2	Box 1-S-3, Hollywood, Richmond, 6/13/72
N							
NABERS, Austin	PVT	20	G	2nd SC CAV	d. Sept. 5	Camp Letterman, Row 7, Grave 13	Magnolia, Charleston, Grave 9, 5/10/71
◆ **NASH, John Miles**	CPL		D	38th GA		Josiah Benner's farm, in meadow along fence	Laurel Grove, Savannah, Lot 853, Grave 10, 9/24/71 as "___ Nash, 38th Georgia"
NASH, James	PVT		C	1st MD BN		Pennsylvania College, in hospital cemetery on north side of main edifice	Box 4-E, Hollywood, Richmond, with 34 others, 5/17/73
NASH, Richard James	PVT	28	G	9th VA	d. Aug. 16	Camp Letterman, Row 2, Grave 27	Box 1-75, Hollywood, Richmond, 6/13/72
NASH, William F.	PVT	27	G	9th GA	d. Aug. 18	Camp Letterman, Row 2, Grave 35; "removed"	Laurel Grove, Savannah, Lot 854, Grave 3
NEAL, Green Berry	PVT	25	D	37th NC	d. Aug. 27 U.S. Gen. Hosp. Chester, PA	Chester Rural Cemetery, Chester, PA	Philadelphia National Cemetery, 1891
NELMS, William C.D.	PVT		C	21st GA	d. July 19 Seminary Hosp. Hagerstown, MD	Old Almshouse Burying Ground, Hagerstown, MD	Probably in "Rose Hill," Washington Cemetery, Hagerstown, MD
NELMS, William F.	PVT	18	B	5th TX	d. July 9	Jesse Worley's farm	Box 3-X, Hollywood, Richmond, 9/10/72
NETTLES, F.L.	SGT	21	E	8th SC	d. Aug. 19	Camp Letterman, Row 3, Grave 31	Magnolia, Charleston, Grave 2, 5/10/71
NEWTON, Ezra	PVT		A	50th GA	k. July 2	George Rose's farm in orchard, near fence; "in orchard near springhouse" "removed"	Laurel Grove, Savannah, Lot 853, Grave 13, 9/24/71
NICHOLS, Charles	PVT	22	C	57th VA	d. Sept. 11	Camp Letterman, Row 7, Grave 29	Box 1-93, Hollywood, Richmond, 6/13/72
NICHOLS, Thomas H.B.	PVT		H	16th GA		John Cunningham's farm, across creek from John S. Crawford's farm; Confederate cemetery was in orchard, south side	Laurel Grove, Savannah, Lot 853, Grave 11, 9/24/71
NICHOLS, William L.	PVT	29	C	1st MD BN	d. Aug. 13	Camp Letterman, Row 1, Grave 14; also, "died at Mrs. Elizabeth Wible's farm"	
NIXON, Archibald	PVT	40	G	52nd NC	d. July 19	Jacob Schwartz's farm, in cornfield, Yard D, Row 1	Box 1-S-22, Hollywood, Richmond, 6/13/72
NIXON, George	PVT	35	G	52nd NC	d. July 20	On hill under walnut tree between Jacob Schwartz's and George Bushman's farms, Yard B, Row 2	Box 1-S-11, Hollywood, Richmond, 6/13/72

Name	Rank	Age	Co.	Regiment	Date	Burial Location	Reinterment
NOBLE, L.R.	PVT		K	3rd AR	d. July 7	John Edward Plank's farm, north side of house under walnut tree; grave covered with stone	Box 2-H, Hollywood, Richmond, 8/3/72
NORMAN, W.Y.	PVT		G	3rd AL	d. July 21 U.S. Gen. Hosp. Harrisburg, PA	None	Soldiers' Lot, Harrisburg, PA, Cemetery, Grave 74
NORRIS, Hardy R.	PVT	22	B	15th AL	d. Aug. 29	Camp Letterman, Row 6, Grave 22	Box 1-73, Hollywood, Richmond, 6/13/72
NORRIS, Moses T.	SGT		B	4th TX		John Edward Plank's farm, north side of house under walnut tree	Box 2-H, Hollywood, Richmond, 8/3/72
NORTON, James P.	PVT		C	8th AL	d. Jan. 11, 1864	U.S. General Hospital, York, PA	Grotto Cemetery, Mount St. Mary's College, Emmitsburg, MD
NOWELL, Ransom G.	PVT	21	K	14th NC	k. July 1	John S. Forney's farm, foot of garden, next to Lt. James Griffith, Co. G, 14th NC	Oakwood, Raleigh, 10/1/71
NUCHOLDS, David R.	PVT	20	B	38th VA	d. Sept. 17	Camp Letterman, Row 8, Grave 13	Box 1-113, Hollywood, Richmond, 6/13/72
NUCKOLS, James A.	PVT	22	B	38th VA	d. Sept. 17/21	Camp Letterman, Row 8, Grave 21	Box 1-95, Hollywood, Richmond, 6/13/72
NUNN, Calton	PVT	24	K	13th NC	d. July 24 U.S. Gen. Hosp. Chester, PA	Chester Rural Cemetery, Chester, PA	Philadelphia National Cemetery, 1891
NUNN, William D.	CPT	21	B	11th MS	d. July 13	Peter Conover's farm	
NUTTING, George W.	PVT		D	5th AL	k. July 1	Moses McClean's farm, south along the lane in cherry thicket	Box 1-186, Hollywood, Richmond, 6/13/72
O							
OAKES, Thomas C.	SGT	28	B	38th VA	d. Aug. 2	On the hill between Jacob Schwartz's and George Bushman's farms, Yard B, Row 2	Box 1-213, Hollywood, Richmond, 6/13/72
OATES, John A.	LT		G	15th AL	d. July 23/24	Michael Fiscel's farm, east of house across creek, next to Lt. B.H. Cody, 15th AL	Box 3-A, Hollywood, Richmond, 9/10/72, with 11 others
ODUM, J.C.	PVT		G	18th GA	d. July 12	John Cunningham's farm, across creek from John S. Crawford's farm; Confederate cemetery was in orchard, south side	Laurel Grove, Savannah, Lot 853, Grave 11, 9/24/71
OLDNER, Philip	PVT			Chesapeake (MD) Artillery	k. July 2	Christian Benner's farm, near Rock Creek, under a walnut tree; also, David Stewart's farm, east of barn and near row of trees	Box 3-286, Hollywood, Richmond, 9/10/72; also, Loudon Park, Baltimore, MD "Confederate Hill," Row F, Grave 43, 1873-1874
OLIVER, Andrew G.	PVT		C	18th GA	k. July 2	John Cunningham's farm across creek from John S. Crawford's Farm; Confederate burial ground was in orchard, south side	Laurel Grove, Savannah, Lot 853, Grave 11, 9/24/71
OLIVER, John C.	1SGT		F	11th GA		Jacob Edward Plank's farm, back of barn	Box 2-H, Hollywood, Richmond, 8/3/72
O'MEARRA, William	PVT		F	5th AL	k. July 1	Moses McClean's farm, south along the lane in cherry thicket	Box 1-187, Hollywood, Richmond, 6/13/72
O'NEAL, James	PVT	27	H	21st NC	d. Sept. 7 U.S. Gen. Hosp. Chester, PA	Chester Rural Cemetery, Chester, PA	Philadelphia National Cemetery, 1891

Name	Rank	Age	Co.	Regiment	Death	Original Burial	Final Disposition
OSBORN, S.W.	SGT		A	14th LA	d. July 25 West's Bldg. U.S. Gen. Hosp. Baltimore, MD	None	Loudon Park, Baltimore, Row C, Grave 72, 7/25/63
OURSLER, W.R.	LT		F	17th MS	k./d. July 2 (?)	Christian Shefferer's farm, on road to Abraham Krise's, near the Negro blacksmith shop west of the "Peach Orchard," "on Eckert's Mill Rd., right side of Blacksmith shop;" "Elliott's Map" places the grave on the north side of the road, just east of Shefferer's farm and the blacksmith's shop	"State Lot" - MS, to Hollywood, Richmond
OUSBY, William C.	CPT	30	F	43rd NC	k. July 1	In "bark coffin" with headboard on grave, somewhere near where he fell, which was southeast of Oak Hill on John S. Forney's farm	Probably in one of six boxes marked "F," to Hollywood, Richmond, 8/3/72, as an unknown
OVERSTREET, Jesse W.	CPL		B	14th VA	d. July 29	None	Winchester, VA, Cemetery, Grave 1171
OVERSTREET, Jesse W.	PVT		C	28th VA	d. July 23 U.S. Gen. Hosp. Chester, PA	Chester Rural Cemetery, Chester, PA, Grave 46	Philadelphia National Cemetery, 1891
OWEN, James P.	PVT		D	17th MS		John S. Crawford's farm, on Marsh Creek, in garden	Box 4-Y, Hollywood, Richmond, 5/17/73
OWENS, John Crowder	MAJ	33	F&S	9th VA	d. July 4	Francis Bream's mill, in woods across Marsh Creek from mill; "a little mound of earth in the center of a triangle of green sward, shaded by waving trees and watered by a flowing stream"	Oakwood Cemetery, Portsmouth, VA
OWENS, Thomas C.	PVT	24	G	9th VA	d. July 9/12	Francis Bream's mill, in woods across Marsh Creek from mill	Oakwood Cemetery, Portsmouth, VA

P

Name	Rank	Age	Co.	Regiment	Death	Original Burial	Final Disposition
PADGETT, Ellis	PVT		E	8th FL		On hill under walnut tree between Jacob Schwartz's and George Bushman's farms, Yard B, Row 2	Box 1-201, Hollywood, Richmond, 6/13/72
◆ PAGE, Everet C.	PVT	25	E	26th NC	d. July 28	John Edward Plank's farm, back of barn	Box 2-H, Hollywood, Richmond, 8/3/72, as "E.F.P., NC"
PAGE, Solomon S.	CPL		D	59th GA	d. Aug. 7 U.S. Gen. Hosp. Harrisburg, PA	None	Soldiers' Lot, Harrisburg, PA, Cemetery, Grave 132
PALMER, William T.	PVT			King William (VA) Artillery	k. July 1	Jacob Hershey's farm, northwest corner of orchard	Box 1-183, Hollywood, Richmond, 6/13/72, as "Capt. W.J. Palmore, 3rd Ala."
◆ PARISH, Samuel	PVT	19	E	28th VA		Probably on Jacob Schwartz's farm	Probably in one of seven boxes marked "S," to Hollywood, Richmond, 9/10/72, as an unknown
PARK, William A.	PVT	22	K	13th MS	d. Aug. 18	Camp Letterman, Row 3, Grave 34	Box 1-42, Hollywood, Richmond, 6/13/72
PARKER, Angus M.	LT		B	11th GA	d. July 21	John Edward Plank's farm under a large locust tree toward John S. Crawford's farm and near road to Bream's Mill; also, "back of barn"	Box 2-H, Hollywood, Richmond, 8/3/72
PARKER, Thaddeus	PVT			Chesapeake (MD) Artillery	k. July 2	Christian Benner's farm, back of Rock Creek under a large walnut tree	Loudon Park, Baltimore, 7/4/73

Name	Rank	Age	Co.	Regiment	Death	Burial Location	Final Disposition
PARKER, William J.	SGT		A	17th MS	d. July 29	Jacob Schwartz's farm, back of barn, Grave 7	Possibly in one of seven boxes marked "S," to Hollywood, Richmond, 9/10/72, as an unknown
PARKS, Andrew P.	PVT		C	17th MS		John S. Crawford's farm, in orchard north of "Walnut Avenue" under apple tree	Box 2-C-Miss, Hollywood, Richmond, 8/3/72; "grave unmarked by then"
PARRISH, Samuel	PVT	16/17	E	57th VA	d. July 17	Jacob Schwartz's farm, in a cornfield near Rock Creek, Yard D, Row 1	Box 1-S-27, Hollywood, Richmond, 6/13/72
PARRISH, Uriah R.	PVT	25	K	2nd NC CAV	d. Aug. 3	Camp Letterman, Row 6, Grave 26	Oakwood, Raleigh, Grave 470, 10/1/71
PARSONS, James T.	PVT		B	1st MD BN	d. July 1 U.S. Gen. Hosp. Chester, PA	Chester Rural Cemetery, Chester, PA	Philadelphia National Cemetery, 1891
PARTIN, Daniel Wilson	PVT	24	D	14th VA	d. July 23	Pennsylvania College, north of main edifice in hospital cemetery	Box 4-E, Hollywood, Richmond, 5/17/73, with 36 others in three boxes
PATE, Thomas B.	PVT	19	A	9th LA	d. July 28	Camp Letterman, Row 1, Grave 12	Box 1-88, Hollywood, Richmond, 6/13/72
PATRICK, James M.	PVT		A	2nd MS		John Horting's farm; "near the garden fence;" and, "corner of orchard under locust tree"	"State Lot" - MS, to Hollywood, Richmond, or Box 4-A, Hollywood, Richmond, 5/17/73
PATTERSON, William B.	LT		E	31st GA	k. July 1	Probably Josiah Benner's farm, in meadow along fence	Laurel Grove, Savannah, Lot 853, Grave 10, 9/24/71
PATTERSON, William M.	PVT		B	8th GA		Jacob Schwartz's farm, along lane near creek under walnut tree; "removed"	Laurel Grove, Savannah, Lot 853, Grave 15
PATTON, Waller Tazewell	COL	27	F&S	7th VA	d. July 21 at "College Hosp."	Possibly buried at Pennsylvania College or taken to Green Mount Cemetery, Baltimore, MD	Stonewall Cemetery, Winchester, VA
PAUL, William C.	PVT	20	D	1st NC	d. July 12	Michael Shealer's farm, in meadow next to Elizabeth Wible's	Box 3-V, Hollywood, Richmond, 9/10/72
PAYNE, Fielding F.	LT		B	8th VA	d. July 13	Jacob Schwartz's farm, in cornfield on Rock Creek, Yard D, Row 3	Box 1-S-58, Hollywood, Richmond, 6/13/72, with 110 others
PAYNE, Joseph T.	PVT		C	38th VA	d. July 22	On hill between Jacob Schwartz's and George Bushman's farms, Yard B, Row 2	Box 1-S-14 Hollywood, Richmond, 6/13/72, with 110 others
PAYSINGER, Henry M.	SGT	23	C	3rd SC	d. Sept. 22	Camp Letterman, Row 7, Grave 12	Magnolia, Charleston, Grave 8, 5/10/71
PEARSON, Robert R.	PVT	20	C	2nd SC	d. July 23	Francis Bream's farm, north of tavern, near graveyard and creek	Magnolia, Charleston, Grave 43, 5/10/71
PEGRAM, William A.	CPT	25	F	21st VA	k. July 6 Williamsport, Maryland	None	Town Cemetery or Public Burying Ground, Williamsport, MD
PENDLETON, Hugh Thomas "Tom"	PVT		2nd Co., Richmond (VA) Howitzers		k. July 3	McClellan's lot near fence on Seminary Ridge, near Elizabeth Shultz's lot, next to Pvt. James R. Maupin. "We buried them on the Ridge." "Battle-field near widow Schultz"	
PENDLEY, Merrit B.	1SGT	33/36	E	6th NC	d. Sept. 18	Camp Letterman, Row 8, Grave 10	Oakwood, Raleigh, Grave 480, 10/1/71
PENNY, Henry Frank	PVT		F	12th GA	d. July 23	"Buried at Gettysburg" Probably Jacob Hankey's farm	Laurel Grove, Savannah, Lot 854, Grave 13, 8/21/71

Name	Rank	Age	Co.	Regiment	Death	Original Burial	Reinterment
PERRY, Joseph E.	PVT	18	G	32nd NC	d. Sept. 27	Camp Letterman, Row 8, Grave 31	Oakwood, Raleigh, Grave 485, 10/1/71
PERRYMAN, Harvey	PVT		K	14th AL		George Bushman's farm; hospital cemetery was east of house	Box 1-225, Hollywood, Richmond, 6/13/72
PERSON, Jesse H.	LT	21	E	1st NC CAV	d. July 2	Presbyterian Church graveyard, Hunterstown, PA	
PETERS, S.W.	PVT		A	50th VA		W. Henry Monfort's farm, Hunterstown Road	Box 3-M, Hollywood, Richmond, 9/10/72
PHILLIPS, Robert S.	PVT		B	42nd MS	d. July 14	Samuel Lohr's farm, next to grave of Lt. G. A. Howze, 42nd MS, both, "well marked"	Probably Box 4-S, Hollywood, Richmond, 5/17/73, as unknown
PICKETT, Jacob W.	PVT		G	13th AL	d. July 28	Camp Letterman, Row 1, Grave 17	Box 1-29, Hollywood, Richmond, 6/13/72
PIKE, John	PVT	29	G	26th NC	"Died in the hands of the enemy"		Rocky River Friends Cemetery, Chatham Co, NC
PINDELL, Philip	PVT	29	A	1st MD BN	d. Aug. 2/21 U.S. Gen. Hosp., Chester, PA	Chester Rural Cemetery, Chester, PA	Philadelphia National Cemetery, 1891; his skull is in the National Museum of Health and Medicine, Specimen #3119
PIPER, George	PVT	17	I	45th NC	d.c. Aug. 11	Probably Jacob Hankey's farm	Oakwood, Raleigh
PITCOCK, Robert	PVT		D	33rd VA	d. July 15	Henry Picking's farm, in field, along fence opposite schoolhouse near road	Box 1-173, Hollywood, Richmond, 6/13/72
PITTMAN, Benjamin F.	PVT	28	C	1st NC	d. Sept. 14	Camp Letterman, Row 8, Grave 5	Oakwood, Raleigh, Grave 478, 10/1/71
PITTMAN, Jesse W.	SGT		I	11th GA	k. July 2	John Edward Plank's farm, under a large locust tree toward John S. Crawford's place and near road to Bream's Mill; also "back of barn"	Box 2-H, Hollywood, Richmond, 8/3/72
PLUMER, James M.	SGT	25	B	1st SC	d. Sept. 4 U.S. Gen. Hosp., Chester, PA	Chester Rural Cemetery, Chester, PA	Magnolia, Charleston, Grave 60, 5/10/71
POAG, Alonzo W.	LT	24	H	12th SC	k. July 3	Along Willoughby's Run near Herr's Tavern	Possibly in one of five boxes marked "F," to Hollywood, Richmond, 9/10/72
POINDEXTER, William G.	PVT		G	28th NC	d. July 5	Jacob Schwartz's farm; "grave still marked in July 1866"	Possibly in one of seven boxes marked "S," to Hollywood, Richmond, 9/10/72, as an unknown
POLK, J.W.	PVT	22	E	2nd SC	k. July 2	George Rose's farm, back of stone barn under cherry tree	Magnolia, Charleston, Grave 15, 5/10/71
POLLOCK, Thomas G.	CPT	24	F Staff, Gen. G. Pickett	60th VA	k. July 3	Near William E. Myers's house at Bream's Mill	Warrenton Cemetery, Warrenton, VA
POOL, Robert W.	SGT	22	B	2nd SC	d. July 3	Francis Bream's farm, north of tavern, near graveyard and creek	Probably in one of two boxes marked "B," with 20 remains to Hollywood, Richmond, 8/3/72
POOLE, William H.	CPL	21	H	9th LA	k. July 3	"Buried by Samuel McCreary on Long Lane"	"Parents [said to have] exhumed his grave after war and returned it to Louisiana."
POORE, Robert Henry	MAJ	40	F&S	14th VA	(Still alive "11 days after the fight")	Francis Bream's tavern; "north of tavern near the McClellan family burial place;" for some reason, it appears his body was later removed to George Bushman's farm	Possibly reinterred in the Charlottesville, or Fluvanna Co., VA, area

Name	Rank	Age	Co.	Regiment	Date	Burial Location	Disposition
POPE, Joseph W.	CPL	25	G	3rd VA	d. July 11	Francis Bream's mill, above William Myers's house by the side of a fence	Box 2-P-Curns, Hollywood, Richmond, 8/3/72, with 33 others
PORTER, Joseph M.	LT		H	15th SC	k. July 2	George Rose's farm, "on the gravl walk in the woods"	Magnolia, Charleston, Common Grave 28, 5/10/71
POTTER, George W.	LT		F	17th GA	d. July 5	John Edward Plank's farm, back of barn	Box 2-H, Hollywood, Richmond, 8/3/72
POWE, Hugh T.	SGT	34	K	5th NC	d. July 26 West's Bldg. U.S. Gen. Hosp. Baltimore, MD	None	Loudon Park, Baltimore, Row C, Grave 62
POWE, Thomas E.	CPT	25	C	8th SC	d. July 22	Francis Bream's farm, north of tavern, near graveyard and creek	Possibly in a box marked "B," with 20 remains to Hollywood, Richmond, 8/3/72
POWELL, Cornelius	CPL		E	9th VA	d. July 21	Jacob Schwartz's farm, back of barn, Grave 17	Possibly in one of seven boxes marked "S," to Hollywood, Richmond, 9/10/72, as an unknown
POWELL, George B.	PVT Color Guard		C	14th TN	d. July 23	Jacob Schwartz's farm, back of barn; A colorbearer, "he fell aparently dead just after crossing the Emmitsburg Road."	Possibly in one of seven boxes marked "S," to Hollywood, Richmond, 9/10/72, as an unknown
POWELL, William Joseph	CPL		F	38th GA	k. July 1	Josiah Benner's farm, in meadow along fence. "all removed"	Laurel Grove, Savannah, Lot 853, Grave 10, 9/24/71
PRESGRAVES, John R.	LT	28	I	8th VA	d. July 15	Jacob Schwartz's farm, in a pine coffin, west of house near bank of creek in woods on Red Hill; buried by one of his brothers; "removed"	Sharon Cemetery, Middleburg, VA
PRESLEY, Thomas N.	PVT		I	7th SC	k. July 2	George Rose's farm, back or north of stone barn	Box 1-152, Hollywood, Richmond, 6/13/72
PRESSON, John A.	CPL		B	53rd GA	d. July 15	John S. Crawford's farm on Marsh Creek	"State Lot" - GA, to Hollywood, Richmond
PRICE, John W.	PVT		E	17th MS		Samuel Pitzer's woods, near Willoughby's Run; John Crawford's farm on Marsh Creek, near William Felix's house along road on left side going to Samuel Pitzer's; from John Edward Plank's to Pitzer's school near a log house on Willoughby's Run; "grave is well marked"	In 1870, Dr. John O'Neal noted that someone was making inquiries about his grave. This person may have taken possession of the remains.
PRIDGEN, Hinton H.	PVT	23	E	18th NC	d. July 15	Jacob Schwartz's farm, in cornfield, Yard D, Row 3	Box 1-S-53, Hollywood, Richmond, 6/13/72
PRINCE, Ephraim	PVT		C	9th GA	d. July 17	John Edward Plank's farm	Possibly in one of 11 boxes marked "H," to Hollywood, Richmond, 8/3/72, as an unknown
PRINCE, William H.	SGT	20	A	5th VA	k. July 3	On Raspberry or Culp's Hill, near breastworks in the flat; "in woods from Union burying ground, back or west of Culp's Hill, near breastworks;" "removed," 1864-1866	Mt. Hebron Cemetery, Winchester, VA; (This cemetery includes a section called "Stonewall Cemetery.")
◆ PRUE, Marshall	PVT		F	5th TX	k. July 2	"Below the rocks, in the lower part of a meadow;" also, "way down in one corner of a field and near the base of the round top;" "his old roundabout [jacket] was lying alongside of his grave"	Possibly in one of four boxes marked "L," to Hollywood, Richmond, 8/3/72, with 49 remains, as an unknown
PUCKETT, William A.	PVT	20	K	55th NC	d. July 23	On hill under walnut tree between Jacob Schwartz's and George Bushman's farms, Yard B, Row 1; "grave still marked in July 1866"	Box 1-4, Hollywood, Richmond, 6/13/72

Name	Rank	Age	Co.	Regiment	Death/Killed	Original Burial Location	Final Location
PUGH, Nathan S.	LT		I	Cobb's (GA) Legion Cavalry	d.c. July 2 in J.L. Grass Hotel	On Hunterstown Road south of Hunterstown, under cherry tree	Laurel Grove, Savannah, Lot 854, Grave 12, 8/21/71
PULLIAM, Robert C.	CPT	34	B	2nd SC	d. July 3	Francis Bream's farm, old burying ground, center, or, north of tavern by graveyard near creek	Magnolia, Charleston, Grave 41, 5/10/71

Q

Name	Rank	Age	Co.	Regiment	Death/Killed	Original Burial Location	Final Location
QUINN, Hillery L.	PVT	20	E	18th MS	d. Sept. 1	Camp Letterman, Row 6, Grave 35	Box 1-25, Hollywood, Richmond, 6/13/72

R

Name	Rank	Age	Co.	Regiment	Death/Killed	Original Burial Location	Final Location
RABER, Henry L.	PVT		A	8th VA	d. Aug. 14 West's Bldg. U.S. Gen. Hosp. Baltimore, MD	None	Loudon Park, Baltimore, Row C, Grave 80, 8/14/63
RACER, James O.B.	1SGT	22	K	7th VA	d. July 15	Jacob Schwartz's farm, in cornfield on Rock Creek, Yard D, Row 3	Box 1-S-55, Hollywood, Richmond, 6/13/72, with 110 others
RAGLAND, Francis M.	SGT		K	17th MS	d. July 7	John S. Crawford's farm, "where Basil Biggs lives;" in garden	Box 4-Y, Hollywood, Richmond, 5/17/73
RAINEY, William W.	CPT	24	C	13th NC	d. July 9	Possibly in the Andrew Heintzelman farm area	Red House Presbyterian Cemetery, Caswell Co., NC
RAINS, Frederick G.	PVT	34	G	51st GA	d. Sept. 9 U.S. Gen. Hosp. Chester, PA	Chester Rural Cemetery, Chester, PA	Philadelphia National Cemetery, 1891
RALSTON, George G.	LT		A	2nd MS	d. July 30 U.S. Gen. Hosp. Chester, PA	Chester Rural Cemetery, Chester, PA	Philadelphia National Cemetery, 1891
RAMSEY, Thomas J.	PVT	33	I	38th NC	k. July 1		Double Springs Baptist Cemetery, Cleveland Co., NC
RAMSEY, W. Frank	PVT	25		Manley's (NC) Battery	k. July 2	John Sachs's place near or on side of barn; also, near William Felix's house on left side of county road toward Samuel Pitzer's	Oakwood, Raleigh, Grave 541, 10/1/71
RAMSEY, William B.	PVT	25	E	14th VA	d. July 25	Jacob Schwartz's farm, back of barn, Grave 3	Possibly in one of seven boxes marked "S," to Hollywood, Richmond, 9/10/72, as an unknown
RANDOLPH, R.J.	PVT		B	16th GA	d. July 5	John Cunningham's farm, in orchard, south side	Box 4-X, Hollywood, Richmond, with 15 other unknown remains, 5/17/73
RAUCH, Henry A. Jr.	LT	21	B	14th SC	d. July 17 RR Depot, Gettysburg	Adam Doersom's farm, in meadow, north of Pennsylvania College; grave "still visible in 1866"	There is no record of his removal, however, he may have been sent to Richmond in May 1873 as an unknown in Box 4-E with other "College Hospital" remains
RAWLS, Charles Cross	LT	30	G	5th NC	k. July 1	Near John S. Forney's house, in field	Possibly in a box marked "F," to Hollywood, Richmond, with 63 other remains
RAWSON, John C.	PVT		K	13th MS		John S. Crawford's farm, in orchard north of "Walnut Avenue" under apple tree	Box 2-C-Miss, Hollywood, Richmond, 8/3/72; "grave unmarked by then"

Name	Rank	Age	Co.	Regiment	Death/Killed	Burial marker / location	Cemetery
RAY, Joseph A.	PVT	26	K	34th NC	d. July 31 DeCamp U.S. Gen. Hosp. David's Island, New York	None	Probably buried in Cypress Hills Cemetery, Long Island, New York
RAY, Thomas N.	PVT		K	22nd GA	d. July 10	Pennsylvania College, in hospital cemetery, north of main edifice	Box 4-E, Hollywood, Richmond, 5/17/73
RAY, William P.	CPL			Taylor's (VA) Battery	k. July 2	Near handboard along county road from Samuel Pitzer's schoolhouse, toward John Sachs's on road to Abraham Krise's, in woods	
REED, Charles W.	1SGT		G	8th VA	d. July 17	Jacob Schwartz's farm, back of barn, Grave 14	Union Cemetery, Leesburg, VA
REED, Joseph D.	PVT		C	16th GA		John Cunningham's farm, across the creek from John S. Crawford's; Confederate cemetery was in orchard, south side	Laurel Grove, Savannah, Lot 853, Grave 1, 9/24/71
REEVES, Isaac	CPL		K	10th LA		W. Henry Monfort's farm, in southeast corner of field, back of barn	Box 3-261, Hollywood, Richmond, 9/10/72
REEVES, John A.	PVT		D	13th GA	d. July 13	Possibly Jacob Kime's farm	Laurel Grove, Savannah, Lot 853, Grave 14, 9/24/71
REEVES, M.	PVT		K	3rd AR	d. July 18	John Edward Plank's farm, north side of house under walnut tree	Box 2-H, Hollywood, Richmond, 8/3/72
REEVES, William R.	PVT		E	16th MS	d. July 19 Probably Seminary Hosp. Hagerstown, MD	Old Almshouse Burying Ground, Hagerstown, MD	Probably "Rose Hill," Washington Cemetery, Hagerstown, MD
REID, Calvin H.	SGT	22	F	7th NC	d. Aug. 12	Camp Letterman, Row 5, Grave 11	Oakwood, Raleigh, Grave 461, 10/1/71
REYNOLDS, John M.	PVT	19	F	2nd SC	k. July 2	George Rose's farm, in meadow, near peach orchard	Magnolia, Charleston, Grave 20, 5/10/71
REYNOLDS, William	PVT		(?)	42nd MS	d. July 19	Jacob Schwartz's farm, in cornfield, Yard D, Row 1	Box 1-S-19, Hollywood, Richmond, 6/13/72
RHIDENHOUR, John W.	PVT	35	F	13th NC	d. Aug. 12 U.S. Gen. Hosp. Chester, PA	Chester Rural Cemetery, Chester, PA	Philadelphia National Cemetery, 1891
RHODES, Edward Averett	LT	22	C	11th NC	k. July 1	Along Willoughby's Run, near Herr's Tavern or the Seminary; "Schoolmasters removed April 26" (c. 1866?); buried next to Lt. Thomas Cooper	Green Mount Cemetery, Baltimore, MD
RHODES, John Dawsey	PVT	20	F	8th SC	k. July 2	George Rose's farm, back or north of stone barn	Box 1-151, Hollywood, Richmond, 6/13/72
RHODES, Theodore A.	SGT	32	H	1st SC	k. July 3	David McMillan's farm, in apple orchard near C.S. fortifications along Seminary Ridge	Magnolia, Charleston, Grave 18, 5/10/71
RICE, Benjamin F.	PVT		C	58th VA	d. Oct. 22 U.S. Gen. Hosp. Harrisburg, PA	None	Soldiers' Lot, Harrisburg, PA, Cemetery, Grave 110

Name	Rank	Age	Co.	Regiment	Status	Burial Notes	Disposition
RICE, James J.	PVT	39	H	38th VA	d. Jan. 13, 1864 West's Bldg. U.S. Gen. Hosp. Baltimore, MD	None	Loudon Park, Baltimore, Row B, Grave 85, 1/14/64, as "J.R.R., Co. H, 38," "'age 39'"
RICE, Napoleon B.	PVT	21	C	11th NC	d. July 17 Jordan Springs Hospital Winchester, VA	None	Stonewall Cemetery, Winchester, VA
RICE, Stephen H.	LT		F	61st GA	k. July 1	Probably on Josiah Benner's farm, in meadow along fence	Laurel Grove, Savannah, Lot 853, Grave 10, 9/24/71
RICE, William	PVT	19	A	52nd NC	d. Aug. 20 U.S. Gen. Hosp. Chester, PA	Chester Rural Cemetery, Chester, PA	Philadelphia National Cemetery, 1891
RICHARDSON, Frederick	CPT	26	F	5th LA	k. July 1/2 "in the charge"	"Lies back of Henry Wantz's house under wild cherry tree;" "buried at midnight by his men"	
RICHARDSON, Robert N.	PVT	41	K	53rd GA	d. Aug. 7/11	DeCamp U.S. Gen. Hospital Cemetery, David's Island, NY, Grave 53	Camp Hill Cemetery, Long Island, NY
RICHARDSON, Samuel R.	PVT		B	17th GA		John Edward Plank's farm, back of barn	Box 2-H, Hollywood, Richmond, 8/3/72
RICHARDSON, William W.	LT	28	B	26th NC	k. July 1	Charles B. Polley's farm	Oakwood, Raleigh, Grave 536, 10/1/71
RICHERSON, William A.	PVT	21	B	9th VA CAV	d. July 5	Buried "3 ½ miles E. or N.E. of Gettysburg along side of Rail Road"	Box 1-219, Hollywood, Richmond, 6/13/72
RICKS, Guilford	PVT	41	C	43rd NC	k. July 2	Lutheran Theological Seminary, back of Dr. C.B. Krauth's house	Box 4-K, Hollywood, Richmond, 5/17/73
RIDDICK, Samuel	PVT	21	A	13th VA CAV	d. July 1	Karl Forney's farm, on the Littlestown pike, near red barn along fence under a locust tree, "100 yards southwest of Hanover, PA," as 2nd NC Cavalry	Said to have been moved by family to "his village graveyard" a year later, c. 1864-1865
RIDDLEMOSER, Joseph	PVT		D	2nd MD BN	d. July 28 U.S. Gen. Hosp. Chester, PA	Chester Rural Cemetery, Chester, PA	Philadelphia National Cemetery, 1891
RIDENHOUR, Anderson J.	PVT	30	F	13th NC	d. Sept. 10 U.S. Gen. Hosp. Chester, PA	Chester Rural Cemetery, Chester, PA	Philadelphia National Cemetery, 1891
RIDENOUR, Amos	PVT			Carpenter's (VA) Battery	k. July 2	George Wolf's farm, York Pike, Camp Letterman grounds, near woods; "along edge of Hospital Woods;" "grave obliterated"	
RIDGEWAY, John C.	PVT	25	B	11th AL	k. July 2	In woods south of Samuel Pitzer's farm and west or back of John Sachs's place, near a run or dry water course	Possibly in a box marked "Y," to Hollywood, Richmond, 8/3/72, with 10 remains, as an unknown
RIDGEWAY, S.C.	PVT		I	7th SC	k. July 2	George Rose's farm, back or north of stone barn	Box 1-155, Hollywood, Richmond, 6/13/72
RILEY, William Newton	PVT	22	F	2nd SC	k. July 2	George Rose's farm, in meadow, near peach orchard	Magnolia, Charleston, Grave 19, 5/10/71

Name	Rank	Age	Co.	Regiment	Death	Burial Location	Final Disposition
◆ RISON, Henry C.	PVT	21	B	7th TN	d. Aug. 5	Camp Letterman, Row 1, Grave 40	Box 1-46, Hollywood, Richmond, 6/13/72, as "H.C. Risen"
ROACH, William J.	PVT	20	A	2nd SC	k. July 2	George Rose's farm, in meadow, near peach orchard	Magnolia, Charleston, Grave 35, 5/10/71
ROARK, Walter	PVT		F	5th AL	k. July 1	Moses McClean's farm, south along the lane in cherry thicket; marked "W.J.R., Co. F, 5th Alabama"	"State Lot"- AL, to Hollywood, Richmond
ROBBINS, Daniel	PVT	22	B	53rd VA	d. July 29	Camp Letterman, Row 1, Grave 7	Box 1-34, Hollywood, Richmond, 6/13/72
ROBBINS, Isaiah S.	LT	25	I	22nd NC	k. July 1	Seminary Woods, southwest corner	Box 4-U, Hollywood, Richmond, with 11 remains, 5/17/73
ROBBINS, James P.	PVT	23	B	53rd VA	d. July 20	On hill between Jacob Schwartz's and George Bushman's farms, Yard B, Row 2	Box 1-S-8, Hollywood, Richmond, 6/13/72 with 110 others
ROBBINS, John B.	CPL		I	8th SC	k. July 2	George Rose's farm, back or north of stone barn; his "left hand stuck out of the grave looking like an old parched well worn buck-skin glove"	Box 1-160, Hollywood, Richmond, 6/13/72
ROBBINS, Rufus, A.	CPL		C	17th MS		John S. Crawford's farm, in orchard, north of "Walnut Avenue" under apple tree	Box 2-C-Miss, Hollywood, Richmond, 8/3/72; "grave unmarked by then"
ROBERTS, Benjamin G.	LT		Chesapeake (MD) Artillery		k. July 2	"Removed from Gettysburg, 1874," probably originally buried on Christian Benner's farm, under a walnut tree	Loudon Park, Baltimore, on "Confederate Hill," Row E, Grave 50
ROBERTS, James F.	PVT	22	A	2nd SC	k. July 2	George Rose's farm, in meadow, near peach orchard	Magnolia, Charleston, Grave 23, 5/10/71
ROBERTS, Whitemel P.	CPL		I	42nd MS	d. Aug. 5 U.S. Gen. Hosp. Chester, PA	Chester Rural Cemetery, Chester, PA	Philadelphia National Cemetery, 1891
◆ ROBERTSON, James	PVT	39	B	45th NC	d. Aug. 13/14	Camp Letterman, Row 1, Grave 29 (from fence)	Oakwood, Raleigh, 10/1/71
◆ ROBERTSON, John N.	PVT		B	5th AL BN		On hill between Jacob Schwartz's and George Bushman's farms, Yard B, Row 1	Possibly Box 1-1, Hollywood, Richmond, 6/13/73, as "J.N. Robertson, Co. B, 4th AL"
ROBERTSON, Robert A.	CPL	25	C	18th VA	d. July 24	Jacob Schwartz's farm, back of barn, Grave 9	Possibly in one of seven boxes marked "S," to Hollywood, Richmond, 9/10/72, as an unknown
ROBINSON, Hugh Y.	SGT	25	E	15th SC	d. July 6	Francis Bream's farm, in old burying ground, center	Probably in one of two boxes marked "B," Hollywood, Richmond, 8/3/72
ROBINSON, J.W.	PVT		D	17th MS		John Crawford's farm, in garden	Probably in Box 4-Y, Hollywood, Richmond, 5/17/73, with 21 remains
ROBINSON, Joseph B.	CPL	22	G	52nd NC	d. Sept. 9	Camp Letterman, Row 7, Grave 25	Oakwood, Raleigh, Grave 476, 10/1/71
ROBINSON, William A.	PVT		C	56th VA	d. July 4	George Bushman's farm; hospital cemetery was east of house	Probably "State Lot" - VA, to Hollywood, Richmond, as "C. Robinson, 56th VA"
ROBNETT, Jesse A.	SGT	21	G	37th NC	d. July 22	On hill under walnut tree between Jacob Schwartz's and George Bushman's farms, Yard B, Row 2	Box 1-S-13, Hollywood, Richmond, 6/13/72
ROLLINS, James J.	SGT	29	H	28th NC	d. July 22	George Bushman's farm; hospital cemetery was east of the house	Oakwood, Raleigh, Grave 528, 10/1/71

Name	Rank	Age	Co.	Regiment	Death	Location	Burial
RONEY, L.H.	LT	33	I	57th NC	k. July 1	Probably on Christian Byers's farm with 23 others, unmarked	Oakwood, Raleigh, Grave 538, 10/1/71
ROSE, William A.	PVT	37	I	7th NC	d. July 20/21	On hill under walnut tree between Jacob Schwartz's and George Bushman's farms, Yard B, Row 2	Box 1-S-12, Hollywood, Richmond, 6/13/72
ROSS, Egbert A.	MAJ	21	F&S	11th NC	k. July 1	South of Frederick Herr's place in woods; buried and marked by Lt. W.B. Taylor, Co. A, 11th NC	"Removed to Charlotte, N.C."
ROTHSCHILD, Albert	CPL		G	8th AL	d. July 17	Jacob Schwartz's farm, in cornfield, Yard D, Row 2	Box 1-S-44, Hollywood, Richmond, 6/13/72
ROUNTREE, Reuben	SGT		A	61st GA	k. July 1	Probably on Josiah Benner's farm, in meadow along fence	Laurel Grove, Savannah, Lot 853, Grave 10, 9/24/71
ROWELL, James H.	PVT		E	42nd MS	d. Aug. 1 Seminary Hosp. Hagerstown, MD	Probably in Old Almshouse Burial Ground, Hagerstown, MD	Probably in "Rose Hill," Washington Cemetery, Hagerstown, MD
ROWEN, Tim	CPL		G	14th LA	d. July 2	W. Henry Monfort's farm	Box 3-M, Hollywood, Richmond, 9/10/72, as "Capt. S.T. Roahn, 14th LA"
ROYSTER, Iowa Michigan	LT	23	G	37th NC	d. July 14	Michael Trostle's farm, corner of woods, south; by the side of Henry Beitler's tenant house, which was just northeast, and across Rock Creek	A skeleton was discovered near this house in the 1940s; it was never removed
ROYSTER, James M.	PVT	29	C	47th NC	d. July 29 Probably U.S. Hospital Frederick, MD	None	Mt. Olivet Cemetery, Frederick, MD, Grave 209
ROZZELL, William F.	LT	23	E	11th NC	d c. July 10	Samuel Lohr's farm, opposite house, in meadow, near pear tree	Box 4-S, Hollywood, Richmond, with 44 others, 5/17/73
RULEAU, Felix	PVT	26	3rd Co., Washington (LA) Artillery		d. July 28	John S. Crawford's tenant house, Samual Johns's place, back of barn	
RUSH, Joseph B.	1SGT		E	10th VA	d. July 14	Martin Shealer's farm, in meadow next to Elizabeth Wible's; Dr. John W. O'Neal listed him as John Huss, no unit	Probably in Box 3-V, Hollywood, Richmond, 9/10/72, as an unknown
◆ RUSSELL, John	PVT		I	8th FL	d. Aug. 7	Camp Letterman, Row 4, Grave 16	Box 1-59, Hollywood, Richmond, 6/13/72
RUSSELL, John W.	PVT	27	E	26th NC		George Spangler's farm, U.S. 11th Corps hospital, with 6 other graves unmarked	
RUSSELL, M.B.	PVT	25	F	12th SC	d. July 31 West's Bldg. U.S. Gen. Hosp. Baltimore, MD	None	Loudon Park, Baltimore, Row D, Grave 55, 7/31/63
RYAN, David R.	SGT	25	E	2nd SC	k. July 2	George Rose's farm, back of barn under cherry tree; before his death, Ryan said, "Tell my mother I fell at my post of duty."	Magnolia, Charleston, Grave 14, 5/10/71

S

Name	Rank	Age	Co.	Regiment	Death	Location	Burial
SANCHEZ, S.J.	SGT		B	2nd FL	d. July 17	Jacob Schwartz's farm, back of barn, Grave 16	Possibly in one of seven boxes marked "S," to Hollywood, Richmond, 9/10/72, as an unknown

Name	Rank	Age	Co.	Regiment	Death	Location	Disposition
SANDERS, Adam	PVT		I	3rd GA	d. July 16	Jacob Schwartz's farm, in cornfield, Yard D, Row 3	Box 1-S-74, Hollywood, Richmond, 6/13/72
SANDERSON, Daniel B.	PVT		H	42nd MS	d. July 16	George Bushman's farm; hospital cemetery was east of house	Box 1-237, Hollywood, Richmond, 6/13/72
SANSOM, John	PVT	40	D	42nd MS	d. Aug. 29	Camp Letterman, Row 6, Grave 21	Box 1-105, Hollywood, Richmond, 6/13/72
SAULS, Richard	PVT	27	E	51st GA	d. Aug. 27	Camp Letterman, Row 6, Grave 10	Laurel Grove, Savannah, Lot 853, Grave 3, 9/24/71
SAUNDERS, James	PVT		H	52nd NC	d. July 19	Jacob Schwartz's farm, in cornfield, Yard D, Row 1	Box 1-S-20, Hollywood, Richmond, 6/13/72
◆ SCHAMMEL, John H.	PVT		C	1st VA	d. July 5	Probably in one of the U.S. 2nd Corps hospital cemeteries on Jacob Schwartz's farm	Probably in one of seven boxes marked "S," to Hollywood, Richmond, 6/13/72, as an unknown
SCARBORO, James Newton	PVT		K	61st GA	k. July 1	Josiah Benner's farm, in meadow along fence	Laurel Grove, Savannah, Lot 853, Grave 10, 9/24/71
SCARBOROUGH, J.S.	CPL		A	2nd LA	d.c. July 3	W. Henry Monfort's farm under locust tree opposite house; "recovered"	Box 3-260, Hollywood, Richmond, 9/10/72
SCLATER, Robert J.	PVT	28	F	44th VA	d. July 28 U.S. Gen. Hosp. Chester, PA	Chester Rural Cemetery, Chester, PA, Grave 64; "mortally wounded near his dead brother, William, at Culp's Hill"	Philadelphia National Cemetery, 1891
SCOTT, Robert R.	LT	35	H	8th AL	d. July 18	Camp Letterman, Row 1, Grave 8	Box 1-86, Hollywood, Richmond, 6/13/72
SCRUGGS, Drury	PVT	23	D	16th NC	d.c. July 3	Peter Conover's farm, a U.S. 1st Corps hospital	
SEALS, James M.	LT		F	42nd MS	d. July 20	On hill between Jacob Schwartz's and George Bushman's farms, Yard B, Row 2	Box 1-203, Hollywood, Richmond, 6/13/72
SENSEBAUGH, William	PVT		E	5th TX	d. July 21	Jesse Worley's farm, with 5 others not marked, near Two Taverns, PA	Box 3-X, Hollywood, Richmond, 9/10/72
◆ SHACKELFORD, John W.	PVT	26	D	9th LA	d.c. June 30 "on march"	David Shriver's farm	Probably in a box marked "A," to Hollywood, Richmond, 6/13/72, with 11 remains, as an unknown
SHANKLE, James W.	PVT	18	I	52nd NC	d. July 6	Jacob Schwartz's farm, in cornfield, Yard D, Row 3	Box 1-S-52, Hollywood, Richmond, 6/13/72
SHARP, E.P.	SGT		F	11th GA		John Edward Plank's farm, back of barn	Box 2-H, Hollywood, Richmond, 8/3/72
SHAW, N.M.	PVT		B	44th GA	k. July 1 (?)	Buried about two miles above Cashtown, PA, in the mountains near John Reed's sawmill	Box 4-A, Hollywood, Richmond, with 11 other remains, as "Lt. Shaw - Georgia," 5/17/73
SHELTON, Josiah W.	PVT		B	57th VA	d. July 27	Jacob Schwartz's farm, back of barn, Grave 5	Possibly in one of seven boxes marked "S," to Hollywood, Richmond, 9/10/72, as an unknown
SHELTON, Thomas A.	PVT		G	18th VA CAV	k. June 29	Near McConnellsburg, PA, "where he had fallen;" by the side of the road on the Mercersburg Pike; "just inside Daniel Fore's meadow alongside the pike;" next to W.B. Moore	The United Daughters of the Confederacy placed a marker near the site in 1929
SHEPHERD, James "Nick"	PVT	24	G	15th AL	d. Aug. 26	Camp Letterman, Row 6, Grave 7	Box 1-35, Hollywood, Richmond, 6/13/72
SHIELDS, Allen R.	PVT	26	E	26th NC	d. July 29 U.S. Gen. Hosp. Chester, PA	Chester Rural Cemetery, Chester, PA	Philadelphia National Cemetery, 1891

Name	Rank	Age	Co.	Regiment	Death	Burial Location	Disposition
SHIFFLETT, Octavius M.	SGT		H	57th VA	d. July 13	Jacob Schwartz's farm, in cornfield on Rock Creek, Yard D, Row 1	Box 1-S-32, Hollywood, Richmond, 6/13/72, with 110 others
SHIRLEY, William R.	PVT	23	I	48th GA	d. July 18 Seminary Hosp. Hagerstown, MD	Possibly in Old Almshouse Burying Ground, Hagerstown, MD	Probably in "Rose Hill," Washington Cemetery, Hagerstown, MD
SHOAF, William N.	PVT		H	33rd NC	d. Aug. 3 U.S. Gen. Hosp. Chester, PA	Chester Rural Cemetery, Chester, PA	Philadelphia National Cemetery, 1891
SHORT, Augustus L.	CPL		C	17th GA	k. July 2	John Edward Plank's farm	Probably in one of eleven boxes marked "H," to Hollywood, Richmond, 8/3/72, as an unknown
SHOUP, Jacob G.	LT	28	H	7th VA CAV		Flohr's Church graveyard, near Cashtown, PA	Box 3-258, Hollywood, Richmond, 9/10/72
SIBERT, Onesinus	PVT		F	2nd VA	d. July 9	Henry Picking's farm, in field along fence, opposite schoolhouse near road	Box 1-175, Hollywood, Richmond, 6/13/72
SIMMONS, George A.	PVT	28	A	2nd NC BN	d. Oct. 26	Camp Letterman Cemetery	Philadelphia National Cemetery, 1891
SIMMONS, Jared	PVT		H	1st TN		Samuel Lohr's farm, near pear tree, east side of pike	Probably in one of four boxes marked "S," to Hollywood, Richmond, 5/17/73, as an unknown
SIMMONS, John L.	PVT		G	8th LA	d. July 3	Elizabeth Wible's farm, back of barn	Box 3-Y, Hollywood, Richmond, 9/10/72
SIMMONS, Thomas N.	CPL	24	C	14th TN	d. July 27	On hill between Jacob Schwartz's and George Bushman's farms, Yard B, Row 1	Box 1-21, Hollywood, Richmond, 6/13/72
SIMMS, Alexander	PVT		G	28th VA	d. July 22 U.S. Gen. Hosp. Chester, PA	Chester Rural Cemetery, Chester, PA, Grave 42	Philadelphia National Cemetery, 1891
SIMONTON, Theophilus J.	PVT		C	44th GA	d. July 2	Possibly Josiah Benner's farm	Laurel Grove, Savannah, Lot 854, Grave 13, 8/21/71
SIMS, Benjamin A.	SGT	29	B	11th MS	d. July 5	Jacob Schwartz's farm	Probably in one of seven boxes marked "S," to Hollywood, Richmond, 9/10/72, as an unknown
SIMS, E.B.	CPL		E	10th AL	d. Sept. 19 U.S. Gen. Hosp. Harrisburg, PA	None	Soldiers' Lot, Harrisburg, PA, Cemetery, Grave 133
SKELTON, Alexander	PVT		A	53rd VA	d. Dec. 4 Ft. Wood, Bedloe's Island, NY	None	Cypress Hill Cemetery, Long Island, New York
SKIPPER, Silas	PVT		G	9th AL		North of Adam Butt's stone farmhouse under cherry tree	Box 1-119, Hollywood, Richmond, 6/13/72, with two others
SLADE, Jesse Franklin	PVT	39	K	13th NC	k. July 1	Michael Crist's farm; also, "at Jacob Hankey's across from David Shriver's under a peach tree;" a "Mr. Boyde" of Troublesome P.O., Rockingham Co., VA searched for body without success	

Name	Rank	Age	Co.	Regiment	Death	Burial Location	Disposition
SLIGH, Thomas W.	PVT	22	E	3rd SC Regt. Orderly	k. July 2	George Rose's farm, "on the gravl walk in the woods;" said to be "witty, very ready and always kind"	Magnolia, Charleston, Grave 28, 5/10/71; Historian Wm. A. Frassanito believes his corpse might be the second from the left on the front cover of this book.
SMITH, Benjamin H.	LT		B	14th VA	d. Aug. 8	Camp Letterman, Row 4, Grave 12	Box 1-71, Hollywood, Richmond, 6/13/72
SMITH, Benjamin R.	PVT		M	7th SC	k. July 2	George Rose's farm, north or back of stone barn	Box 1-158, Hollywood, Richmond, 6/13/72
SMITH, David G.	PVT		I	11th NC	d. July 19 West's Bldg. U.S. Gen. Hosp. Baltimore, MD	None	Loudon Park, Baltimore, Row D, Grave 49, 7/20/63
SMITH, Doctor E.	PVT	20	D	28th NC	d. Aug. 21 U.S. Gen. Hosp. Chester, PA	Chester Rural Cemetery, Chester, PA	Philadelphia National Cemetery, 1891
SMITH, Ebenezer F.	CPL		E	Cobb's (GA) Legion Cavalry	d. July 2	On Hunterstown Road under cherry tree near Hunterstown	Laurel Grove, Savannah, Lot 854, Grave 12, 8/21/71
SMITH, George W.	PVT			Jordan's (VA) Battery		John S. Crawford's farm, southeast of Samuel Johns's barn (tenant), east of house	Magnolia, Charleston, Grave 34, 5/10/71, listed also as "Co. E, 21st SC;" also, Box 2-255, Hollywood, Richmond, 8/3/72
SMITH, John	PVT		F	14th TN		Jacob Schwartz's farm; "grave still marked in July 1866"	Possibly in one of seven boxes marked "S," to Hollywood, Richmond, 9/10/72, as unknown
SMITH, John S.	PVT	36	A	11th NC	d. July 15	Jacob Schwartz's farm, in cornfield, Yard D, Row 3	Box 1-S-54, Hollywood, Richmond, 6/13/72
SMITH, Maurice T.	LTC	35	F&S	55th NC	k. July 1	Smith Farm, Granville Co., NC	
SMITH, Thomas	PVT		H	14th LA	d. July 16	Camp Letterman, Row 2, Grave 31; "from Ireland"	Box 1-58, Hollywood, Richmond, 6/13/72
SMITH, William	CPL	18	K	1st LA	d. Nov. 3	Camp Letterman Cemetery	"State Lot" - LA, to Hollywood, Richmond
SMITH, William H.	SGT	26	K	26th NC	d. July 18	Jacob Schwartz's farm, in cornfield, Yard D, Row 2	Box 1-S-48, Hollywood, Richmond, 6/13/72
SMITH, William P.	1SGT		C	10th AL		North of Francis Bream's house in field near woods alongside of Adam Butt's woods near road; "south of house"	Box 1-138, Hollywood, Richmond, 6/13/72
SMITHER, George W.	PVT		F	55th VA		Samuel Lohr's farm, probably opposite house in meadow near pear tree	Box 4-S, Hollywood, Richmond, 5/17/73
SNELLGROVE, John C.	PVT		M	6th AL	k. July 1	Seminary Woods, southwest corner	Box 4-U, Hollywood, Richmond, 5/17/73
SNIPES, Jeter J.	CPL	21	G	11th NC	d. July 19 U.S. Gen. Hosp. Chester, PA	Chester Rural Cemetery, Chester, PA	Philadelphia National Cemetery, 1891
SOLLEY, Seabron	PVT		C	47th AL	d. July 5	Opposite John Group's farm, on Edward B. Buehler's farm "NW corner of field near country road"	Box 4-293, Hollywood, Richmond, 5/17/73
SOREY, Dorsey W.	CPL	22	H	12th NC	d. July 11	Jacob Hankey's farm	Oakwood, Raleigh, Grave 523, 10/1/71

Name	Rank	Age	Co.	Regiment	Death	Location	Burial
SOUTHALL, Valentine W.	LT	23	B	23rd VA	d. July 20	Widow Elizabeth Wible's farm, in fence corner above or southeast of house; disinterred by Dr. John O'Neal, for $5.25 on 8/10/69; remains shipped to Virginia	In cemetery on family plantation "Selma," near Amelia in Amelia Co., VA. "The South had no better soldier… cheerful, generous, brave, he was beloved by all."
SOWERS, John S.	PVT		L	4th VA	d. July 25	Henry Picking's farm, possibly "opposite schoolhouse"	Box 1-239, Hollywood, Richmond, 6/13/72
SPAINHOWER, Jacob P.	PVT	22	D	53rd NC	d. July 25	Probably Jacob Hankey's farm	Oakwood, Raleigh, Grave 514, 10/1/71
SPARKS, Hiram	PVT		H	17th GA	d. July 8	John Edward Plank's farm, under large locust tree toward John S. Crawford's and near road to Bream's Mill; also "back of barn"	Box 2-H, Hollywood, Richmond, 8/3/72
SPARKS, Stephen Smiley	PVT		B	59th GA	d. July 4	John Edward Plank's farm, under large locust tree toward John S. Crawford's and near road to Bream's Mill; also "back of barn"	Box 2-H, Hollywood, Richmond, 8/3/72
SPEARS, J.T.	SGT	21	H	15th SC	k. July 2	George Rose's farm, "on the gravl walk in the woods"	Magnolia, Charleston, Common Grave 28, 5/10/71
SPENCER, John M.	LT		G	42nd MS		Jacob Schwartz's farm; "grave still marked in July 1866"	Possibly in one of seven boxes marked "S," to Hollywood, Richmond, 9/10/72, as an unknown
STALLINGS, Joseph T.	PVT	31	B	47th NC	d. "after July 5"	Samuel Lohr's farm, opposite house, in meadow near pear tree	Box 4-S, Hollywood, Richmond, 5/17/73
STAMPS, Isaac D.	CPT	35	E	21st MS	d. July 3	John S. Crawford's homestead on Marsh Creek, north side of "Walnut Avenue;" also, "in a wheat field under a medium sized oak"	Removed by Mary E. Stamps to family cemetery, Rosemont Plantation, Woodville, MS, in Dec. 1863; also, Box 2-C, Hollywood, Richmond, 8/3/72
STANCILL, John	SGT		C	8th SC	d. July 25	Francis Bream's farm, north of tavern, near graveyard and creek	Magnolia, Charleston, Grave 46, 5/10/71
STEEL, Robert C.	PVT	30	I	7th NC	d. Aug. 27	Camp Letterman, Row 6, Grave 12	Oakwood, Raleigh, Grave 468, 10/1/71
STEELE, Robert	PVT	26	E	5th VA	d. July 18	Henry Picking's farm, in field, along fence opposite schoolhouse near road	Box 1-171, Hollywood, Richmond, 6/13/72
STEGER, Thomas E.	1SGT	20	F	17th MS		Camp Letterman Cemetery	"State Lot" - MS, to Hollywood, Richmond
STEIN, John	PVT	20	B	14th LA	d. July 30 U.S. Gen. Hosp. Chester, PA	Chester Rural Cemetery, Chester, PA	Philadelphia National Cemetery, 1891
STEPHENS, John F.	PVT		C	9th GA	k. July 2	East of Philip Snyder's house and the Emmitsburg Road, "near staked and ridered fence in a wheatfield;" and west of George W. Weikert's house [J.W. Timber, tenant]; "a little way out in field;" east of Snyder's house	
STEVENS, James W.	PVT		F	38th VA	d. July 29	On the hill between Jacob Schwartz's and George Bushman's farms, Yard B, Row 2	Box 1-200, Hollywood, Richmond, 6/13/72
STEVENS, William E.	PVT	18	E	5th TX	d. Sept. 4	Camp Letterman, Row 7, Grave 11	Box 1-81, Hollywood, Richmond, 6/13/72
STEVENSON, S.V.	PVT		H	5th TX	d. Aug. 7 West's Bldg. U.S. Gen. Hosp. Baltimore, MD	None	Loudon Park, Baltimore, Row C, Grave 80, 8/7/63

Name	Rank	Age	Co.	Regiment	Death	Original Burial	Final Burial
STEWART, J. Rial	PVT		G	23rd NC	d. July 1 evening	Buried by K.W. Coghill, probably in field near where he fell, which was southeast of Oak Hill on John Forney's farm	Possibly in one of six boxes marked "F," to Hollywood, Richmond, 8/3/72, as unknown
STEWART, John Walter	LT	23	F	18th NC	d. July 19	Jacob Schwartz's farm, in cornfield, Yard D, Row 1	Box 1-S-21, Hollywood, Richmond, 6/13/72
STEWART, Joseph W.	PVT		E	3rd SC BN	k. July 2	George Rose's farm, west of barn, under large cherry tree; "grave deep, with board cover with 6 others"	Magnolia, Charleston, Grave 24, 5/10/71
STEWART, S.W.	PVT		G	22nd GA	k. July 2	Near Adam Butt's brick schoolhouse on Fairfield Road	Laurel Grove, Savannah, Lot 854, Grave 12, 8/21/71
STOCKTON, John B.	LT	19	H	4th NC	k. July 1	Negro graveyard, outside of fence, near Long Lane	
STOKES, Ellwood R. Jr.	SGT	23	F	3rd SC BN	k. July 2	George Rose's farm, west of barn, under large cherry tree	Probably in one of 15 boxes marked "L," with 157 remains to Hollywood, Richmond, 8/3/72, as an unknown
STOKES, William	PVT		D	5th AL	d. Aug. 28 U.S. Gen. Hosp. Chester, PA	Chester Rural Cemetery, Chester, PA	Philadelphia National Cemetery, 1891
STONE, Benjamin H.	PVT	21		Page's (VA) Battery		David Shriver's farm, north of house, under peach tree	Box 1-184, Hollywood, Richmond, 6/13/72; also, "removed by his brother to Ashland, Hanover Co., Va."
STRADER, John A.	PVT	19	H	45th NC	d. July 20	George Bushman's farm; hospital cemetery was east of house	Oakwood, Raleigh, Grave 526, 10/1/71
STRICKER, John M.	SGT		E	21st MS	k. July 2	In woods on road to Abraham Krise's near Pitzer's Schoolhouse, near three other graves	
STRICKLAND, Noah C.	PVT		C	Cobb's (GA) Legion Cavalry	d. July 2/3	On Hunterstown Road under a cherry tree near Hunterstown	Laurel Grove, Savannah, Lot 854, Grave 12, 8/21/71
STROUD, William	PVT		H	8th AL	d. July 21	Jacob Schwartz's farm, back of barn	Possibly in one of seven boxes marked "S," to Hollywood, Richmond, 9/10/72, as an unknown
STUART, William D.	COL	32	F&S	56th VA	d. July 29 C.S. Hospital Staunton, VA	None	Thornrose Cemetery, Staunton, VA
SUDDERTH, George H.	PVT	26	I	26th NC	k. July 1	1. "Frederick Herr's old place, corner of garden" 2. German Reformed Churchyard, Gettysburg	Oakwood, Raleigh, Grave 549, 10/1/71
SUIT, Johnson	PVT	18	D	6th AL	d. Aug. 28 Probably U.S. Gen. Hosp. Frederick, MD	None	Mt. Olivet Cemetery, Frederick, MD, Grave 215
SULLIVAN, John	PVT		E	1st MD BN	d. Aug. 1	David Stewart's farm, east of barn	Box 3-N, Hollywood, Richmond, 9/10/72
SUTHER, Robert J.	PVT	27	C	33rd NC		Camp Letterman Cemetery, possibly as "Franklin Suther, Co. B, 52nd NC"	
SUTTON, Francis M.	PVT		K	2nd MS	d. July 19 Probably Seminary Hosp. Hagerstown, MD	Probably Old Almshouse Burying Ground, Hagerstown, MD	Probably in "Rose Hill," Washington Cemetery, Hagerstown, MD

Name	Rank	Age	Unit	Co.	Death	Location	Disposition
SWANNER, James	PVT	25	5th AL	A		Camp Letterman, Row 2, Grave 25	Box 1- 49, Hollywood, Richmond, 6/13/72
SWEETLAND, William A.	LT		16th VA CAV	K	k. July 3	Isaac Miller's farm	Possibly "State Lot" - VA, to Hollywood, Richmond
SWINSON, John A.	CPL	19	11th GA	G	d. July 10	Probably John Edward Plank's farm, back of barn; "died in field hospital near Gettysburg"	Possibly in one of 11 boxes marked "H," to Hollywood, Richmond, 8/3/72, as an unknown
T							
TABER, Ferdinand D.	PVT	27	1st LA	A	d. Aug. 10	Camp Letterman, Row 4, Grave 7	Box 1-39, Hollywood, Richmond, 6/13/72
TALBOT, Wallace P.	LT	28	7th LA	E	k. July 3	John Crist's farm	
TALIAFERRO, John W.	SGT		42nd MS	A	d. July 2/3	Back of Elizabeth Shultz's house, near Emanuel Pitzer's farm; also back of Zachariah Myers's lot and above the garden	Possibly in a box marked "D," to Hollywood, Richmond, 6/13/72, with 9 other remains, as an unknown
TALLY, James R.	PVT	21	26th NC	E	d. July 11	Samuel Lohr's farm	Box 4-S, Hollywood, Richmond, 5/17/73
TATE, Enos R.	PVT		15th GA	C	d. July 5	John Edward Plank's farm, under large locust tree toward John S. Crawford's and near road to Bream's Mill; also, "back of barn"	Box 2-H, Hollywood, Richmond, 8/3/72
TATE, Hugh A.	PVT	22	11th NC	D	d. Aug. 25	Camp Letterman, Row 6, Grave 3	Grace Episcopal Church Cemetery, Burke Co., NC
TAYLOR, Adam	PVT		37th VA	A	d. July 3	Martin Shealer's farm	Box 3-V, Hollywood, Richmond, 9/10/72, with 10 remains
TEDDER, Newton J.	PVT		17th MS	D		John S. Crawford's farm, on north side of "Walnut Avenue"	Box 2-C-Miss, Hollywood, Richmond, 8/3/72, with 6 others
TELLY, William	PVT		53rd VA	G	d. Aug. 9	Camp Letterman Cemetery	
TENNEY, Nathaniel B.	LT	27	11th NC	G	k. July 1	Along Willoughby's Run, possibly near Herr's Tavern; buried near Lts. E.A. Rhodes and J.H. McDade	Possibly to Green Mount Cemetery, Baltimore, with several others, or, in one of five boxes marked "F," to Hollywood, Richmond, 9/10/72, as an unknown
TERRELL, Henry	PVT		1st Co., Richmond (VA) Howitzers			John S. Crawford's homestead on Marsh Creek, north side of "Walnut Avenue"	Box 2-C-Miss, Hollywood, Richmond, 8/3/72, with 6 others
TERRELL, Joseph R.	PVT		Woolfolk's (VA) Battery		k. July 3	In front of Nicholas Codori's brick house on the Confederate artillery line, northeast of Joseph Sherfy's, in edge of woods. "He died on the field of battle at his post."	Possibly in one of 21 boxes marked "P," to Hollywood, Richmond, 8/3/72, as an unknown
TERRELL, William P.	PVT	27	45th NC	H	d. July 7	Jacob Hankey's farm	Oakwood, Raleigh, Grave 492, 10/1/71
TEW, Ashley B.	PVT	28	20th NC	E	d. July 3	Probably Jacob Hankey's farm, or nearby	Oakwood, Raleigh, Grave 516, 10/1/71
THEUS, Simeon B.	SGT		59th GA	F	d. July 8	North side of John Edward Plank's house under walnut tree	Box 2-H, Hollywood, Richmond, 8/3/72
THIBAUT, Louis	PVT		Louisiana Guard Artillery		"k. July 1"	Elizabeth Wible's farm, back of barn	Box 3-Y, Hollywood, Richmond, 9/10/72
THOMAS, Abraham J.	PVT		38th VA	D	d. July 9	Jacob Schwartz's farm, in cornfield, Yard D, Row 3	Box 1-S-60, Hollywood, Richmond, 6/13/72, with 110 others
THOMAS, William R.	LT	27	3rd SC	K	d. July 4	Francis Bream's farm, old McClellan family burying ground, center	Magnolia, Charleston, Grave 42, 5/10/71

Name	Rank	Age	Co.	Regiment	Death	Burial	Final Disposition
THOMASSON, George L.	SGT	28	H	37th NC	d. Aug. 16 U.S. Gen. Hosp. Chester, PA	Chester Rural Cemetery, Chester, PA	Philadelphia National Cemetery, 1891
THOMPSON, A.L.	PVT		(?)	21st NC	d. July 24 Seminary Hosp. Hagerstown, Maryland	Probably Old Almshouse Burying Ground, Hagerstown, MD	Probably in "Rose Hill," Washington Cemetery, Hagerstown, MD
THOMPSON, John W.	PVT	38	G	10th AL	d. Sept. 19	Camp Letterman, Row 8, Grave 14	Box 1-110, Hollywood, Richmond, 6/13/72
THOMPSON, Risden N.	PVT	20	I	52nd NC	d. Sept. 24	Camp Letterman, Row 8, Grave 25	Oakwood, Raleigh, Grave 484, 10/1/71
THOMPSON, Samuel	CPL			Dement's (MD) Battery	k. July 2	George Wolf's farm, near woods and Camp Letterman hospital grounds; "removed"	Supposedly removed to a Baltimore area cemetery
THOMPSON, Thomas B.	SGT	29	G	52nd NC	d. Aug. 10	Camp Letterman, Row 4, Grave 10	Oakwood, Raleigh, Grave 484, 10/1/71
◆ THOMPSON, William R.	CPT	25	A	7th LA	d. July 21 Jordan Springs Hospital Winchester, Virginia	None	Stonewall Cemetery, Winchester, VA
THORN, Thomas J.	LT	25	D	16th NC	d. July 30 U.S. Gen. Hosp. Chester, PA	Chester Rural Cemetery, Chester, PA	Philadelphia National Cemetery, 1891
TICE, James R.	SGT	21	B	42nd VA	d. July 6	W. Henry Monfort's farm, back of barn on north border of field	Box 3-263, Hollywood, Richmond, 9/10/72
TIFFANY, John	LT	21	D	27th VA	d. July 23	Henry Picking's farm, across from schoolhouse	Sharon Cemetery, Middleburg, VA
TILLEY, Robert P.	SGT	20	G	53rd NC	d. July 4	Probably on Jacob Hankey's farm	Oakwood, Raleigh, Grave 509, 10/1/71, as "Robt. Timbly, Co. G, 53rd NC"
TINEY, N. (or W.) C.	CPL		F	21st VA	k. July 6 Williamsport, Maryland	None	Town Cemetery or Public Burial Ground, Williamsport, MD
TODD, R.L.	PVT	19	D	11th NC	d. July 26	On hill under walnut tree between Jacob Schwartz's and George Bushman's farms, Yard B, Row 2	Box 1-S-5, Hollywood, Richmond, 6/13/72
TOMPKINS, Thomas B.	LT		A	45th GA	d. July 3	Adam Doersom's farm, in meadow, north of college	Possibly in Box 4-E, Hollywood, Richmond, as an unknown
TORRENCE, Leonidas	CPL		H	23rd NC	d. July 7	Probably Jacob Hankey's farm	Possibly in one of eight boxes marked "N," to Hollywood, Richmond, 8/3/72, as an unknown
TRAYLOR, Albert J.	LT	25	C	7th SC	d. July 3/8	On Isaac Rife's farm, Cashtown, PA, under chestnut tree	Box 1-235, Hollywood, Richmond, 6/13/72
TRAYNHAM, William B.	SGT	24	B	20th NC	d. July 9	Jacob Hankey's farm	Oakwood, Raleigh, Grave 522, 10/1/71
TRAYWICK, William H.	PVT	46	A	8th AL	d. Sept. 4	Camp Letterman, Row 7, Grave 10	Box 1-96, Hollywood, Richmond, 6/13/72

Name	Rank	Age	Co.	Regiment	Death	Burial Location	Notes
TREDWAY, Thomas B.	SGT	18	I	53rd VA	d. July 13	Jacob Schwartz's farm, in cornfield, Yard D, Row 1	Box 1-S-31, Hollywood, Richmond, 6/13/72
TUCKER, James G.	1SGT		F	53rd VA	d. Aug. 12	Camp Letterman, Row 5, Grave 7	Probably to Oakwood, Raleigh, Grave 459, 10/1/71, as "James T. Tucker, Co. I, 53rd NC"
TURNBOW, James M.	LT	24	G	4th AL	k. July 2	John Slyder's farm, near barn, "front of row"	
TURNER, T.J.	PVT		G	2nd NC	d. Aug. 1/8	Camp Letterman, Row 4, Grave 8	Magnolia, Charleston, Grave 3, 5/10/71, as "Sgt. T.J. Turner, Co. G, 22nd SC;" also, Oakwood, Raleigh, 10/1/71, as "T.J. Turner, 2nd NC"
TWEEDY, George D.	PVT	21	C	11th VA	d. July 3	Francis Bream's mill dam, back of John Curren's farmhouse, buried by one of his brothers northeast of Curren's house in the corner of a field on the edge of the woods and on the south bank of dam; "mark indistinct"	Box-2-248, Hollywood, Richmond, 8/3/72

V

Name	Rank	Age	Co.	Regiment	Death	Burial Location	Notes
VANDERFORD, Hampton	PVT	33	H	15th SC	d. July 11	Francis Bream's farm, north of tavern, near graveyard and creek	Magnolia, Charleston, Grave 47, 5/10/71
VAUGHAN, John L.	PVT		B	56th VA	d. July 29	Camp Letterman, Row 1, Grave 5	Box 1-32, Hollywood, Richmond, 6/13/72
VEHORN, Elias	PVT		F	13th SC	d. Oct. 13 U.S. Gen. Hosp., Chester, PA	Chester Rural Cemetery, Chester, PA	Philadelphia National Cemetery, 1891
VERMILLION, Levi H.	PVT		G	24th VA	d. July 9	Francis Bream's mill, above William E. Myers's house at the side of a fence	Box 2-P-Curns, Hollywood, Richmond, 8/3/72, with 33 others
VEST, Willis M.	SGT	21	C	57th VA	d. Aug. 18 West's Bldg. U.S. Gen. Hosp. Baltimore, MD	None	Loudon Park, Baltimore, Row D, Grave 63, 8/19/63
VICK, William H.	PVT	23	D	32nd NC	d. July 2-4	Jacob Hankey's farm	Oakwood, Raleigh, Grave 507, 10/1/71
VICTORY, John	SGT		B	1st TX		John Edward Plank's farm, north of house under walnut tree	Box 2-H, Hollywood, Richmond, 8/3/72

W

Name	Rank	Age	Co.	Regiment	Death	Burial Location	Notes
WADDELL, William D.	PVT		H	1st VA	d. Aug. 12 U.S. Gen. Hosp. Chester, PA	Chester Rural Cemetery, Chester, PA, Grave 146	Philadelphia National Cemetery, 1891; his right tibia and fibula are in the National Museum of Health and Medicine, Specimen #2910
◆ **WADDY**, George R.	PVT		D	55th VA	d. July 9	Samuel Lohr's farm	Possibly in one of four boxes marked "S," to Hollywood, Richmond, 5/17/73, as an unknown
WADE, Littleton R.	PVT	19	E	32nd NC	d. July 7	Jacob Hankey's farm	Oakwood, Raleigh, Grave 499, 10/1/71
WADE, Thaddeus M.	PVT	26	D	28th VA	d. Sept. 16 U.S. Gen. Hosp., Chester, PA	Chester Rural Cemetery, Chester, PA, Grave 199	Philadelphia National Cemetery, 1891

Name	Rank	Age	Co.	Regiment	Death	Original Burial	Reburial
WAESNER, Solomon E.	PVT	28	E	28th NC	d. Aug. 18	Camp Letterman, Row 3, Grave 29	Oakwood, Raleigh, 10/1/71
WAGGY, Henry	PVT	21	F	25th VA	d. July 2	W. Henry Monfort's farm	Box 3-M, Hollywood, Richmond, 9/10/72, with 46 others
WALKER, Anderson W.	PVT	28	D	4th AL	d. Sept. 20	Camp Letterman, Row 8, Grave 17	Box 1-111, Hollywood, Richmond, 6/13/72
WALKER, Benjamin F.	PVT	31	I	30th NC	d. Aug. 12	Camp Letterman, Row 5, Grave 3	Oakwood, Raleigh, 10/1/71
WALKER, Charles L.	LT	43	F/D	26th GA	d. Sept. 4	Camp Letterman, Row 7, Grave 5	Laurel Grove, Savannah, Lot 854, Grave 12, 8/21/71
WALKER, James H.	CPL	33	H	57th NC			Rocky River Presbyterian Cemetery, Cabarrus Co., NC
WALKER, John M.	PVT		E	12th AL		George Culp's farm, near Willoughby's Run, as "Walters, Ga."	Possibly Box 4-295, Hollywood, Richmond, 5/17/73
WALKER, Marshall H.	CPL	21	H	6th NC	d. July 1-3	Elizabeth Wible's farm	Oakwood, Raleigh, Grave 540, 10/1/71
WALKER, Nathan W.	PVT	35	I	18th VA	d. Aug. 8	Camp Letterman, Row 4, Grave 17	Box 1-69, Hollywood, Richmond, 6/13/72, as "H.W. Walker, Co. I, 18th Fla."
WALKER, P.E.	LT	27	A	7th SC	d. July 8 Possibly Seminary Hosp. Hagerstown, MD	Possibly in Old Almshouse Burying Ground, Hagerstown, MD	Possibly in "Rose Hill," Washington Cemetery, Hagerstown, MD
WALKER, Robert R.	PVT		G	8th GA		William Douglas's farm, under a large oak tree to the rear of the extreme Confederate right	Box 4-L, Hollywood, Richmond, with 11 others, 5/17/73
WALKER, Thomas B.	SGT		F	21st VA	k. July 6 Williamsport, Maryland	None	Town cemetery or Public Burial Ground, Williamsport, MD
WALLACE, Stephen A.	PVT	26	B	3rd AR	d. Aug. 21	Camp Letterman, Row 4, Grave 35	Box 1-44, Hollywood, Richmond, 6/13/72
WALLACE, William P.	PVT	25	C	23rd NC	d. July 21	George Bushman's farm; hospital cemetery was east of his stone house	Possibly to Oakwood, Raleigh, Grave 527, 10/1/71, as "J.A. Wallace"
WALLER, John R.	PVT	29	I	52nd NC	d. July 23	On hill under walnut tree between Jacob Schwartz's and George Bushman's farms, Yard B, Row 1	Box 1-9, Hollywood, Richmond, 6/13/72 as "John R. Walar, Co. I, 57th NC"
WALLER, William W.	PVT	33	F	2nd SC	k. July 2	George Rose's farm, in meadow, near peach orchard	Magnolia, Charleston, Grave 21, 5/10/71
WALROND, John P.	LT	22	D	28th VA	d. July 31	Camp Letterman, Row 2, Grave 22	Box 1-28, Hollywood, Richmond, 6/13/72
WALTERS, James F.	PVT		I	3rd GA	d. July 22 U.S. Gen. Hosp. Chester, PA	Chester Rural Cemetery, Chester, PA	Philadelphia National Cemetery, 1891
WALTHALL, J.J.	SGT		E	5th TX	d. July 5 wounded accidentally	John Edward Plank's farm, north of house under walnut tree	Box 2-H, Hollywood, Richmond, 8/3/72
WARD, Eliza Alonzo	PVT		C	60th GA	d. Oct. 5	Camp Letterman, Row 8, Grave 1	Laurel Grove, Savannah, Lot 854, Grave 3, 8/21/71

Name	Rank	Age	Co.	Regiment	Death	Original Burial	Reinterment/Final Location
WARD, Michael	PVT		I	3rd GA	k. July 6 Williamsport, Maryland	None	Town cemetery or Public Burial Ground, Williamsport, MD
WARD, Patrick	PVT		I	3rd GA	d. July 7 Williamsport, Maryland	None	Town cemetery or Public Burial Ground, Williamsport, MD
WARE, George W.	PVT	33	K	13th NC	k. July 2	Jacob Schwartz's farm, in cornfield, Yard D, Row 1	Box 1-S-50, Hollywood, Richmond, 6/13/72
WARE, Thomas L.	PVT	25	G	15th GA	k. July 2	Michael Bushman's farm; "removed"	Laurel Grove, Savannah, Lot 853, Grave 12, 9/24/71
WARREN, Thomas J.	CPT	39	D	15th SC	k. July 2	George Rose's farm, under pear tree; opposite the house in orchard	Magnolia, Charleston, Grave 53, 5/10/71
WASDEN, Joseph	COL		F&S	22nd GA	k. July 2	Nicholas Codori's farm, Emmitsburg Road, in a single grave, south of barn, east of road; picket fence around grave; buried by 2nd RI Inf., Capt. Thomas Foy in attendance; a Freemason, Wasden's grave was marked by local Masons	Box 5 to Laurel Grove, Savannah, Lot 853, Grave 14, 9/24/71, with 7 other Georgians and Col. David Winn
WATKINS, Aurelius A.	LT	23	C	18th VA		Andrew Heintzelman's tavern, east of, and near peach tree	Possibly Box 3-281, Hollywood, Richmond, 9/10/72, as "Watson, Lt., Unknown"
WATKINS, Charles A.	SGT	19	H	45th NC	k. July 2	Jacob Hankey's farm	Oakwood, Raleigh, Grave 501, 10/1/71
WATSON, A.A.	PVT		K	11th GA	k. July 2	South of George Rose's house, edge of woods	Possibly to Laurel Grove, Savannah, Lot 853, Grave 13, 9/24/71, as "Irvine H. Watson, Co. K, 11th Ga."
◆ WATSON, James F.	CPL		B	11th GA	d. July 14	John Edward Plank's farm	"State Lot" - GA, to Hollywood, Richmond
WATSON, Samuel H.	PVT	21	E	5th TX	d. Sept. 11	Camp Letterman, Row 8, Grave 3; his last words to a nurse were, "I did my duty, and died for my country."	Box 1-100, Hollywood, Richmond, 6/13/72
WATTS, William B.	PVT		C	1st SC Rifles	d. Aug. 8 Gen. Hosp. Frederick, MD	None	Mt. Olivet Cemetery, Frederick, MD, Grave 211; also, "Rose Hill," Washington Cemetery, Hagerstown, MD
WATTS, William T.	PVT	26	G	4th VA	d. Aug. 27	Southwest corner of Seminary Woods	Box 4-U, Hollywood, Richmond, 5/17/73
WEAVER, John A.	PVT			Purcell's (VA) Battery	k. July 3	In area of Emanuel Pitzer's farm, "under a Pin Oak tree in Pitzer's woods;" buried by Wm. P. Broy	Box 3-271, Hollywood, Richmond, 9/10/72
WEBB, Ferdinand H.	PVT	19	D	28th VA	d. July 25 U.S. Gen. Hosp. Chester, PA	Chester Rural Cemetery, Chester, PA, Grave 77	Philadelphia National Cemetery, 1891
◆ WEBB, William H.	1SGT	21	K	55th NC	d. Sept. 21 U.S. Gen. Hosp. Chester, PA	Chester Rural Cemetery, Chester, PA	Philadelphia National Cemetery, 1891; his right tibia is in the National Museum of Health and Medicine, Specimen #899
WEEDEN, Robert A.	CPL	24	K	47th NC	d. July 23	Peter Conover's farm	Oakwood, Raleigh, Grave 544, 10/1/71
WEEKLY, John T.	PVT		I	50th GA	d. July 2	George Rose's farm, in orchard near fence, "in the orchard near the springhouse," "removed"	Laurel Grove, Savannah, Lot 853, Grave 13, 9/24/71

Name	Rank	Age	Co.	Regiment	Death	Original Burial / Marker	Final Location
WELDON, Eli	PVT	21	I	57th NC	d. July 2-3	Probably Christian Byers's farm, with 23 others not marked	Oakwood, Raleigh, Grave 524, 10/1/71, as "E. W. Walker"
WELDON, J.W.	PVT		G	53rd GA	k. July 2	George Rose's farm, between the two apple trees behind the washhouse	Laurel Grove, Savannah, Lot 853, Grave 13, 9/24/71
WELSH, John P.	CPT	32	B	27th VA	d. July 15 Hospital Williamsport Maryland	None	Catholic Cemetery, Williamsport, MD
WELSH, Willis W.	PVT		E	7th VA	d. July 3	John F. Currens's farm, east of house under peach tree	Box 2-247, Hollywood, Richmond, 8/3/72, as "Welsh, Va."
WERTHIEM, Hyman	LT		E	8th SC	k. July 2	George Rose's farm, north or back of stone barn	Box 1-162, Hollywood, Richmond, 6/13/72
WESSINGER, Wesley F.	SGT	24	I	15th SC	d. July 4	Francis Bream's farm, north of tavern near the graveyard along the creek	Magnolia, Charleston, Grave 50, 5/10/71, as "Lt. W.F. Wissen"
WEST, Henry H.	PVT	20	A	3rd NC	d. July 6 Gen. Hosp. Frederick, MD	None	Mt. Olivet Cemetery, Frederick, MD, Grave 201; also, possibly, "Rose Hill," Washington Cemetery, Hagerstown, MD
WEST, Lloyd Jr.	PVT	24	H	20th NC	k. July 1	Probably John S. Forney's farm, in field south of house	West Cemetery, Sampson Co., NC
WEST, William J.	PVT	25	B	13th MS		John S. Crawford's farm, in orchard north of "Walnut Avenue," under apple tree	Box 2-C-Miss, Hollywood, Richmond, 8/3/72; "grave unmarked by then"
WHAM, Benjamin F.	LT	32	B	42nd MS	d. Sept. 3	Camp Letterman, Row 7, Grave 1	Box 1-85, Hollywood, Richmond, 6/13/72
WHEELER, Artemus H.	PVT		K	5th FL	d. July 17	Jacob Schwartz's farm, back of barn, as "Thomas Wizell, Co. K, 8th Fla."	Possibly in one of seven boxes marked "S," to Hollywood, Richmond, 9/10/72, as an unknown
WHEELER, Council	PVT		A	3rd GA	k. July 2	Near Adam Butt's brick schoolhouse	Laurel Grove, Savannah, Lot 853, Grave 12, 9/24/71
WHITE, Clinton	PVT	20/25	H	1st NC	d. July 23	Camp Letterman Cemetery. "First death at Camp Letterman"	
WHITE, George W.	PVT	24	2nd Rockbridge (VA) Artillery		k. July 3	"In woods near Jacob Lott's [Ephraim Wisler's] place right of Trostle's Mill road;" west of "Mr. Whisler's" in wood bottom, "blaze on tree;" "grave well marked"	Box 1-217, Hollywood, Richmond, 6/13/72
WHITE, Henry	PVT	26	C	55th NC	d. Aug. 8	Camp Letterman, Row 4, Grave 13	Oakwood, Raleigh, 10/1/71
WHITE, Henry P.	PVT		G	57th VA	d. July 27	Jacob Schwartz's farm, Yard B, Row 2, on hill toward George Bushman's farm	Box 1-3, Hollywood, Richmond, 6/13/72
WHITE, James	PVT	21	F	11th NC	d. July 10 West's Bldg. U.S. Gen. Hosp. Baltimore, MD	None	Loudon Park, Baltimore, Row D, Grave 43, 7/10/63
WHITE, Joseph H.	PVT		F	49th VA	k. July 3	Almshouse farm, in orchard; "still marked in 1866"	
WHITE, William P.	SGT		E	13th GA	d. July 1	Almshouse, on hill back of graveyard	Possibly to Laurel Grove, Savannah, Lot 853, Grave 13, as "J.R. White - Georgia"

Name	Rank	Age	Co.	Regiment	Death	Original Burial	Reburial / Present Location
WHITFIELD, George B.	PVT	22	K	4th AL		John Edward Plank's farm under large locust tree toward John S. Crawford's, near road to Bream's Mill	Box 2-H, Hollywood, Richmond, 8/3/72
WHITLEY, Henry	PVT	20	F	1st NC	d. July 17/ Aug. 3 Seminary Hosp. Hagerstown, MD	Probably Old Almshouse Burying Ground, Hagerstown, MD	Probably in "Rose Hill," Washington Cemetery, Hagerstown, MD
WHITLEY, John J.	PVT		E	2nd MS	d. July 16	Jacob Schwartz's farm, in cornfield on Rock Creek, Yard D, Row 3	Box 1-S-71, Hollywood, Richmond, 6/13/72
WHITTEN, Craven	PVT		H	17th GA	k. July 2	John Edward Plank's farm	"State Lot" - GA, to Hollywood, Richmond
WHITTLE, Joel M.	PVT	18	B	14th SC	d. Aug. 19 U.S. Gen. Hosp. Chester, PA	Chester Rural Cemetery, Chester, PA	Magnolia, Charleston, Grave 58, 5/10/71
WHYTE, Solomon H.	CPT	24	G	32nd NC	d. July 13	Jacob Plank's farm, back of barn, Grave 9	Box 3-P, Hollywood, Richmond, 9/10/72
◆ WICKER, Louis M.	PVT	32	H	30th NC	k. July 1	Moses McClean's farm, south of house, in meadow	Box 1-190, Hollywood, Richmond, 6/13/72
WIER, John A.	PVT		K	3rd VA	d. July 8	Francis Bream's mill above William Myers's house at the side of a fence	Box 2-P-Cums, Hollywood, Richmond, 8/3/72, with 33 others
WILCOX, Albert J.	LT		F	5th AL	k. July 1	Moses McClean's farm, south along the lane in cherry thicket	Box 1-185, Hollywood, Richmond, 6/13/72
WILCOX, Harmon H.	PVT	18	H	26th NC	d. July 2	Probably near or on the Charles B. Polley farm	Oakwood, Raleigh, Grave 537, 10/1/71
WILEY, William J.	PVT		H	11th GA	d. Jan. 2, 1864 U.S. Gen. Hosp. York, PA	Possibly in a temporary grave at the hospital, Jan. 3, 1864, or directly to Prospect Hill	Probably Prospect Hill Cemetery, York, PA, as an unknown
WILKERSON, Henry W.	PVT	27	H	2nd SC	k. July 2	George Rose's farm, back of barn, under cherry tree	Magnolia, Charleston, Grave 13, 5/10/71
WILKINSON, Neill	PVT	32	B	53rd NC	k. July 3		Presbyterian Church Cemetery, Mecklenburg Co., NC
WILLEY, Frederick W.	PVT			Carpenter's (VA) Battery	k. July 2	George Wolf's farm, near woods, and the Camp Letterman U.S. Gen. Hosp. grounds; "along edge of hospital woods;" "grave obliterated"	Box 2-T, Hollywood, Richmond, 8/3/72, with 12 others
WILLIAMS, Charles W.H.	PVT	30	E	56th VA	d. July 8	Jacob Schwartz's farm, in cornfield on Rock Creek, Yard D, Row 1	Box 1-S-42, Hollywood, Richmond, 6/13/72
WILLIAMS, David	CPL	27	D	20th NC	k. July 1	Probably on John S. Forney's farm, in field south of house	Some believe he is buried in the National Cemetery, Gettysburg, PA, in Conn. Plot B-8, as "Williams, Co. D, 20 Ct"
WILLIAMS, Henry L.N.	MAJ	27	F&S	9th LA	d. July 5	John or Michael Crist's farm under gum tree near railroad	Box 3-280, Hollywood, Richmond, 9/10/72
WILLIAMS, James A.	PVT		E	56th VA	d. July 19	Jacob Schwartz's farm, in cornfield on Rock Creek, Yard D, Row 1	Box 1-S-18, Hollywood, Richmond, 6/13/72
WILLIAMS, James M.	SGT		B	22nd GA	d. Oct. 25 U.S. Gen. Hosp. Harrisburg, PA	None	Soldiers' Lot, Harrisburg, PA, Cemetery, Grave 137

Name	Rank	Age	Co.	Regiment	Death	Location	Reinterment
WILLIAMS, James M.	PVT	21	I	6th NC	k. July 2	Peter Conover's farm; however, "Elliott's Map" places him just northeast of where the railroad tracks cross Stratton Street in Gettysburg	Oakwood, Raleigh, Grave 547, 10/1/71
WILLIAMS, James W.	LT	24	G	11th NC	k. July 1	1. Frederick Herr's old place or tavern on turnpike, corner of garden 2. German Reformed Church Cemetery, Gettysburg	Oakwood, Raleigh, Grave 550, 10/1/71
WILLIAMS, John Bennett	SGT	32	A	40th VA	d.c. July 1	Samuel Lohr's farm, opposite house, in meadow near pear tree	Box 4-S, Hollywood, Richmond, 5/17/73
WILLIAMS, John T.	PVT	25	H	3rd NC	d. July 2-3	Martin Shealer's farm, under little apple tree; in same grave as Pvt. E.A. Littleton, 3rd NC.	Box 3-V, Hollywood, Richmond, 9/10/72
WILLIAMS, John W.	PVT	27	A	7th TN	d. Sept. 8	Camp Letterman, Row 7, Grave 23	Box 1-23, Hollywood, Richmond, 6/13/72
WILLIAMS, Lewis	CPL	20	A	47th VA	k.c. July 1	In John Herbst's woods, west of Lutheran Seminary; buried next to M.M. Littrell, Co. A, 47th VA	Possibly in Box 3-U, Hollywood, Richmond, or Box 3-T, Hollywood, Richmond, 9/10/73, as an unknown, or Box 4-U, Hollywood, Richmond, 5/17/73, as an unknown
WILLIAMS, Lewis B. Jr.	COL	29	F&S	1st VA	d. c. July 9	Jacob Schwartz's farm, or possibly directly to Green Mount Cemetery, Baltimore, MD	Reinterred from Baltimore to Hollywood, Richmond, 2/16/1896
WILLIAMS, W.H.	PVT	26	B	5th LA	d. July 4	John Crist's farm	
◆ **WILLIAMS, W.R.**	PVT	25	C	53rd VA	d. Aug. 4	Camp Letterman, Row 3, Grave 21	Box 1-72, Hollywood, Richmond, 6/13/72
WILLIAMS, William	PVT		B	60th GA		Probably in the area of the Almshouse farm, or out toward Jacob Kime's farm	Laurel Grove, Savannah, Lot 853, Grave 13, 9/24/71
WILLIAMS, William A.	SGT	24	I	45th NC	d.c. July 6	John Reed's place, at foot of South Mountain, two miles above Fairfield; "body recovered by Dr. Weaver"	Oakwood, Raleigh, Grave 534, 10/1/71
WILLIAMSON, James	PVT	24	F	11th VA	d. July 4	Francis Bream's mill, "on hill from Bream's Mill," above William Myers's house	Box 2-P-Currus, Hollywood, Richmond, 8/3/72, with 33 others
WILLIAMSON, Peter G.	PVT	24	D	5th TX	d. Sept. 6	Camp Letterman, Row 7, Grave 15	Box 1-82, Hollywood, Richmond, 6/13/72
WILLIFORD, Thomas	PVT	19	G	2nd NC	d. Aug. 5	Camp Letterman, Row 3, Grave 15	Oakwood, Raleigh, 10/1/71
WILLIS, Thomas W.	CPL	24	C	7th SC	k. July 2	George Rose's farm, possibly "on the gravl walk in the woods," or "North West of Rose's Barn under a Peach Tree"	Possibly to Magnolia, Charleston, 5/10/71, Grave 29, as "_____ Wilson, Captain, 2d S.C.V."
WILLOUGHBY, John B.	PVT	20	G	38th GA	d. Aug. 31	Camp Letterman, Row 6, Grave 31	Laurel Grove, Savannah, Lot 854, Grave 3, 8/21/71
WILSON, Andrew T.	PVT	23	G	17th MS	k. July 2	Christian Shefferer's farm, northwest corner of barn near Emmitsburg Road	Box 3-279, Hollywood, Richmond, 9/10/72, as "A.J. Wilson, Co. I, 13th Miss."
WILSON, David	PVT		D	11th GA	d. Aug. 30 DeCamp U.S. Gen. Hosp. David's Island, New York	None	Probably Cypress Hill Cemetery, Long Island, NY
WILSON, Francis C.	LT	20	F	20th NC	k. July 1	Probably John S. Forney's farm, in field south of house	Wilson Cemetery, Sampson Co., NC

Name	Rank	Age	Co.	Regiment	Death	Burial Location	Disposition
WILSON, James Thomas	PVT		L	2nd FL	d. July 7	Pennsylvania College campus, in hospital cemetery, north of main edifice	Possibly in Box 4-E, Hollywood, Richmond, with 35 remains, 27 unknown, 5/17/73
WILSON, John	PVT	28	B	12th NC	d.c. July 12	Jacob Hankey's farm	Probably in one of eight boxes marked "N," to Hollywood, Richmond, 8/3/72, as an unknown
WILSON, John A.	PVT		D	5th VA	d. July 18	Henry Picking's farm, in field, along fence opposite schoolhouse near road	Box 1-172, Hollywood, Richmond, 6/13/72
WILSON, Nathaniel C.	MAJ	24	F&S	28th VA	d. July 3	John F. Curren's farm, in meadow under a walnut tree	Remains removed to "old burying ground at home," Fincastle, Botetourt Co., VA, after the war
WILSON, William	CPT	22	B	26th NC	k. July 1	About two miles out the Chambersburg Pike, east of a stately walnut tree, 100 yards north of road; 75 yards northeast of a medium size stone farmhouse, and across road from a large yellow barn; alongside H. Burgwyn, C. Iredell and W. McCreery	Oakwood, Raleigh, Grave 535, 10/1/71
WINCHESTER, William H.	LT	23	I	13th NC	d. Aug. 1 U.S. Gen. Hosp. Chester, PA	Chester Rural Cemetery, Chester, PA	Philadelphia National Cemetery, 1891
WINGATE, John A.	SGT		F	8th FL	d. Aug. 1	Camp Letterman, Row 2, Grave 12	Box 1-51, Hollywood, Richmond, 6/13/72
WINN, David R.E.	LTC	32	F&S	4th GA	k. July 1	David Blocher's farm under a tree behind the barn; "under a tree near house;" "still marked in 1866." (Prior to shipment, his "gold plate and teeth" were removed by the Blocher family who requested $10 to return the dental set.)	Oak Grove Cemetery, Americus, GA, then to Laurel Grove, Savannah, Lot 853, Grave 14, 9/24/71
WINTERS, Leonard	PVT		K	50th GA	d. Sept. 30 U.S. Gen. Hosp. Chester, PA	Chester Rural Cemetery, Chester, PA	Philadelphia National Cemetery, 1891
WITHERINGTON, M.	PVT		D	50th GA	d. Oct. 17 U.S. Gen. Hosp. Harrisburg, PA	None	Soldiers' Lot, Harrisburg, PA, Cemetery, Grave 136
WOLFE, Frederick or R.J.	PVT/CPL		C/D	2nd FL	d. July 8	Pennsylvania College, in hospital cemetery north of main edifice	Possibly in Box 4-E, Hollywood, Richmond, with 35 remains, 27 unknown, 5/17/73
WOLFF, Milton Y.	SGT		D	3rd SC BN	k. July 2	George Rose's farm, west of barn, under large cherry tree; "grave deep, with board cover with 6 others"	Magnolia, Charleston, Grave 24, 5/10/71
WOMACK, Charles Henry	PVT	28	H	14th VA	d. Aug. 16	Camp Letterman, Row 2, Grave 30	Box 1-60, Hollywood, Richmond, 6/13/72
WOOD, David	PVT		H	33rd VA	d. July 17	Henry Picking's farm, in field, along fence opposite schoolhouse near road	Box 1-176, Hollywood, Richmond, 6/13/72
WOOD, George W.	LT		B	60th GA	d. July 23	Andrew Weikert's farm, Fairfield Road	Laurel Grove, Savannah, Lot 853, Grave 14, 9/24/71
WOODS, John J.	SGT	20	K	19th VA	d.c. July 30	Pennsylvania College; north of main edifice, in hospital cemetery	Probably in Box 4-E, Hollywood, Richmond, with 35 remains, 27 unknown, 5/17/73
WOOTEN, Oscar	PVT	20	E	55th NC	d. Sept. 22 U.S. Gen. Hosp. Chester, PA	Chester Rural Cemetery, Chester, PA	Philadelphia National Cemetery, 1891

Name	Rank	Age	Co.	Regiment	Death	Burial Location	Final Location
WORKMAN, George	PVT	21	I	32nd NC	d. July 1-3	Jacob Hankey's farm; "truly a brave man"	Oakwood, Raleigh, Grave 508, 10/1/71
WORLEY, James M.	PVT		F	21st MS	d. July 3	John S. Crawford's farm, "where Basil Biggs lives;" in garden	Box 4-Y, Hollywood, Richmond, 5/17/73
WRIGHT, Jesse M.	PVT		K	44th GA	d. July 8 or Sept. 1	Jacob Hankey's farm	Laurel Grove, Savannah, Lot 854, Grave 13, 8/21/71
WRIGHT, Thomas J.	CPL	20	B	16th VA	k. July 2	John Horting's farm, near Willoughby's Run, under walnut tree in southeast corner of garden	Box 4-A, Hollywood, Richmond, 5/17/73
WRIGHT, William	PVT	44	B	11th MS	d. July 17 in hospital at Hagerstown or Williamsport, Maryland	Possibly Old Almshouse Burying Ground, Hagerstown, MD	Possibly in "Rose Hill," Washington Cemetery, Hagerstown, MD
WYANT, James C.	CPT		H	56th VA	d. July 31 U.S. Gen. Hosp. Chester, PA	Chester Rural Cemetery, Chester, PA, Grave 90	Philadelphia National Cemetery, 1891
WYCHE, James	PVT	18	G	47th NC	d. Aug. 12 U.S. Gen. Hosp. Chester, PA	Chester Rural Cemetery, Chester, PA	Philadelphia National Cemetery, 1891

Y

Name	Rank	Age	Co.	Regiment	Death	Burial Location	Final Location
YANCEY, S. Peter	PVT		D	12th NC	d. July 26	Jacob Hankey's farm	Oakwood, Raleigh, Grave 518, 10/1/71, as "Peter Yancey, Co. E, 21st NC"
YAWN, George W.	PVT		B	11th GA	d. July 5/15	John Edward Plank's farm	"State Lot" – GA, to Hollywood, Richmond
◆ **YEARGER**, William P.	PVT		E	22nd GA	d. Aug. 11 U.S. Gen. Hosp. Chester, PA	Chester Rural Cemetery, Chester, PA, Grave 139	Philadelphia National Cemetery, 1891
YOUNG, Beverly D.	PVT	33	I	11th MS	d. Aug. 29 DeCamp U.S. Gen. Hosp. David's Island New York	Cypress Hill Cemetery, Long Island, NY, Grave 78	"reinterred in 1864 to unknown location"
YOUNG, Franklin J.	PVT		C	6th AL		David Shriver's farm, Mummasburg Road, north of house, corner of orchard	Possibly Box 1-134, Hollywood, Richmond, 6/13/72, as "R.S. Young, Co. C, 6th Ala."
YOUNG, George P.	SGT	24	K	48th GA	d. July 13	Jacob Schwartz's farm, in cornfield on Rock Creek, Yard D, Row 2	Box 1-S-35, Hollywood, Richmond, 6/13/72
YOUNG, Henry H.	PVT		C	2nd GA BN	d.c. July 2	Near Adam Butt's farm or schoolhouse off Fairfield Road	Possibly in Box 1-119, Hollywood, Richmond, 6/13/72, with Pvt. Silas Skipper and one other soldier
YOUNG, John A.	CPT		G	8th GA	d. July 10	John Edward Plank's farm	"State Lot" – GA, to Hollywood, Richmond
YOUNG, John R.	CPL	40	G	3rd NC	d. July 25	Presbyterian Graveyard, High Street, Gettysburg	

Name	Rank	Age	Co.	Unit	Death	Burial	Reburial
YOUNG, Samuel M.	LT	25	K	11th NC	d. July 7	Samuel Lohr's farm, opposite house, in meadow near pear tree	Box 4-S, Hollywood, Richmond, 5/17/73
YOUNG, William	CPL		A	61st GA	k. July 1	Jacob Kime's farm, Harrisburg Road in orchard under peach tree	Laurel Grove, Savannah, Lot 853, Grave 12, 9/24/71

Z

Name	Rank	Age	Co.	Unit	Death	Burial	Reburial
ZEIGLER, Thomas F.	PVT		D	24th VA	d. July 16	Francis Bream's mill, above William Myers's house by side of fence	Box 2-P-Curns, Hollywood, Richmond, 8/3/72, with 33 others
ZIMMERMAN, Israel	PVT	35	F	26th NC	d. July 24/25 Seminary Hosp. Hagerstown, MD	Probably Old Almshouse Burying Ground, Hagerstown, MD	Probably in "Rose Hill," Washington Cemetery, Hagerstown, MD

THE END

NOTE: The approximately 1,400 men on this roster represent only about 30 percent of the Confederates who died as a result of the Battle of Gettysburg.

ROSTER ADDITIONS

| HILL, Peter | PVT | B | 3rd SC BN | d. July 3 | Buried west of George Rose's barn under a large cherry tree, deep grave with board cover, with 6 others as "P.H.T.T., Co. B, 3rd S.C. Bn." | Magnolia , Charleston, Common Grave 24, 5/10/71, as "O. Hill, Co. B, 3rd S.C. Bn." |

APPENDIX I

BURIAL ROSTER NOTES

The roster in this book delineates several names which are preceded by and accentuated with the symbol of a diamond such as this: ♦. That symbol applies to this section and helps to clarify certain points or questions which could not be referenced in the roster itself.

Frequently, it was found that the Gettysburg Confederate burial information compiled by Doctors O'Neal and Weaver, and others over the years, does not coincide with outside sources, such as state or federal "compiled service records," etc. This appendix attempts to explain a few of those discrepancies.

If anyone is interested in additional personal information on some of the Southerners who died as a result of the battle, there are 100 more detailed accounts in my two books, *Wasted Valor* and *Confederates Killed in Action at Gettysburg*.

ANDREWS, T.C. — He was wounded and captured in the action at Williamsport, Maryland on July 6, 1863. Many other soldiers shown in hospitals in Williamsport or Hagerstown, Maryland, were also casualties at Falling Waters and other actions nearby.

ATKINS, T.W. — The Roster of Georgia Confederate Soldiers indicates he resigned in May, 1862.

BEVERAGE, J. — He was a resident of Highland County, Virginia. Other sources state he died at Williamsport, Maryland, and was later buried in the Spotsylvania (Virginia) Court House Cemetery, in October, 1864.

BOYD, J.A. — His name is also listed as "James A.," his age "27," and his rank "corporal."

BRENAN, P. — This name is also spelled variously as "Brannon," and "Branan."

BRITTAIN, W. — This man's burial location closely matches that of the skeletal remains found in March, 1996, (see page 125) on the Gettysburg battlefield by Park Ranger Curt Johnson. However there was positively nothing in the grave which could point to the soldier being in the Union or Confederate army.

BROCKENBROUGH, A. — Adjutant and inspector general of Davis' Brigade, he was mortally wounded while commanding a battalion of sharpshooters from his brigade.

CARTER, B.F. — It would certainly seem that a man as prominent in Austin, Texas, as Colonel Carter was in the years prior to the Civil War, would have had his remains shipped home to Texas. However, after making several inquiries, I could find nothing to prove this ever happened, even though his wife and one child are buried in that city.

CHODMAN, J. — Also listed as "Chadman," and "Godman." He was probably a slave or freedman attached to the army in some capacity.

CLARK, J. or A. — According to the grave's headboard and the family history, one son was killed on July 1 with his father, and the second son died in the attack against Cemetery Ridge on July 3. Moreover, the family is at odds as to which son died first, but the consensus seems to be it was Albert Henry. One account states that the headboard was found "on the old McPherson Farm."

RELIC.—Mrs. Clayton Hoke, some time ago, found, near the Chambersburg turnpike, a piece of white pine board, about nine inches square, marked as follows.

Capt. J. M. Gaston.
Capt. T. G. Clark and Son.
42d Miss. Vols.
Killed July 1st, 1863.

The marking is very distinct; looks as if the letters had first been cut with a sharpbladed pocket knife, and the lines afterwards followed by a pointed piece of iron or coarse wire heated. This notice of the relic is made with the hope that it may meet the eye of some one directly interested.

(ACHS)

This headboard was found in the 1880s, but the graves had long since disappeared.

COCKE, J.M. — Adjutant Robert Cole of the 4th Alabama says in his memoir that a "James H. Cooke" of Co. G was killed while acting as litter-bearer to Lt. Col. L. H. Scruggs on July 2. Cocke is probably that man.

COOPER, T.W. — He and another man were buried near Lt. Edward Rhodes. Rhodes' mother had her son moved to Green Mount Cemetery in Baltimore, Maryland. There is evidence that she also had Cooper, and possibly one or two other soldiers, transported there as well.

COX, S.N. — Cox has been included on my roster, but I am not totally convinced that the "S C" on Dr. Weaver's list is Samuel Cox, 10th Georgia, although he is noted as such in the modern "Hollywood Roster" of Confederate dead. It could have happened, but seems unlikely, that a Semmes' Brigade (McLaws' Division) soldier would be in a Hood's Division hospital.

CREECY, W.P. — The Louisiana service record on this soldier mentions he was wounded at Gettysburg, but it also states he was still present with his unit in 1864.

DALTON, L. — Although the 29th Virginia was not present as a unit at Gettysburg, a few troops from General Corse's Brigade accompanied General Lee's Army into Pennsylvania. Dalton may have been one of those men.

DANLEY, H. — The North Carolina rosters record his name as "Danielly."

DIXON, J.E. — Two comrades of this soldier, while hunting for the material to make his headboard, discovered a large sum of money in the bake oven on the farm of Samuel Pitzer. For more on this story, see *Confederates Killed in Action*.

EARLY, H.F. — Georgia's records say he died on July 23 at DeCamp U.S. General Hospital, David's Island, N.Y.

EASTRIDGE, J. — His Virginia service record places his death at a hospital in Culpeper, Virginia.

FOSTER, H.H. — The 18th Virginia regimental history states he died in Baltimore, Maryland, on July 17. Dr. Weaver lists him as a lieutenant.

GRAVES, T.J. — Georgia's records say he was killed on July 2. A Confederate hospital register for the wounded cared for in the Williamsport and Hagerstown areas in Maryland, notes he was wounded on July 2 and died on July 22. Another source claims he died September 8, and is buried in the Gettysburg National Cemetery, Plot D-30 as "J. Graves, Co. C, 1st Pa."

HENKLE, M.P. — This is a possibility only. After checking all deaths in the Chesapeake Battery and in the infantry regiments that fought nearby, Lieutenant Henkle came the closest to fitting this burial. The "Co. A" is also a clue that the lieutenant was not an artilleryman.

HINDMAN, N.B. — There are some who believe he is buried in the Gettysburg National Cemetery, Mass. Plot E-10, as "S. Hindman, 15th Mass."

KOINER, C.H. — A sergeant in his regiment states that Koiner was mortally wounded in the abdomen at the Battle of Hanover, Pennsylvania. However, his service records say he died of disease in the military prison at Fort Delaware.

LONG, J.E. — There was also an "Isaac J. Long" in the 42nd Mississippi who could be the correct burial in this instance.

LOTT, J.B. — According to Vol. 9, p. 134, of the *Confederate Veteran* magazine, Lott's brother, George, was still searching for his burial spot even as late as 1901.

LOVE, J.E. — His canteen was found near Little Round Top after the battle. For more on his story, see *Confederates Killed in Action*.

McCULLOUGH, J.T. — His compiled service record in the National Archives in Washington, D.C., lists him as a sergeant. The Georgia rosters and a Camp Letterman Confederate death roster show him to be a private.

McGLEMRE, J.W. — This name was spelled "McGlemore" in some sources.

McHONE, M. — State records indicate he was buried in North Carolina.

MAGRUDER, J.B. — J. Howard Wert of Gettysburg claims the colonel died about July 20 on the Jacob Schwartz farm, which was contiguous to that of Mr. Bushman. It was common for field hospitals to overlap.

MATHIS, W.W. — Georgia does not list Mathis in their records, but his federal "combined service record" shows him as a member of Co. B, "State Guards," 8th Georgia Infantry. Dr. Weaver wrote his company as "H."

MILAN, J.C. — In the Georgia rosters he is shown as a sergeant in Company H and spelled "Milam." His combined service record lists him as "Sergeant Major Milan."

MILLER, W.T. — There were two "John Millers" who were members of units which could have used Bream's Mill, or the Curren's farm as a field hospital. They were the 38th Virginia Battalion, and the 28th Virginia Infantry Regiment. However, those two men were not reported as "killed in action." Therefore, William T. was the best candidate, and even though William died of battle wounds, he still may not be the correct individual.

MILLS, J. — His military record indicates he died of wounds on December 2. John Edward Plank's farm was no longer in use as a hospital at that time. So, either the date or place of his death is incorrect.

MOORE, H.M. — Dr. Weaver recorded this man as "H.K. Moore, Co. F, 14th Va." Dr. O'Neal also says "H.K." Moore's Virginia military record states he was "returned to duty" after his Gettysburg wound on April 13, 1864, and was "killed in action," May 10, 1864. Another source shows him "exchanged from Chester U.S. General Hospital." There is also a "Corp. George T. Moore, Co. D, 14th Va." on file who was killed at Gettysburg.

NASH, J.N. — Records indicate he was wounded in the left arm on July 1st, arm amputated, but was "at home, wounded, close of war."

PAGE, E.C. — The present day Hollywood Cemetery roster shows Page as the man shipped in Box 2-H. That identification is very meager, i.e., "E.F.P., NC," and may not be correct. Unfortunately, this is not an unusual case; in recent years, some of the barely identifiable remains have had complete names affixed to them by parties unknown.

PARISH, S. & PARRISH, S. — Dr. O'Neal was the first to list "Sam'l Parish." He was shown to be buried on the Schwartz farm in Yard D as a member of the 57th Virginia. Dr. Weaver cataloges the same soldier as "Samuel Parrish," also of the 57th. The federal "combined service records" in the National Archives, indicate two men with similar names: "Samuel Parish, Co. E, 28th Va.," and "Samuel Parrish, (no company listed), 57th Va." In checking the published regimental histories of these two units, one finds a "Samuel Parish, Co. E, 28th Va.," as "killed in action" at Gettysburg on July 3, and a "Samuel Parrish, Co. E, 57th Va.," who died of wounds near Gettysburg on July 17. J. Howard Wert, a local citizen of Mt. Joy Township, Adams County, Pennsylvania, places Samuel Parrish's burial (of the 57th), "in a trench with 20 others in one of the fields of the Schwartz farm."

PRUE, M. — In the vicinity where Prue was buried, Dr. Weaver recovered 49 unidentified remains and shipped them to Richmond, Virginia, on Aug. 3, 1872, in four large boxes marked "L." He added a remark that in this swampy area, "many...[others] have been washed away." These recoveries were similar to the 580 unknown remains from the Codori farm, and the 189 from Culp's Hill, in that the Federals buried them mostly in large trench graves, without the benefit of headboards, or other identification.

RISON, H.C. — Sometimes his name is spelled "Risen," or "Raison." The military record shows Rison's death on August 1 at the U.S. General Hospital in Chester, Pennsylvania.

ROBERTSON, J. — His name is also shown as spelled "Roberson."

ROBERTSON, J.N. — Dr. O'Neal lists him as a "sergeant," Dr. Weaver demotes him to a "private," the official military record says "private," and Krick's roster shows him as a "lieutenant."

RUSSELL, J. — Dr. Weaver has him buried at Camp Letterman as "John Rusell," but the federal rosters do not show a John "Rusell," "Russell," or "Russel," or any other close spelling, as having been a member of Co. I, 8th Florida. However, he is in Krick's book, (who may have gotten his name from Dr. Weaver), and on a roll of Confederates who died at Camp Letterman U.S. General Hospital at Gettysburg. This register is in the National Archives in RG 94, Stack 9W3, Rows 8 and 12.

SCHAMMEL, J.H. — A friend in the regiment, Lt. John Dooley, states in a memoir that Schammel died at the U.S. 2nd Corps Hospital on the Schwartz farm. However, his service record claims he was captured in April, 1865, during the Battle of Five Forks, Virginia.

SHACKELFORD, J.W. — Dr. O'Neal was called to David Shriver's farm just prior to the battle to attend to this soldier. Shackelford died shortly afterwards from "over exhaustion" while on the march, probably on or about June 30. He was from "Rocky Mount," Bossier Parish, Louisiana, and his mother was Mary A. Shackelford, same address.

THOMPSON, W.R. — In the Louisiana rosters he is listed as a first lieutenant. In his combined service record, he is recorded as "William P." and his rank is captain.

WADDY, G.R. — Krick's "Gettysburg Death Roster" lists him as a private in Co. D. But both the Virginia and the federal records on this soldier show him as a captain in Co. L.

WATSON, J.F. — His Georgia military record chronicles the fact that he died on July 14 at Camp Letterman near Gettysburg. Yet, they also show that his widow, Leila Watson, when filing for a pension in 1937, proved that James died in Americus, Georgia, on March 1, 1900.

WEBB, W.H. — A Chester Hospital patient ledger indicates he was a lieutenant and his name was "William H. Jr." He is not listed in the North Carolina rosters. Krick's book records him as "Sergeant William Henry Graham Webb."

WICKER, L.M. — His service record in the National Archives shows him to be a sergeant. North Carolina's rosters say he was reduced to a private from the rank of sergeant early in the war.

WILLIAMS, W.R. — The rolls of the 53rd Virginia indicate two men by the name of "Williams" who died at Gettysburg. They were "W.R." and "David R." David, of Co. F, was wounded and died as a prisoner in a field hospital, "after July 25."

YEARGER, W.P. — John Y. Foster, a volunteer nurse from Philadelphia, wrote a memoir of his experiences at Gettysburg shortly after the battle. In it, he claimed that Yearger died at the U.S. 2nd Corps Hospital on the Schwartz farm sometime after July 10.

APPENDIX II

THE NUMBER OF CONFEDERATE WOUNDED

Below is a very rough estimate of the number of Southern wounded left behind by General Lee's Army in some of the major Union and Confederate field hospitals in and around Gettysburg, prior to the establishment of the U.S. General Hospital at Camp Letterman. This list was made just after the battle and is not complete, but the total figure comes close to the official calculation of 6,802.

Confederate Army Field Hospitals

Cashtown	171
Samuel Lohr's	700 [1]
Jacob Hankey's	800 [2]
Pennsylvania College	700
Elizabeth Wible's & W. Henry Monfort's	311 [3]
Fairfield	50
Jacob Plank's	259
Andrew Weikert's	300 [4]
Other farms along Fairfield Road	135
Adam Butt's	111 [5]
Francis Bream's	700 [6]
John S. Crawford's & John Edward Plank's	515

Union Army Field Hospitals

White Church, Peter Conover's, & Jonathan Young's	260
Jacob Schwartz's & vicinity	1,250
George Bushman's	300
Michael Fiscel's & Jesse Worley's	75
Borough of Gettysburg	300
Total	6,937

1. This might also include the Andrew Heintzelman farm area.
2. Possibly includes David Shriver's farm.
3. May or may not include Henry A. Picking's place.
4. Although Mr. Weikert claimed this number, it is probably too high; however, it does closely match the total wounded of Gordon's Brigade.
5. This probably includes the Butt Schoolhouse casualties.
6. We do not know if this encompasses John Curren's farm and the Bream's Mill area as well.

APPENDIX III

A REGISTER OF GETTYSBURG CONFEDERATE BURIAL SITES

The following descriptions may help the reader to better pinpoint the initial grave locations of more than 1,000 identified Confederate dead that lay in the vicinity of Gettysburg between 1863 and 1873. The majority of these places are designated in relation to the landscape features of the 1860s. For more precise information on these sites, see the *1858 Adams County Map* by G. M. Hopkins, C.E., the 1868-69 *Map of the Gettysburg Battle-Field* by Brevet Major General G.K. Warren, Major of Engineers, U.S. Army, the *1872 Atlas of Adams County* by D.J. Lake, C.E., and the "Sergeant E.B. Cope 1863 map of the Gettysburg battlefield," Plate XL, in *The Official Military Atlas of the Civil War*. (Arno Press, New York, 1978). In a number of cases, where material is presented in parenthesis, ( ), this denotes that the farm or other premises may have been in use as a field hospital or aid station by a particular military unit or units. Likewise, some postbattle farm names are provided. This is due to the practice, in the years following the war, of Doctors O'Neal and Weaver listing the current property owners where Confederate graves still remained.

ALMSHOUSE, farm and cemetery. Known as the "Adams County Almshouse" or "Poorhouse," this large farm complex sat on the west side of Harrisburg Road just north of Gettysburg, and was occupied by Jacob Culp and his family, as well as a number of mental patients and indigent persons of the county. The cemetery was situated a little further northward on a small hill southwest of Rock Creek, often called "Blocher's Knoll." Two adjacent burial locations associated with the Almshouse were "Baugher's lot" and "Jacob Codori's." Both were situated just north of the "brickyard" which was to the east of Harrisburg Road, north of the borough. Codori was likely the postwar owner of John S. Crawford's farm and brick house during the Civil War years. Crawford's place stood on the west side of Harrisburg Road, and northeast of the college. "Baugher" was probably Rev. Henry L. Baugher.

ARNOLD, George — See "Horting," "Forney," and "Plank, J.E."

BENNER, Christian, farm. South of Hanover Road and the Daniel Benner farm, and east of Culp's Hill and Rock Creek. (C.S. – Ewell's Corps)

BENNER, Daniel H., farm. East of Rock Creek on the south side of Hanover Road, and northeast of Benner's Hill. (C.S. – Artillery Battalions, Ewell's Corps)

BENNER, Josiah, farm. On the west side of Harrisburg Road, just across Rock Creek. (C.S. – Smith's & Gordon's Brigades, Early's Division, Ewell's Corps)

BLACK HORSE TAVERN — See "Bream."

BLISS, William, farm. South of Gettysburg, and situated between Seminary Ridge and Cemetery Ridge, and west of Emmitsburg Road. The buildings were burned by the Federal army on the morning of July 3.

BLOCHER, David, farm. Across Blocher's Run, and east of Carlisle Road at the "Y" intersection, and west of Rock Creek.

BREAM, Francis, farm and tavern. On Fairfield Road, north side, just at Marsh Creek on the east bank, and often referred to as the "Black Horse Tavern." The old William McClellan family burial ground was north of the stone tavern building and adjacent to the creek. Most of the Confederate dead were interred in this vicinity. Francis Bream told Dr. Weaver that "all at that hospital were South Carolinians." Mr. Bream also owned the "Mineral Mills," which was further southward on Marsh Creek. Sometimes the burials on this farm and that of Adam Butt overlapped. (C.S. – Kershaw's Brigade, McLaws' Division, Longstreet's Corps)

BREAM, Francis, mill. Known as the "Mineral Mills," it stood south of Bream's farm and tavern on the east bank of Marsh Creek. The mill was operated by master miller William E. Myers, who lived in a house nearby. Burials here often overlapped with those at

The old McClellan family cemetery on the Bream farm was the center of a large Confederate burial area.

John Crawford's farm. Possibly known as "Weigle's Mill" in the 1870s. (C.S. – Armistead's and Kemper's Brigades, Pickett's Division, Longstreet's Corps)

BRINKERHOFF, Jacob, farm. Possibly east of Daniel Lady's farm on the north side of Hanover Road, in the vicinity of what is today called "Brinkerhoff's Ridge." The 1858 Adams County Map shows an "H. Brinkerhoff" in this locality, but no "Jacob." The 1868 Warren Map has no Brinkerhoffs living in this area.

BUSHMAN, George, farm. Due to a bend in the watercourse, Bushman's can be seen as situated both north and west of Rock Creek, and a short distance northwest of its junction with White Run. A medical attendant placed the hospital's cemetery "east of the stone farmhouse" and said it was divided into sections for both Union and Confederate dead. (U.S. – 12th Army Corps)

BUSHMAN, Michael, farm. East of Emmitsburg Road and west of the Round Tops, on the very southern end of the battlefield. The Warren Map identifies this farm as "H. Bushman," but it is sometimes listed as the "George Bushman" place.

BUTT, Adam, farm and schoolhouse. Northeast of Francis Bream's tavern, and north of Fairfield Road. The brick school was right along the road, and Butt's stone farmhouse was further to the north. The burials here and on the farm of Francis Bream often overlapped. (C.S. – Wright's and Wilcox's Brigades, Anderson's Division, Hill's Corps)

BYERS, Christian, farm. West of Marsh Creek, on the north side of Fairfield Road, and north of the Jacob Plank farm. The original house was built circa 1766, and may have been one of the oldest in the county. (C.S. – Hoke's and Smith's Brigades, Early's Division, Ewell's Corps)

CAMP LETTERMAN. Established about the middle of July as a U.S. General Hospital, this large medical facility stood one mile northeast of Gettysburg on the south side of York Pike. The hospital's cemetery was located atop a ridge on the southern edge of the camp and had provisions for the separate burial of patients who died from both armies. "Elliott's Map" places the Federal dead on the north side of the graveyard in two rows, and the Confederates on the south side in four rows. Approximately 175 Southerners were interred in this cemetery. Disbanded by early December, 1863, the locality was often referred to as "Hospital Woods," or "Wolf's Woods," because it occupied land owned by George Wolf.

CODORI, Jacob – See "Almshouse."

CODORI, Nicholas, farm. Located on the east side of Emmitsburg Road, and southwest of Cemetery Hill, it was a tenanted property in 1863. Over 580 Confederate remains were reported removed from the vicinity between 1872-1873 by Dr. Weaver, and almost all of them were unidentified.

COLLEGE – See "Pennsylvania College"

CONOVER, Peter, farm. Just past White Church, on the south side of Baltimore Pike between White Run and Two Taverns, Pennsylvania. Also known as "Cownover's." (U.S. – 2nd Division, 1st Army Corps)

CRAWFORD, John S., farm. On the east bank of Marsh Creek, and south of Francis Bream's tavern, it was owned by a Gettysburg attorney, and was possibly tenanted in 1863 by Basil Biggs. One of the described burial sites on this property was near a place called "Walnut Avenue." This was probably a row of trees lining the farm lane leading to the stone house, or something similar. Crawford owned at least one other tenant farm in the area, believed to be that of Samuel Johns. He also had a farm with a large brick house situated just northeast of Gettysburg on the west side of Harrisburg

1986 view near Camp Letterman's hospital cemetery.

Road. At times the descriptions of graves at Crawford's overlap or become confused with burials at Bream's Mill. (C.S. – Barksdale's Brigade, McLaws' Division, Longstreet's Corps)

CRISE - See "Krise."

CRIST, John, farm. Northwest of Michael Crist's farm, also on the west side of Willoughby's Run. Crist's farms are absent from most of the above cited maps. However, John Crist is noted on E.B. Cope's map. (C.S. – Pender's Division, Hill's Corps)

CRIST, Michael, farm. West of Willoughby's Run, on the north side of Chambersburg Pike and northeast of Herr's Tavern. In 1863, Crist's stone farmhouse sat on the north side of the unfinished railroad grade. (C.S. – Hays' Brigade, Early's Division, Ewell's Corps)

CULP, George, farm. South of Fairfield Road, on the west side of Willoughby's Run, and west of Emanual Pitzer's farm. Closely associated with the J.E. Plank farm hospital. (C.S. – Hood's Division, Longstreet's Corps)

CULP, Henry, farm. East of the Gettysburg borough limits, and south of Hanover Road. An "H. Culp" farm is also listed as a burial site, "in the orchard under an apple tree," for a member of the 16th North Carolina. This latter "H. Culp" may represent a separate place, because a soldier from Scales' Brigade would not normally have been interred in the former locale.

CUNNINGHAM, John, farm. South of Francis Bream's tavern, and almost directly west and across Marsh Creek from the John S. Crawford farm. One source placed the hospital's cemetery in an orchard, on a little hill, generally north of the house. The Confederate graves were dug on the south side of the orchard, and Mr. Cunningham tended them as carefully as he did the few Union soldiers who died on his farm. (C.S. – Wofford's Brigade, McLaws' Division, Longstreet's Corps)

CURRENS, John F., farm. Northeast and adjacent to Bream's Mill, and south of Bream's "Black Horse Tavern," on the east side of Marsh Creek. Sometimes designated as "Curn's." (C.S. – Pickett's Division, Longstreet's Corps)

DIEHL, Isaac M., farm. South of the Baltimore Pike bridge over Rock Creek, and west of the stream.

DOERSOM, Adam, farm. North of Pennsylvania College, on the east side of Mummasburg Road. This farm may have been the location of the burial yard associated with the hospital at Pennsylvania College.

DOUGLAS, William, farm. Southwest of Joseph Sherfy's "Peach Orchard," and a little over one half mile south, southeast of Pitzer's School. It was also just south of John Biesecker's farm, and may have been known as "Slonaker's farm" after the war.

DOUGLAS, William, house and lot. Just east of the Lower Marsh Creek Church, across the road leading northward, and on the north side of Fairfield Road.

DURBORAW, Samuel, farm. Northeast of Baltimore Pike at Two Taverns, Pennsylvania. Sometimes listed as "Squire Duborow's," "Durberow's," or "formerly Baubalitz." The burials here and on the Jonathan Young farm appear to overlap in some descriptions.

FELIX, William H., farm. On a piece of land situated in the fork made by the junction of Willoughby's and Pitzer's Runs, and north of Samuel Pitzer's farmhouse. In 1863, this 2.4 acre lot may have been owned by Levi D. Maus, as it was sold by him to Sarah A. Felix in September, 1864. Sarah's husband, William Henry, was not mentioned in the deed. During the battle, it is possible that Sarah and William were tenants of Levi Maus. Often noted in postbattle sources as the "S.A. Felix," or the "J. Felix" place. (C.S. – Artillery Battalions, Army of Northern Virginia)

FISCEL, Michael, farm. South of White Run and the Jacob Schwartz farm, and east of Rock Creek. A hospital cemetery was described as being east of the house, across a branch or creek, possibly Little's or Lousy Run. The name is sometimes spelled "Fissel," and the farm has been seen referred to as "Little's." (U.S. – 3rd and 5th Army Corps)

FLOHR'S Church and Cemetery. On the west side of the old Cashtown/Chambersburg Pike, southeast of Cashtown, Pennsylvania. There was a small, separate cemetery across the road, north of the church, which may have contained the Confederate burials.

FORNEY, John S., farm. The first farm west of Oak Ridge on Mummasburg Road, and south of Oak Hill. The remains of 64 Confederates, all unknowns at that time, were removed from "John Forney's field" by Dr. Weaver in the summer of 1872. One account claimed this field held individual graves and not trenches or "pits." It was also noted that most of these graves had headboards placed on them following the battle. Unfortunately, if that was true, by the time Dr. Weaver exhumed these burials nearly 10 years later, the identifying marks were gone.

FREY, Peter, farm. A tenant farm, with its partial stone house, and located on the west side of Taneytown Road, south of Evergreen Cemetery and Cemetery Hill.

GENERAL HOSPITAL – See "Camp Letterman."

GROUP, John, farm. Situated on the south side of a road leading east off of Taneytown Road, and southwest of the George Spangler farm. The Jacob and Franklin Swisher homesteads were both located nearby, and in post-war years, Confederate burials were often said to be on these farms under the names of "Eichelberger," "J. Ekenrode," and "E.B." or "Edward B. Buehler."

HALL, Dr. Samuel E., farm. On a crossover road north of Adam Butt's farm, between Fairfield Road and Chambersburg Pike. His stone house sat on the west side of the road.

HANKEY, Jacob, farm. On the south side of Mummasburg Road just across Willoughby's Run, and northwest of David Shriver's farm. In postwar accounts, this site was often described as the "Dave," "David," or "P.D.W. Hankey" place. The remains of 98 Confederates were shipped to Richmond from here by Dr. Weaver in August, 1872. (C.S. – Daniel's, Doles' and Iverson's Brigades, Rodes' Division, Ewell's Corps)

HARMAN, Emanuel, farm. Directly west of the Lutheran Seminary, and across Willoughby's Run. A "gatehouse," or "tollhouse" stood just to the north, on the south side of Chambersburg Pike.

HEINTZELMAN, Andrew, farm and tavern. On the north side of Chambersburg Pike in the village of Seven Stars, and just west of Samuel Lohr's farm. Mr. Heintzelman's is the great mystery of Confederate burial sites. Although Dr. Weaver removed 91 remains from this farm in 1872, all but one or two were listed as "unknowns." Since this was one of General Hill's major field hospitals, and it remained in Southern hands for four days, all of the deceased should have had proper headboards. Strangely, that does not seem to be the case. So either the attendants failed to identify the bodies, or the headboards were destroyed and the graves were plowed over between 1863 and 1872. (C.S. – Pender's Division, Hill's Corps)

HERBST, John, farm. West, southwest of the Lutheran Seminary, and east of Willoughby's Run. Herbst owned a "woodlot," now known as McPherson's or Reynold's Woods, and it was north of his farmhouse and south of Chambersburg Pike.

HERR, Frederick, farm and tavern. Westward, and across Willoughby's Run on the south side of Chambersburg Pike. Joseph Wible may have owned this farm or some other land nearby after 1860. The site is referred to in some postwar sources as "Herr's old tavern," "Hare's," and "Ireland's."

HERSHEY, Jacob, farm. East of David Shriver's farm on a crossover road, east side, and just northeast of the junction with Mummasburg Road.

HORTING, John, farm. East of Willoughby's Run, on the south side of Fairfield Road. This was a tenant farm owned by Gettysburg businessman George Arnold. Sometimes listed as "Arnold's," "Hartung's," "Hueting's" or "Hurting's." (C.S. – Davis' Brigade, Heth's Division, Hill's Corps)

JOHNS, Samuel, farm. About midway between the John S. Crawford farm and the John Edward Plank farm, and situated on ground in the midst of Marsh Creek and Willoughby's Run. Often called "Crawford's tenant house," during and after the war. (C.S. – Artillery Battalions, Longstreet's Corps)

KIME, Jacob, farm. Across Rock Creek, on the west side of Harrisburg Road, and just beyond the Josiah Benner farm. (C.S. – Gordon's Brigade, Early's Division, Ewell's Corps)

KRAUTH, Charles B. — See Lutheran Theological Seminary.

KRISE, Abraham, farm. Positive location unknown. However, there is a good possibility that it sat along the county road which led west and southwest from Joseph Sherfy's "Peach Orchard," and past Pitzer's Schoolhouse toward Willoughby's Run and Middle Creek. This lane, in the postwar years, commonly went by the name of "Eckert's Mill Road." Oddly, some descriptions place Krise's in close proximity to Christian Schefferer's farm and James Warfield's buildings. Dr. O'Neal wrote the name as, "Abraham Crise, near Marsh Creek." Sometimes referred to as "Crise's."

LADY, Daniel, farm. East of Rock Creek on Hanover Road, the stone farmhouse sat on the north side of the road. The burials here included seven on the south side of the house near the road, and at least one "back of the barn." (C.S. – possibly Artillery Battalions, Ewell's Corps, and Jones' Brigade, Johnson's Division, Ewell's Corps)

LEAS, Joseph, farm. Just southwest of the "Granite Hill," and south of York Pike, and northeast of Isaac Miller's farm. Sometimes spelled "Lease." Also, a "P. Hann's" farm and a "Mr. Lott's," "four miles east of Gettysburg" were in this area, and held burials of a few of General Stuart's Confederate cavalrymen, as was the nearby graveyard on Abraham Tawney's farm. (C.S. – Stuart's Cavalry Division, Army of Northern Virginia)

LOHR, Samuel, farm. Just west of Marsh Creek on both the north and south sides of Chambersburg

Pike. The original chestnut log farmhouse sat on the south side of the pike between the creek and a nearby intersection. Often cited as "Major Lohr's," the original spelling was "Loahr." (C.S. – Heth's Division, Hill's Corps)

LUTHERAN THEOLOGICAL SEMINARY. Directly west of Gettysburg on Oak Ridge, or what is now called "Seminary Ridge." The Charles P. Krauth house stood north of the main edifice, and the "Seminary Woods" was situated in front, or along the west side of the ridge. Surgeon Henry Janes, who was in charge of the military hospitals in the Gettysburg area, reported in late August that during the battle "a number of Confederate soldiers [had been] buried...in one hole immediately to the rear of the [main seminary] building." Janes said they were later removed to "the graveyard," which may mean the burial yard at Camp Letterman. In addition, he reported that several Rebel graves were still "scattered in the grove back of the building," but these were "well buried."

McCLEAN, Moses, farm. East of Mummasburg Road, and on the southeastern base of Oak Hill. In the postwar era, this farm was owned by James J. Wills, and the burials on the two homesteads, which were near each other, are often confusing to the researcher.

McMILLAN, David, farm. Along Seminary Ridge, south of Fairfield Road and Elizabeth Shultz's brick house.

MARSHALL, Benjamin A., farm. North of Fairfield, Pennsylvania, on the east side of the road to Cashtown. Hugh Culbertson's farm was just to the north. (C.S. – Jones' Brigade, Stuart's Cavalry Division)

MILLER, Isaac, farm and tannery. On the cavalry battlefield east of Gettysburg, and just north of the John Rummel farm. Another farm associated with Confederate cavalry burials is that of George Howard, who lived south of Miller along Hanover Road. Two Southerners were interred there, "under an apple tree." (C.S. – Stuart's Cavalry Division)

MILLERSTOWN ROAD. Now called Fairfield Road, it was also known in 1863 as Hagerstown Road.

MINERAL MILLS — See "Bream."

MONFORT, W. Henry, farm. His large, brick barn and house stood northeast of Gettysburg on the west side of Hunterstown Road. (C.S. – Johnson's Division, Ewell's Corps)

MYERS, William E., house. His residence stood on the grounds of Francis Bream's "Mineral Mills," very near to and east of Marsh Creek. Myers was the master miller of this enterprise.

NEGRO Church and Cemetery. In the southwest section of the Gettysburg borough, east of Washington Street. The church and cemetery were situated on the east side of "Long Lane."

PATTERSON, Sarah, farm. Along the east side of Taneytown Road, south of Michael Frey's, and southwest of the Granite Schoolhouse. (U.S. – 2nd Army Corps)

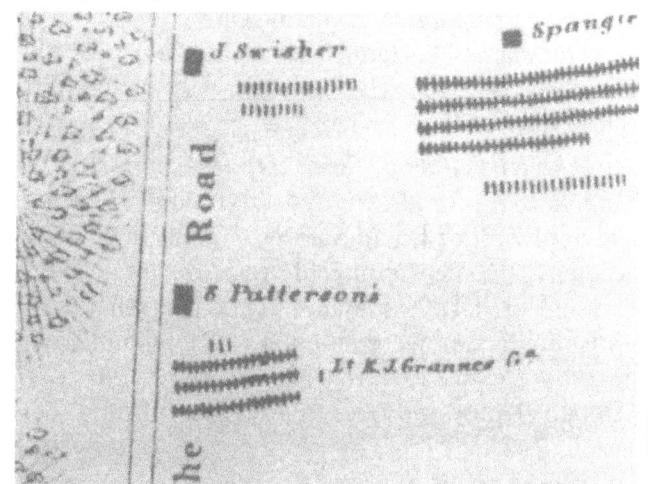

The grave of Lt. Ed. Granniss, 2nd Georgia Battalion, shown on the Elliot map, near Sarah Patterson's farm.

PENNSYLVANIA COLLEGE. Northwest of the Gettysburg town square, the school contained three structures. At one point there may have been between 700 and 900 Confederates recuperating here. The hospital's cemetery was north of the main edifice out toward Adam Doersom's farm. (C.S. – mainly Perry's Brigade, Anderson's Division, Hill's Corps)

PICKING, Henry A., farm and school. The buildings sat on the west side of Hunterstown Road, above the W. Henry Monfort farm. The hospital's cemetery was on a little knoll across the road from the schoolhouse. (C.S. – Walker's "Stonewall" Brigade, Johnson's Division, Ewell's Corps)

PITZER, Emanuel, farm. South of Fairfield Road at the head of Pitzer's Run, and between Willoughby's Run and Emmitsburg Road. Emanuel, father of Samuel Pitzer, died a few weeks prior to the battle. On occasion, a "Myers's lot" is noted nearby, which is Zachariah Myers.

PITZER, Samuel, farm. West of Emmitsburg Road, east of Willoughby's Run, and just north of Pitzer's Schoolhouse. A "John Pitzer" may have been associated with this farm in the years following the Civil War.

PITZER'S SCHOOL. Just east of Willoughby's Run, on the north side of the crossover road that ran from Joseph Sherfy's "Peach Orchard," westward.

PLANK, Jacob, farm. South of Fairfield Road, a short distance west of Marsh Creek and Francis Bream's tavern and farm. A notation in one source states that the graves here, the identified as well as eight "unknowns," were "all plowed over." (C.S. – possibly Daniel's Brigade, Rodes' Division, Ewell's Corps)

PLANK, John Edward, farm. West side of Willoughby's Run, south of Fairfield Road, and east, southeast of Francis Bream's tavern. Following the Civil War, this place was often referred to as the "William" or "Abe" Plank farm, as well as by the surnames of "Altoff," "Arnold," "Butt," and "Ogden." There may have been a "Cornel Dougherty" nearby, during or after the war. (C.S. – Hood's Division, Longstreet's Corps)

POLLEY, Charles B., farm. North side of Chambersburg Pike, and west of Frederick Herr's tavern. Postwar, it was sometimes called the "Emanuel D. Keller" or "Keller" farm, also listed as "near Dougherty's" or "Doughterties." A "James Grimes" lived nearby, and his place may have contained some Confederate graves. (C.S. – Pettigrew's Brigade, Heth's Division, Hill's Corps)

POORHOUSE — See "Almshouse."

RIFE, Isaac, farm. On the eastern outskirts of Cashtown, Pennsylvania, and along the north side of the old Chambersburg Pike.

ROSE, George W., farm. East of Emmitsburg Road, and south of Joseph Sherfy's "Peach Orchard," on the southern end of the Gettysburg battlefield. It was farmed in 1863 by John P. Rose, who was probably a brother of the owner. Between 33 and 35 graves of General Kershaw's South Carolina dead were located behind or north of Rose's stone barn. And according to Dr. O'Neal, besides the 65 or so identified Confederates buried on this property, there were "graves of 40 or 50 others in trenches not marked." One of the burial locations was noted as "on the gravl walk in the woods," which was along a path running southeastward toward the G.W. Weikert farm.

SACHS, John, farm and mill. East of the John Cunningham and John S. Crawford farms, between Marsh Creek and Willoughby's Run. Very often referred to as "Sock's" farm or mill.

SCHWARTZ, Jacob, farm. Southwest of White Church on Baltimore Pike, and west of White Run, just north of Michael Fiscel's farm. Often referred to as the "Schwartz Estate," "Widow Schwartz's" or the "Moses Schwartz" farm. This field hospital complex contained several cemeteries, or burial "yards." One was "back of the barn." Others included "Yard B," which was on a hill between Schwartz's and George Bushman's.

This little knoll on Mr. Picking's farm became a Confederate graveyard.

The farm of John Edward Plank was General Hood's division hospital, where many of his men were buried.

A large number of Confederates were buried north or in back of George Rose's stone barn.

121

"Yard D" was in a cornfield on Rock Creek. Another, "Yard C," was laid out too, but it had only four identified graves, and the exact location is still unclear. Dr. O'Neal places it in "a cornfield," like that of Yard D. Additionally, several Confederates were interred on "Red Hill" and/or "Slaty Ridge," a place or area probably out behind, or northwest of the barn.

Besides those listed in the roster, at least 34 unidentified Confederate graves were removed from this farm. One source stated that this facility contained 952 Confederate wounded, 192 of this number died there. (U.S. – 2nd and 3rd Army Corps)

SEMINARY – See "Lutheran Theological Seminary"

SHEALER, Martin, farm. Just off of Hunterstown Road, northeast of the W. Henry Monfort farm, and southeast of the crossroad. Interestingly, in 1863, Shealer's barn still had a "thatched roof." (C.S. – Steuart's Brigade, Johnson's Division, Ewell's Corps)

SHEFFERER, Christian, farm. Across from James Warfield's place, on the north side of the crossover road that lead westward from Joseph Sherfy's "Peach Orchard" toward Pitzer's Schoolhouse. There are several other spellings noted for his surname.

SHERFY, Joseph, farm. On the west side of Emmitsburg Road, just north of the first crossroad. Across the road from Sherfy's brick house, and just southward, was John Wentz's log house, which was surrounded by Sherfy's "Peach Orchard." A burial trench was dug for some Confederate corpses in Wentz's garden by a detail from the 16th Michigan Infantry. It was said to be "to the left, and in front of the house, near the road." According to one source, Dr. Weaver claimed that all of the Confederate remains he found in the Gettysburg area between 1871 and 1873 were removed and shipped to the South, "except for 40 bodies in Sherfy's peach orchard."

SHRIVER, David, farm. On the north side of Mummasburg Road just past Herr's Ridge, and southeast of Jacob Hankey's farm. (C.S. – Daniel's, O'Neal's and Iverson's Brigades, Rodes' Division, Ewell's Corps)

SHULTZ, Elizabeth F., house and lot. On Seminary Ridge, just south of the Lutheran Seminary and Fairfield Road. Shown as the "Widow Shultz or Schultz" in some sources. It appears that a "J.E. Culp," a "McClellan," and a "Zachariah Myers" owned land or lots nearby.

SLYDER, John, farm. On the southern end of the Gettysburg battlefield, west of Big Round Top, and east of the Emmitsburg Road. It was known in 1863 as the "Granite Farm."

SNYDER, Philip, house. A small log structure, northwest of Michael Bushman's farmhouse, on the west side of Emmitsburg Road.

SOCKS – See "Sachs"

SPANGLER, George, farm. South of Power's Hill, east of Taneytown Road, and west, southwest of Baltimore Pike bridge over Rock Creek. (U.S. – 11th Army Corps)

SPANGLER, Henry, farm. Just east of Seminary Ridge, north of Joseph Sherfy's, and west of Emmitsburg Road. It was a tenant farm in 1863. "Spangler's Woods" was located just to the northwest of the house. A "Zachariah Myer's" property or buildings were noted in the vicinity after the war.

STEWART, David, farm. Along Fairfield Road, south side, west of Marsh Creek and the farms of Jacob Plank, Christian Byers, and Andrew Weikert.

TROSTLE, Abraham, farm. East of Joseph Sherfy's and the Emmitsburg Road on the Gettysburg battlefield. Sometimes identified as the "Peter or Catherine Trostle" farm.

TROSTLE, John, farm. South, and along Rock Creek, and west of Michael Fiscel's farm. A burial site on this farm was on a hillside in the vicinity of a large sycamore tree on Rock Creek, and opposite a place called "Walnut Row." For some unknown reason, this old, but perfectly good, tree was cut down a few years ago. (U.S. – 3rd, 5th, and 6th Army Corps)

U.S. GENERAL HOSPITAL – See "Camp Letterman."

UTZ, Henry, house. On East Middle Street in Gettysburg, it was a brick structure on the second block, southside. In the 1860 census, Utz was listed as a farmer, and may have been renting the house from the school board.

WANTZ, Henry, house. On Carlisle Street in Gettysburg, second block, east side, just north of the railroad depot. Wantz died in January, 1863, and the building was occupied by tenant Alexander Spangler in that year. Sometimes noted as "Wants' place" on the burial rosters.

WARFIELD, James, farm and blacksmith shop. On the south side of the crossover road that ran westward from Joseph Sherfy's "Peach Orchard." One burial site was in the garden near the shop. "Elliott's Map" indicates 13 graves on the east side of the house, all were Mississippians from Barksdale's Brigade. Sometimes referred to as the "Negro blacksmith shop."

WEIKERT, Andrew, farm. On Fairfield Road, across Marsh Creek, it was west of the Christian Byers and Jacob Plank farms. The stone farmhouse, a barn, and other outbuildings, stood on the north side of the road. (C.S. – Gordon's Brigade, Early's Division, Ewell's Corps)

WIBLE, Elizabeth, farm. Northeast of W. Henry Monfort's farm, and southeast of the crossroads on Hunterstown Road. Often called the "Widow Wible or Weible" farm, or "William Weible's." A "Captain Wible," and a "Joseph Wible" appear to be associated with this site, however Joseph lived further south along York Pike. "J. Walter's" name also comes up in connection with this burial area, but it is thought to be a prewar owner. (C.S. – Nicholl's and Steuart's Brigades, Johnson's Division, Ewell's Corps, and possibly Hoke's Brigade, Early's Division, Ewell's Corps)

WISLER, Ephraim, farm and blacksmith shop. North side of Chambersburg Pike, east of Marsh Creek, and just west of Charles B. Polley's. Also known as "Whistler's," or "Whisler's." The postwar name associated with this site was "J." or "Jacob Lott's."

WHITE CHURCH. On the south side of Baltimore Pike, east of White Run. Known as "Mark's German Reformed Church," after Nicholas Mark who lived nearby and donated the land for the structure around 1790. The cemetery was on the southwest side of the building. (U.S. – 1st Division, 1st Army Corps)

WILLS, James J., farm. East of the Michael Crist farm and Willoughby's Run, and north of Chambersburg Pike. Also northwest of the "railroad cut" on the Gettysburg battlefield. In postwar years, it was referred to as "Clarkson's," or "Clarkson's old place," and "Bender's." The Confederate burial locations associated with the Moses McClean and Wills' farms are often confusing due to their proximity, and their ownership in the years after 1863.

WOLF, George, farm. East of Gettysburg, across Rock Creek, and south of York Pike. The U.S. General Hospital, or "Camp Letterman," covered a portion of this farm, and was located east of Wolf's house.

WORLEY, Jesse, farm. South of Baltimore Pike, below Two Taverns, Pennsylvania, on the west side of the road leading southwestward. (U.S. – 3rd Division, 5th Corps)

YOUNG, Jonathan, farm. North of Baltimore Pike, and south of White Run, also east of the "Low Dutch Road." Referred to as "Widow Young's," the burials here appear to overlap onto the farm of Samuel Durboraw. (U.S. – 3rd Division, 1st Army Corps)

Note: For more complete documentation of these and other burial sites, plus maps and photographs, see my 1990 book, *Wasted Valor: The Confederate Dead at Gettysburg*, pp 57-106.

The Evergreen Cemetery burial plot order for Hooper Caffey.

Appendix IV

Were Any of the Confederate Dead Left Behind?

Between the years 1871 and 1873, Dr. Rufus Weaver exhumed the remains of 3,320 Confederate soldiers and forwarded them by rail or steamer to various places in the South. From that massive undertaking, both on and off the battlefield, a question naturally arises. Did Dr. Weaver, in this tremendous work, find all of the Southern graves? The answer, of course, is no; he did not discover, and could not have collected, every single soldier.

We know for certain that up to now, the names of more than 4,700 Confederates who are known to have died as a result of the three-day fighting at Gettysburg. (But this is not to imply, in any way, that more than 1,380 Confederate graves still remain on the battlefield.) Of these 4,700 or so casualties, the majority were either "killed in action," or later expired from wounds. We are also aware that in the years after the Union dead were removed in 1863 and 1864, and the Confederates from 1871 to 1873, there followed a long period when the skeletons of soldiers from both armies were often found by farmers plowing fields, workmen digging ditches, or visitors walking on the old battleground after a heavy rain. In fact, the last such discovery was made in the early spring of 1996, when a park visitor named Curt Johnson stumbled upon the bones of a soldier near the "railroad cut," just northwest of Gettysburg. Perhaps the most incriminating statistic is that if you total the known Confederates cataloged by Doctors O'Neal and Weaver, there are 235 known buried individuals who show no evidence of ever having been removed. In a similar vein, there are 21 localities, out of about 100 such places, that definitely once held Southern remains, but existing records do not indicate any were exhumed. It has already been stated that we have information where Dr. Weaver did not ship to Hollywood, for some reason, the bodies of 40 Southerners buried in Joseph and Mary Sherfy's peach orchard. Dr. Weaver also wrote on one of his shipment records that in a marshy area on the battlefield near Devil's Den, "many [bodies] were buried in the swamp or at its edge which have been washed away." There can be no doubt that this situation existed in other localities, where flooding was commonplace. Then there were the many single, unmarked graves that in that first autumn, and in successive years, were covered by fallen leaves, obliterated by the blades of plowmen, or were purposefully kept hidden by farmers who did not want inquiring strangers on their property.

To put a figure on the number of these lost graves would not be possible. It is enough to say that Confederate remains are still present in the ground near Gettysburg. These Southerners have stories much like the one of a young Georgian, "a mere boy," who died in a field hospital of the U.S. Second Army Corps. Sergeant Frank Nickerson, also wounded, lay on a blanket next to the Georgian for some time before the youth drew his last breath. In 1884, Nickerson visited the old farm where he thought the Georgian had been laid to rest. When asked about the incident, and if any Confederates had been brought onto his land, the owner replied, "Yes, one boy, and I buried him across that little rolling by the fence. I miss the place when I plow. He is there."

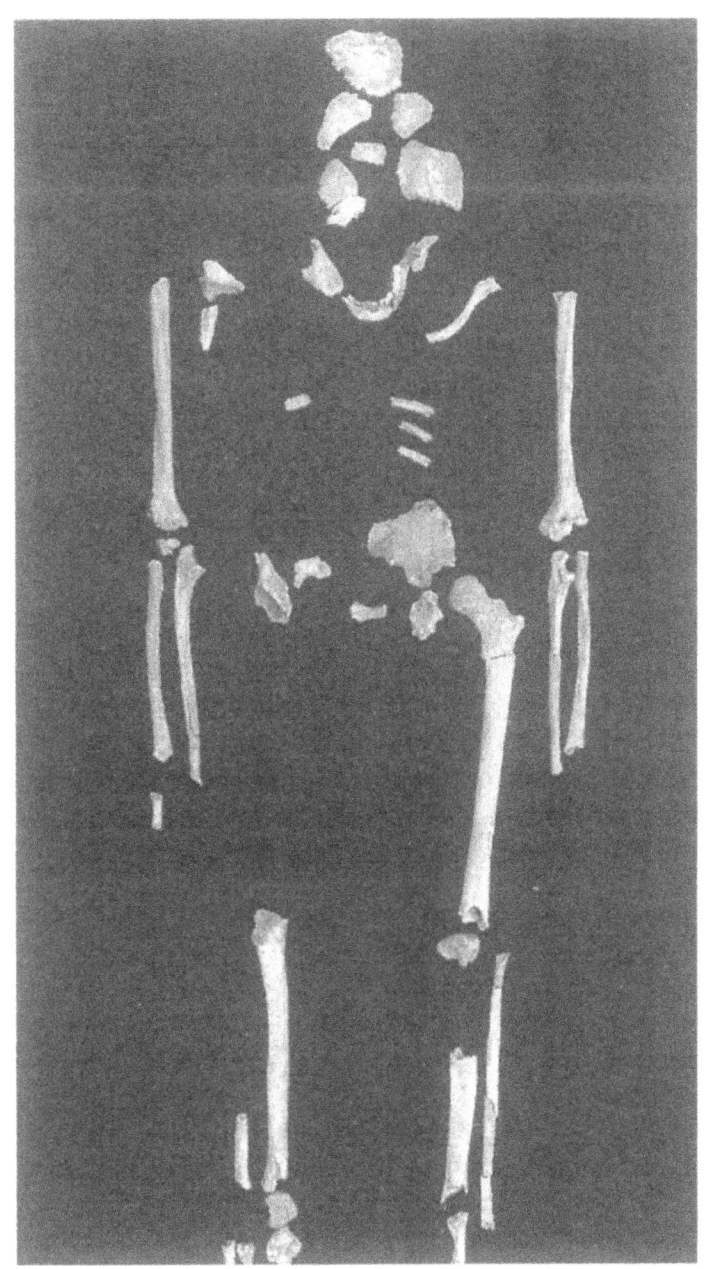

Skeleton of unknown soldier discovered in 1996 near the old railroad grade west of Gettysburg.

APPENDIX V

"ELLIOTT'S MAP"

During the period from July, 1863 to June of 1864, a map was produced which showed the general terrain and other historic aspects of the Gettysburg battlefield. One of the most unusual features of this map was that it appeared to indicate the location of almost every soldier's burial place in a 20-square-mile area surrounding the town. The cartography was likely done by S. G. Elliott and Company, of Philadelphia, and a lithograph was printed prior to June 10, 1864 by F. Bourgran and Company, of the same city. Unfortunately, the map only listed the names of a few of the "marked" graves on the field, and it exaggerated the number of burials in some areas. The following names are the only identified Confederates who appear on what is now called, "Elliott's Map."

BUTLER, William R.	4th Georgia
GIBSON, Hardy V.	13th Alabama
GRANNISS, Edward J.	2nd Georgia Battalion
LAW, Josiah H.	4th Georgia
LEIGH, Benjamin W.	Staff, Gen. Ed. Johnson
MEACHAM, R. W.	13th Georgia
MORTON, Allan	1st Co., Richmond (Va.) Howitzers
OURSLER, W. R.	17th Mississippi
WASDEN, Joseph	22nd Georgia
WILLIAMS, James M.	6th North Carolina
WINN, David R. E.	4th Georgia

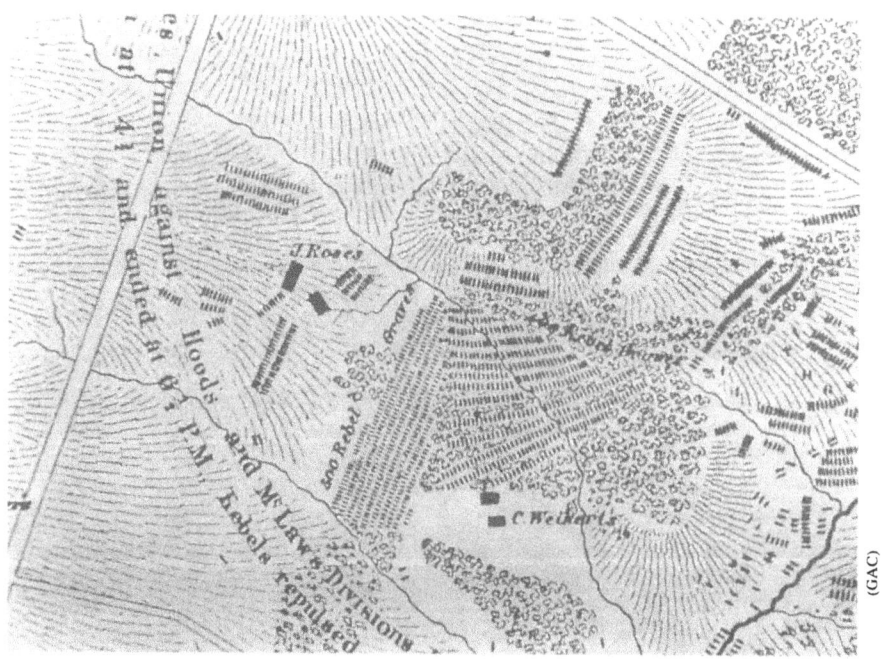

A portion of "Elliott's Map" showing an overestimate of the burials on the Rose Farm.

Greg Coco speaking with servicemen in the Gettysburg National Military Park
Soldiers' National Cemetery on July 19, 2005 *(Katie Lawhon, NPS)*.

About the Author

Gregory Ashton Coco, born and raised in Louisiana, lived in the Gettysburg area for nearly 35 years.

In 1972, after serving in the U.S. Army, he earned a degree in American History from the University of Southwestern Louisiana. While in the military, Greg spent a tour of duty in Vietnam as a prisoner of war military interrogator and infantry platoon radio operator with the 25th Infantry and received, among other awards, the Purple Heart and Bronze Star.

During his years in Gettysburg, Greg worked as a National Park Service Ranger and a Licensed Battlefield Guide. He wrote sixteen books and a dozen scholarly articles on Gettysburg and the Civil War. His book *A Strange and Blighted Land. Gettysburg: The Aftermath of a Battle* was voted #12 in the Top 50 Civil War Books ever written.

Greg died at age 62 in February of 2009. In his words, he was "the happy husband of Cindy L. Small for 26 years. He was the fortunate father of daughter Keri E. Coco. He loved them both with all his heart." Keri is married to Cail MacLean and they have a daughter, Ashton MacLean Coco.